Langbord
9 Walmer Road
ronto, Ontario, Canada
5R 2Y3

Athens greece May/77.

THE FILM DIRECTOR
AS SUPERSTAR

THE FILM DIRECTOR
AS SUPERSTAR

JOSEPH GELMIS

SECKER & WARBURG · LONDON

First published in England in 1971 by
Secker & Warburg Ltd
14 Carlisle Street, Soho Square, London WIV 6NN

Copyright © 1970 by Joseph Gelmis

SBN 436 17370 0
Printed in Great Britain by Stephen Austin Ltd

A Shadows Book

To Bill McIlwain and Allan Wallach,

who made it possible.

CONTENTS

INTRODUCTION   viii

PREFACE   ix

ACKNOWLEDGMENTS   xi

PART ONE: THE OUTSIDERS

BEYOND THE UNDERGROUND   3

Jim McBride   5
Brian De Palma   21
Robert Downey   33

THEIR OWN MONEY, THEIR OWN SCENE   41

Norman Mailer   43
Andy Warhol   65
John Cassavetes   75

PART TWO: THE EUROPEAN EXPERIENCE

THE UNDEREMPLOYED INDEPENDENT   91

Lindsay Anderson   93
Bernardo Bertolucci   111

THE SOCIALIST FILM SCHOOLS   121

Milos Forman   123
Roman Polanski   139

PART THREE: FREE AGENTS WITHIN THE SYSTEM

TRANSITIONAL DIRECTORS   159

Roger Corman   161
Francis Ford Coppola   177

INDEPENDENTS WITH MUSCLE   191

Arthur Penn   193
Richard Lester   231
Mike Nichols   265
Stanley Kubrick   293

ACKNOWLEDGMENTS

I am indebted to Audi Marks and Ruth Gelmis for their assistance and moral support and to my editor, Bill Whitehead, for his encouragement, tact, and astute suggestions.

PREFACE

A patient spent an hour telling his psychoanalyst in elaborate detail all the dreams he had dreamt the previous week. When his patient was leaving, the psychiatrist said: "That was a very interesting session we had today." The patient laughed scornfully and said: "Well, that shows how little you really know about me. The joke is on you. Everything I told you was a complete lie." The psychiatrist replied: "Ah, *that's* even more interesting."

I cannot guarantee that what you are about to read by the sixteen dreamers presented here is the truth. But I don't think that it is possible for a man to spend a number of hours discussing himself and his work and his life without revealing a kind of personality profile. And since this book is concerned as much with life styles as with film styles, one man's evasiveness can be as eloquent as another man's candor.

This book does not attempt to present a critical overview of the directors—except, inescapably, by my having selected them and through an occasional slip of the tongue. My questions, in almost every case, have been trimmed down from what may have been originally a conversation to simple shorthand cues wherever possible. What I have tried to do, to paraphrase Bernardo Bertolucci in his discussion of actors, is to make documentaries of my directors.

The director is in vogue today, due to a complex set of social and economic circumstances. The premise of this book is that the phenomenon will not soon peak and pass. Rather, I suggest that we are on the threshold of a technological and aesthetic revolution in movies which will inevitably restructure human consciousness and understanding. Accessibility of the means of production and changes in distribution and exhibition will democratize movies so there will be thousands made every year instead of just hundreds. And the independent filmmaker, whether he's working in Super 8 or 70-mm Panavision, will be the nexus of the change to come.

Spokesmen for the new sensibility are already at work. Jean-Luc Godard, Stanley Kubrick, Michelangelo Antonioni, Richard Lester, Arthur Penn, Roman Polanski, Mike Nichols, Norman Mailer are, rightly or wrongly, superstars to a generation of would-be filmmakers and those just interested in finding a meaningful life style.

In preparing this book, I chose filmmakers who hadn't been interviewed in other collections—which eliminated, for example, the New Wave Directors. The sixteen interviews that follow are a cross section of independent directors—from outsiders like Jim McBride, whose

$2500 first film still hadn't been shown theatrically two years after he made it, to Stanley Kubrick, who spent $10,500,000 on the most awesome underground movie ever made, 2001: A *Space Odyssey.*

The directors come from a variety of backgrounds—poetry, the novel, painting, TV, the stage, documentaries, shorts, film school, criticism, and still photography. Whether they use their own money or a studio's, they are determined to make films their own way and to maintain complete artistic control. And, unlike the older generation of directors, every filmmaker in the book—except Roger Corman, who has been picked as a transitional figure—learned his craft outside the studio and didn't have to serve an apprenticeship on B films.

This book is not a defense of cinema versus movies, nor is it a brief for underground films versus Hollywood. Personal films are not the invention of the amateur with his 16-mm Arriflex and Nagra tape recorder slung across his shoulder. Every great film has issued from a great nature. But I suspect there is some validity in the assertion of young directors that they are reinventing the language of film through their trial and error. They are, with their portable equipment, closer to D. W. Griffith and film's origins than to the studios where technique had become institutionalized and the apprentice merely learned the house rules. In their ardor, they are the first authentic film generation.

I have tried in the interviews to find a balance between what would be comprehensible to the general reader and yet would still be useful to the film student and buff. The questions cover broad areas of aesthetics, technique, how the director got his start, advice to new filmmakers, what he was trying to do when he made his films and what they meant to him.

INTRODUCTION

"To me," says Roman Polanski, "the director is always a superstar. The best films are best because of nobody but the director. You speak of *Citizen Kane* or *8½* or *Seven Samurai*, it's thanks to the director who was the star of it. He makes the film, he creates it."

Film has long been the director's medium in Europe. But Hollywood is only now—reluctantly—starting to give directors real authority. In the feudal studio system, the director was usually a hireling along with the writer, the cameraman, the actor, and the wardrobe lady. He was apprenticed at the studio, where he got his tutoring in the company way, and he tunneled as best he could through someone else's choice of cast, script, and editor.

There were a handful of exceptions, such as Billy Wilder, George Stevens, Alfred Hitchcock, Otto Preminger, William Wyler, and John Ford, but most of them were hyphenates—producer-director. The rule was that the producer ran the show and the studio put *its* stamp on each film. Directors were interchangeable. The formulas were sacred.

It was, in retrospect, rather miraculous that even gifted men like René Clair, Ernst Lubitsch, Josef von Sternberg, and others were able to put their personalities into films made under such impersonal, factory conditions. Like any oversimplification, this view of the studio system doesn't take into account the fact that some men thrived under the system, that others were court favorites or had special status because of their success at the box office or with the intelligentsia.

But some unique, intractable geniuses like Eric von Stroheim and Orson Welles were misfits in that milieu. Welles was sent, in effect, into exile because he was presumptuous and there was no room for so large an ego and talent within a studio system dominated by tycoons and producers.

Yet, now, Hollywood—which in its decline has become a euphemism for banks, backlots full of TV series, and overseas production— is so desperate to find ways to please fickle audiences, it is willing to give the director the kind of control and money to make personal films that Welles needed to survive.

Richard Lester, who enjoys such complete artistic control over his movies, says: "A director's job in this period of filmmaking—and I know that this may change, as it has in the past—is to be an absolute dictator and produce a personal vision on a subject that he has chosen. He is paid too much because he has that responsibility, and what the people who pay him are buying is that personal vision. He must be absolutely ruthless in producing an accurate vision. He must be a dilettante and interfere in every part of the production and it must finally succeed or fail on the success or failure of his own personal vision."

There are a growing number of directors, in and out of Hollywood, who make films their own way—who develop the script with the writer(s), choose their own cast (which means they are not at the mercy of the star who has chosen them), don't have the studio looking over their shoulder to unnerve them while they are shooting, and then have final cut. Obviously, the issue of control where millions are at stake in Hollywood is usually a correlative of the "muscle" a director can flex at the box office.

After the success of *Dr. Strangelove*, Stanley Kubrick spent three and a half years and $10,500,000 to make *2001: A Space Odyssey*. There were no stars in the cast and no presold property. Yet the film was financed—and will earn $25,000,000 in the United States and Canada alone—on the strength of Kubrick's name and M-G-M's faith in his vision.

Mike Nichols got an Oscar for directing *The Graduate*, which—in the absence of any other Oscars for the cast or film—was interpreted in some quarters to be an award for the year's best performance by a director. *The Graduate* had already grossed $40,000,000 domestically by early 1969, when Nichols began shooting *Catch-22* with $11,000,000 and the kind of absolute control (he didn't even have to show rushes to the studio) that Welles was given just once, with *Citizen Kane*.

The new personal directors differ in a crucial way from the old superstars. Unlike the traditional director who worked within the studio as a film editor or a camera operator or an assistant director, the new breed of personal filmmaker come—like Welles—from other media and haven't learned their craft as apprentices.

And, in a very real sense, they are still outsiders who either keep their distance from Hollywood—like Lester and Kubrick working in London—or keep returning to work in other forms—like Nichols and Arthur Penn in the legitimate theater. With a few exceptions, like Polanski—who has adopted Hollywood as the fulfillment of his boyhood dreams—the new superstar is suspicious of authority and keeps his distance. Kubrick, for instance, is as independent as he was when he raised the money for his first film, *Fear and Desire*, and shot it his way. The difference is that now he makes more expensive films and gets the money for them from M-G-M or United Artists, rather than his father or uncle or friends.

Whether he is supported by a major studio or a student grant, the independent filmmaker in 1970 demands the same prerogatives. Except for the way he gets his money, he shares the same general concerns and credo—that his work be as honest an expression of himself as he is capable of making.

Jim McBride, who had made his first film, *David Holzman's Diary*, with $2500 of his own money when he was twenty-five, and then hadn't been able to get it shown in a theater for two years, says: "Traditionally, the director is the guy who tells the cameraman where to put the camera and tells the actors how to say their lines. But that's not what I am. I just don't think that that means anything—to be a 'director.' I prefer to think of myself as a 'filmmaker'—as someone who uses people and equipment as tools to make an expression of himself . . .

"Maybe all a director is is someone who chooses people, chooses all these elements and throws them together. I assure you that Mailer's new film, *Maidstone*—which had ten thousand people in it and was shot on a wild orgiastic weekend with twenty cameras and a loose improvised situation—I assure you that it's going to be the epitome of the personal film. It will be a perfect expression of Mailer's sensibilities . . .

"What interests me about movies is seeing them as expressions of a man's sensibilities: of seeing a person through his art. I don't particularly put too much value on learning technique. On learning the meaning of a tracking shot, for example. All you have to know is that tracking shots exist, that it's possible to track with a camera. Because the only thing that a movie can really be is an expression of yourself . . . Take the example of even a rotten, hack director. His films are dishonest and pretentious. Yet they're a perfect expression of what he is. Because he made them. And you see him through them. He's a false person."

And the young Italian director, Bernardo Bertolucci, says: "I am making always just one film. The filmmakers I love have made only one film. Godard started with *Breathless* and continued with the same film that proceeds along with his life. It's one film, even if it has many titles or many chapters. It's the same film and it walks along with him. To make film is a way of life. If we take out the title of the film and THE END and put the films all together, we will have the figure of one man, of an auteur, the life of an auteur, transferred in many characters naturally."

Some of the differences between the independents who can't get studio financing and those who can are due almost entirely to economics. McBride would work differently if he had a bigger budget, because he wants to make story films with a number of characters, sets, and situations. However, some filmmakers would make the same films, no matter what the budget. For example, Norman Mailer's filmmaking technique—multiple cameras shooting a scene without a script in which he is both director and star and host and general—is an improvisatory one which is an extension of his own temperament.

"The way I look at the movie business," says Mailer, "is that the commercial directors are mining one end of the tunnel and I'm mining the other. What they're saying is that I'm crazy and that I'm digging holes like an earthworm and I'm going to drown in my own stuff. And what I'm saying is I'm digging in from the other end and we're going to meet in the center of the tunnel and we're going to come in so close that we won't be an inch apart. Now, if not me, another. What I do know and they don't is that a movie can be made this way."

Mailer, like John Cassavetes and other independent filmmakers, is able to make his films his way by paying for them with his own money. And, as in the case of Cassavetes and Andy Warhol, Mailer is interested in filming his own scene—the friends and ideas that reflect facets of his own personality—so that his pictures become a kind of self-analysis.

Actually, distinctions between *Hollywood* and *underground* films are no longer really valid, except as a handy catchword. Kubrick's 2001 was an underground film; Cassavetes' home movie, *Faces*, became a Hollywood film. There are independent or personal directors and there are directors for hire. There are student filmmakers and there are home movie makers. Every independent film financed by the director is a home movie, whether it's made by Mailer, Warhol, McBride, or Cassavetes. There are only differences today in intentions, seriousness of purpose, and method of financing.

Making feature films had become a sort of religious sacrament available only to the initiates in Hollywood, especially since the era of the talkies. It was expensive and complicated and mysterious. In the early 1950s, Kubrick helped demystify the experience by making *Fear and Desire* outside the studios for $39,000. The audacity of his Promethean theft earned notoriety beyond what, he says, his film deserved. It was the novelty of his just going out and doing it that astonished everyone. He had shown that filmmaking was accessible to a young amateur from the Bronx—and, therefore, available to everyone who could also get financing from their family and friends.

The underground and a few aboveground independents continued with indifferent results to make films for the next decade. And out of that came some interesting films, like *The Little Fugitive, Shadows, The Brig, Nothing But a Man, Crazy Quilt*, and the documentaries of Lionel Rogosin, Shirley Clarke, the Maysles brothers, and D. A. Pennebaker. Showcases and money for new films were scarce.

Then several things happened toward the end of the 1960s. Film schools began to graduate hundreds of semiskilled filmmakers every year—virtually all of them automatically unemployable. And at the same time, the manufacture of high-quality portable equipment at moderate prices provided access to the tools of filmmaking for anyone seriously motivated to finance and shoot his own film.

The developments of the past few years are pointing to staggering conclusions. As film becomes a second language for the young and as the tools become even cheaper and current problems of distribution and exhibition are resolved, it will be possible to make commercially viable personal movies in the same way one writes a book or makes a painting. The proliferation of films is bound to affect the sensibilities of the public and the filmmaker alike.

It would give impetus to the emergence of an independent film movement unlike anything that has ever been conceived before. Up until now, if the filmmaking process can be compared to publishing books, it's as if a privileged class of literate and semiliterate editors had the power to limit production of new books to several hundred a year instead of several thousand.

Up until now, there hasn't been enough talent available to provide a steady supply of good new low-budget films upon which to build a viable and self-sustaining system of distribution and exhibition. The film school graduates, being prepared for jobs that don't exist, are certain to create their own.

The film school graduate—whose hero is Godard, because Godard has bent the French system to serve his needs—is faced with either going Hollywood and working as an employee, if he's asked, like Noel Black (*Pretty Poison*) or Francis Ford Coppola (*Finian's Rainbow*), and tunneling, perhaps, or maybe just getting deflowered. Or of staying a virgin, outside the system, embittered, making an occasional documentary or short.

Given an untenable situation, the economic structure will change. The independents have tried co-operatives—which are fairly successful in handling experimental shorts but have been ineffective in trying to market feature films. The newest development is the merger of publishing houses with small film distributors—like McGraw-Hill, which bought Pathé Contemporary—or for a company like Grove Press to start its own film division, buy up the archives of Cinema

xvi   INTRODUCTION

16, and make deals for distributing independent films (like *Beyond the Law* or *Warrendale*). Grove operates its own one hundred forty-five seat theater, the Evergreen, in Greenwich Village to make sure it has an outlet for its films.

There are perhaps a dozen other new firms—some with limited funds for making films—moving into this field of independent distribution. The market they all aim at first is the nation's university campuses, where interest in films is probably more intense than anywhere else. Reportedly, this is a lucrative market. Several thousand film societies—the bulk of them affiliated with the American Federation of Film Societies—are already a kind of concert circuit for one-night performances of classics and some new films. Potentially, they may be a profitable showcase system for medium-budgeted independent films. The distributors which use the college circuit include the Canyon Cinema Co-op in San Francisco, and the New Line Cinema, Janus Films, Grove Press, New York Review Presentations, Contemporary Films, and Paradigm Films—all in New York. Paradigm Films, an ex-subsidiary of a giant videotape company, is a prototype of the small, flexible outfit that plans to produce, buy, distribute, and show low-budget films in little theaters it hopes to buy in New York, San Francisco, Los Angeles, and Boston.

Changes in distribution are evolving to meet specific needs. But there is a technological revolution in the offing which is far more incredible. It's a total transformation of the process by which films will be seen. TV has already caused neighborhood theaters to be metamorphosed into supermarkets. But there is still enormous waste energy and expense involved in the logistics of getting films to their potential audience.

One of the first significant innovations will be in the UHF TV stations—mostly operated by universities—that will be a showcase for new filmmakers whose work may never be shown in theaters. And, most significant of all, there are systems such as EVR (Electronic Video Recording) which will make it possible for films to be recorded on the equivalent of the present tape recorder cartridge. They will be rented or sold at the local drug store or shipped through the mails. They will offer everything from *Citizen Kane* to a selection of Super 8 and 16-mm independent films. They will be played through our TV set, which eventually will have a huge wall screen. Presumably, the function of the critic will be comparable to what the LP music critic does now—to be an advisor on the best of the new tape and record products.

The technicians assure us this is all going to be happening in the 1970s. Movie theaters will probably continue to exist, serving social and psychological needs. They'll provide an excuse to dress up, get out of the house, mingle with people, possibly for the special effects of the feelies—utilizing electrical impulses transmitted through an armrest and enabling the moviegoer to be not only a voyeur, which we have already become, but, through the electrodes, a participant, plugged into the event itself. Musical and outdoor spectaculars will be shown in 3-D on cyclorama screens. And the drive-in theaters will continue to appeal to their patrons' special tastes.

The Motion Picture Association of America estimated that in 1968 there were 85,000 students in 205 colleges taking 3000 undergraduate and graduate film courses. Even if only a fraction of the courses involved actual film production, there was the likelihood that an audience was being prepared for these new personal films of the coming years. Over half the movie tickets sold today are bought by moviegoers between the ages of sixteen and twenty-five. They know what a director is, what he does, and what he's done.

Since the unions and studios have been unwilling or unable to initiate effective training programs, the film schools at American universities have tried to fill the gap. Instruction is uneven. Results are problematic. But enrollment has been increasing by about twenty per cent a year. One source suggests that the student who might have majored in English ten years ago with the vague expectation of becoming a writer or a teacher is majoring in film and going into secondary school education.

The state film schools of Poland, Czechoslovakia, Hungary, and Russia are superlative. There is nothing like them in the United States, in terms of the quality of instruction. The Lodz film school in Poland, for instance, has a five-year curriculum in which students learn every aspect of photography and directing and make a half dozen shorts. The Prague school is part of the university's fine arts program and students study the humanities as well as film technique.

There is some debate in this country about the value of film schools. Richard Lester, for example, thinks they are a waste of time. "Get out and work in a job for a year and earn money to buy yourself a camera and film and shoot your own film," he says. "Time is wasted in film school that should be spent making films." Roger Corman, who has helped finance the first films of several young directors, thinks that if he had gone to film school he would have saved a lot of time and bother in learning fundamentals.

Both Milos Forman, a graduate of the Czech film school, and Roman Polanski, who attended the Polish school, think that film school is a good idea—as long as one gets plenty of opportunity to make short films. Kubrick believes that film school is an alternative only if you can't raise money to make your own films. And Bernardo Bertolucci insists, "The only school for the cinema is to go to the cinema, and not to waste time studying theory in film school. The best school of cinema in the world is the Cinémathèque of Paris. And the best professor is Henri Langlois."

Everyone agrees that would-be directors must see as many films and expose as much footage as possible. Schools offer some opportunities for shooting shorts and documentaries. But the work usually has to be supplemented with outside projects to be meaningful. Some foundations and government agencies commission short films. One of the most respected of these is the United States Information Agency, whose films are only shown abroad—which does cause some ego problems.

The American Film Institute, created on June 5, 1967, is one major link between students, independent filmmakers, and Hollywood. With headquarters in Washington, D.C., AFI was funded with matching $1,300,000 grants by the National Council on the Arts, the Ford Foundation, and the Motion Picture Association of America. The AFI is the funnel through which most of the establishment's money is passed along to deserving filmmakers.

In the five programs involving filmmakers, the following grants were made in 1968: (1) twenty-two independent filmmakers received from $500 to $15,000 to help finance films ranging in length from five minutes to ninety minutes; (2) fifteen film students received from $500 to $2500 for film projects undertaken as part of university course work; (3) eight scholarships were awarded to outstanding film and television students for tuition and other expenses apart from specific film projects; (4) a total of eight interns between 1968–69 were assigned as part of a tutorial program to watch films being directed by men like Mike Nichols, Sam Peckinpah, Elia Kazan, and Arthur Penn, and (5) five screenwriting grants of $2000 each were awarded for the development of scripts that might be produced by the AFI on a budget of up to $400,000.

The feature film production program is being underwritten by fourteen film companies who will rotate as sponsor and distributor —with an option to turn down any script they feel is unsuitable. The National Association of Theater Owners has assured the AFI that any films it produces will be exhibited commercially. Eighteen months after the program was announced in May 1968, there had been about three hundred applications. None was accepted. Instead, the screenwriting grants were added to help support the filmmakers whose projects were being most seriously considered.

In 1969 the AFI planned to have started production on its first

feature film and to begin funding a number of films for television
with the aid of a $100,000 grant from the Corporation for Public
Broadcasting. And, in its most ambitious move, it was scheduled to
open the AFI Center for Advanced Studies at an old rehabilitated
mansion in Beverly Hills called Graystone. Frantisek Daniel, the
dean of the Czech film school, was enlisted to spend a year at the
new Center to help set up the program.

AFI Director George Stevens Jr. described the two-year Center
as a sort of conservatory where fifteen apprentices would progress
under the tutelage of a master while doing their work. People like
Hitchcock and Jean Renoir would participate in the tutorial program.

"The ideal," said Stevens, "is to create a situation where a person
can learn about the process of filmmaking, mature his thinking, and,
by experience with other artists, become more quickly a filmmaker.
I certainly don't think it's essential to becoming a filmmaker that
one has training. Yet, for an example of the effect of proper training,
just look at the filmmakers produced in the Czechoslovakian film
school."

In making its grants to students and independent filmmakers, the
AFI operates on the premise that the short film has been "a training
ground for feature filmmakers from Antonioni to Zinnemann." Says
Stevens, "You've got to practice someplace. You just can't come
full-blown and say: 'I'm a movie director.' Kubrick's two documentaries taught him enough to make a feature. *Fear and Desire*
might have fit into our short independent film program. Robert
Kramer (director of the New Left film *The Edge*) may come up
with *Fear and Desire* or better. We've given him $12,000. Truffaut,
Godard, Skolimowski, Polanski, Dick Lester, Lindsay Anderson, Milos Forman, they've all learned their craft by making short films
first. And they have material which is evidence they can complete
some work.

"The directors in the early days mostly started as cameramen
assistants and then started directing short films. Leo McCarey, Willie
Wyler, my father, and Frank Capra would make two short films
a week. Not one student film which they'd labor over for nine
months. They'd do it here today and then gone tomorrow. Zinnemann worked with Robert Flaherty and then went into the shorts
department as a director at M-G-M. So there was a system. And
there was a great deal of work going on which gave these people
practice. And the good ones emerged as important artists. Today
it's entirely different. There's never been anything like the student
film programs and the democratization of the utensils, the equipment

—the accessibility of the filmmaking process. Today you can get an 8-mm camera. People are making films when they're seven, ten, twelve, fourteen years old. So they're getting that sense of film grammar."

There is no one best way to learn the language of film. The backgrounds of sixteen representative directors who are making personal films in England, Europe, and the United States is a study in diversity. Kubrick was a still photographer for *Look* magazine. Lindsay Anderson was a film critic. Coppola was a film student, as were Forman, Polanski, and Jim McBride. Cassavetes is an actor. Arthur Penn was a TV director. Lester directed live TV and commercials. Warhol was a painter. Mailer is a novelist and para-journalist. Roger Corman had a degree in engineering, worked his way up within the studio system starting as a $32.50-a-week messenger boy. Nichols was a performer in a Chicago cabaret and a Broadway director. Robert Downey was a prep school dropout who wrote and acted in off Broadway plays and waited on tables. Brian De Palma was a science major at Columbia and started making shorts on his own. Bertolucci was a prize-winning poet.

Eight of these sixteen directors made their first feature film when they were in their twenties. And thirteen of them were under thirty-five. Of the three who were older, Penn left TV at thirty-six as dramatic anthology shows were on the wane, Anderson made *This Sporting Life* at thirty-nine after a career as a director of documentaries and shorts, and Mailer was forty-five and an established novelist when he got hooked on filmmaking.

Whatever their backgrounds or ages or credit rating, the personal filmmakers share at least one thing in common—an almost obsessional need to make films. Norman Mailer, after losing large investments in his first two films, was editing his third film when he asserted: "The point is not to make a living making films. The point is to participate in the experience, which is an extraordinary one . . . Moviemaking is like sex. You start doing it, and then you get interested in getting better at it."

PART ONE:
THE OUTSIDERS

BEYOND THE UNDERGROUND

JIM MCBRIDE

"A filmmaker uses people and
equipment as tools to make an
expression of himself."

*Jim McBride was twenty-five when he made the prize-winning fea-
ture film* David Holzman's Diary, *and two years later he still hadn't
been able to get it opened in a theater. Penniless, with two films
completed and unreleased, he confides: "I didn't know what the
hell I was doing." He feels defeated by existing systems of film
distribution and exhibition.*

*A film school graduate who discovered that his diploma was worth-
less, he got jobs afterwards "that I could have gotten just walking
in off the street, having absolutely no experience with film whatsoever."*

*As a frustrated outsider, McBride sees the commercial system of
production and distribution as an insuperable, anachronistic hierarchy placed between the filmmaker and his potential audience.
He suggests as an alternative an effectively administered filmmakers'
cooperative for feature films which would be a service owned by
the filmmakers themselves. And his ideal is a collaborative project
that offers a living wage and possible profit-sharing if the film is a
success.*

*Born September 1941 in New York, McBride, in his words, had
"a normal middle-class, half-Jewish, half-Irish upbringing. I went to
public schools and a private high school, Fieldston. Then I went
to Kenyon College. After two years of that, I spent my junior year
in Brazil on an exchange program. I spent those eight months in
Brazil just trying to escape getting educated. I saw a lot of movies
at fifteen cents apiece. I came back and finished up at NYU."*

*McBride belongs to the growing ranks of unemployed film school
graduates, though he is luckier than most—having made two features
so far.* David Holzman's Diary *was shot for $2500 in 16-mm black
and white, sound, runs seventy-four minutes and won prizes at Mannheim and Pesaro. It covers nine days in the life of an auto-voyeur
who is trying, in Godard's phrase, to discover truth at twenty-four
frames per second. He aims his trusty Eclair camera at himself, and
we can see him growing monomaniacal. He films his girl friend
while she is asleep and naked on his bed. She awakens and leaves
him. He films his acerbic friend, a pop artist, who wants to be left*

*alone, and chides: "Your life is a bad script." And, in accordance
with the Heisenberg principle of physics, he is unable to reflect his
reality because in the process of trying to measure it he deflects and
changes it.*

*His second film, My Girl Friend's Wedding, which may end up
being called Clarissa, was shot for Paradigm Films on a budget of
under $10,000 in sound and color on 16 mm. He describes the film
in the following interview, which took place in New York in March
1969. In the fall, McBride began work for an independent producer
on a $240,000 science fiction drama about the aftermath of a nuclear
war.*

FILMOGRAPHY:

DAVID HOLZMAN'S DIARY ('67)
MY GIRL FRIEND'S WEDDING ('69)

GELMIS: What led you into filmmaking?

McBRIDE: When I was studying English at NYU, I got interested in movies. At that time, NYU was one of the few universities in the country that had a film department. I majored in film, graduated, and had lousy jobs.

G: What kind of training did you have in film at NYU?

MCB: They had essentially two kinds of courses. They had pragmatic courses and bullshit courses. The bullshit courses were things like history of film, scriptwriting and theory of film editing, which were totally useless and were mostly taught by people who couldn't make it as filmmakers and had become teachers instead.

But they did have one practical course, a production course where you formed into groups of six people and each group made a ten-minute film. The process of how people were chosen to be director, editor, and so on was, in the worst sense, political. It depended on who the teacher liked. Most of the films were pretty lousy.

But you really experienced what it meant to make film, which is an extraordinary experience. That's how you learn. I was the editor, for no good reason. They had one production course during the school year and a concentrated one in the summer time. And that was the really good one. It was six weeks of intensive work, of just making movies.

The whole school was indoctrinated with a liberal, New York, social consciousness, documentary philosophy. Ultimately, that was a very powerful influence on the films that we made. I was there two years and I edited two films. One was about a community workshop on the Lower East Side that taught ghetto kids how to play steel drums. The other one was a parable about a carpenter who makes a cross for a church and has all sorts of unpleasant experiences in the process of delivering it to the church.

G: What do you believe now that is at odds with the training you got at the NYU film school?

MCB: I'd have to illustrate by telling you the things that weren't appreciated, that were looked down upon. Any kind of underground filmmaking was absolutely déclassé. Hollywood filmmaking of any kind was felt to be absolutely *not* where it's at. They felt it was impossible for art to come out of Hollywood. Certain kinds of foreign films were highly regarded. Certain kinds of classic American films—like *Citizen Kane*—were admired.

But most highly regarded were socially conscious documentaries. I don't put them down. But that's where *they* were at. Cinéma vérité was beginning to come into vogue at the time. And even that was looked down on. They put all sorts of sanctions against learning about what they felt were unacceptable film styles.

The best movie course that I can imagine would be one that let you see movies all the time. That's how you learn about movies. I had to get out of NYU before I started my film education. After I left, I used to see fifteen movies a week. At some point I had a revelation—that there were all sorts of other films and filmmaking than the kind I had been taught at NYU.

And I guess it was partly from reading *Cahiers du Cinéma* that I got interested in American movies again. I had been going to see mostly foreign movies up until then. I began to rediscover American movies.

So I had this revelation that everything I had learned before was useless. NYU had a narrow perspective in which they tried to define what it was about movies that made them different from all of the other art forms; what it had to offer that was unique. I don't share that view. Film is a terribly complex art form. It's complex because it has its roots in all the other arts, as well.

G: Is there an ideal film school?

MCB: The ideal film school would let you see every kind of movie there is—good, bad, Hollywood, underground, whatever—and let you make films, too.

G: Is there an alternative? Would you have done it differently, on the basis of what you know now?

MCB: There is an alternative that few people ever thought of then, I suppose. You don't need to go to film school to learn about movies. You just have to go to the movies as much as you can. Then you get yourself an 8-mm camera and you make movies. Lots of people are doing that. There are only two things you need, it seems to me, if you want to learn how to make films. You've got to see how other people have made them. And you need to handle the apparatus involved in the filmmaking process—a camera and a Movieola.

Every family has an 8-mm movie camera. Everybody makes home movies. Somebody is just going to see what it all means when he picks up the 8-mm movie camera to shoot his baby sister—and he may make a genius film. There are probably genius films all over the place.

I go to movies every chance I get. What interests me about movies is seeing them as expressions of a man's sensibilities, of seeing a person through his art. I don't particularly put too much value on learning technique. On learning the meaning of a tracking shot, for example. All you have to know is that tracking shots exist, that it's possible to track with a camera. Because the only thing that a movie can really be is an expression of yourself. If you have an idea of what you want to express, figuring out how to express it will come naturally to you.

If you feel strongly about that telephone, if it has some real meaning to you, you'll pick up your camera and you'll shoot the telephone. And somehow the way you frame it, and whether you move the camera or you don't move the camera, whether you zoom in or zoom out, how long the shot lasts, what else is in the shot, will just come, because that's the way you feel about the thing you want to film.

G: Do you believe that it's not necessary to know about exposures, lenses, composition, graphics, sound?

MCB: There's a difference between technique and technical things. You obviously have to know how to work a camera in order to expose your film. That you must learn, even if you teach yourself. In terms of aesthetic considerations like framing and camera movements, it's good to learn about them but they get you more screwed up than they help you.

Student films are just overwhelmed with technique. The camera flies all around the place. There's fancy cutting. All of it totally useless. It doesn't have anything to do with what the film is supposed to be about. People begin to feel that the thing about making good movies is to be flashy, to show technique. But that doesn't have anything to do with it, really.

If you shoot that telephone and you get your rushes back, you'll see whether that shot conveys to you what you felt about it in the first place. And if it doesn't, then you realize that you framed it wrong so you go back and reshoot it from a slightly different angle.

G: But doesn't personal expression have limitations? I can teach somebody how to use the alphabet and how to use my typewriter. Can you assume that everybody is a poet and has something to express that's worth listening to? By teaching somebody some of the technical things about the use of a camera and a movieola does it mean that you're going to get something on film worth expressing? Isn't it true that just a few people have anything interesting to say or an original way of saying it?

MC B: I don't know about that. I distinguish only between people who are *more*—or *less*—honest with themselves. I don't think that you can avoid expressing yourself through what you do. Take the example of even a rotten, hack director. His films are dishonest and pretentious. Yet they're a perfect expression of what he is. Because he made them. And you see him through them. He's a false person. If he were a more open and real person, more honest with himself, he would make good films instead of bad films. Because every person is unique, is interesting, has value.

I think that talented people are those who get closer to themselves somehow. They're able to be more direct and uncompromising. Some people are artists and some people aren't. It's not what's in their heads, but in their relation to themselves. It may be a terribly tortured, neurotic relationship, but the honesty comes through, somehow.

G: Is a bad film, therefore, simply one in which a director is kidding himself or is not able to know himself?

MC B: Yes, for me, that's absolutely the test.

G: When did you decide this is how you felt about films?

MC B: Yesterday.

G: How are you going to feel tomorrow?

MC B: Who knows?

G: What happened to you after you were graduated from the film school?

MC B: Nothing happened. There was absolutely no correlation between the education or the degree you got from film school and the real world outside. There had been the implication within the movie department that they had all kinds of great connections with the industry and everybody was going to get a job and go right to the top. It just wasn't true at that time, which was about seven years ago. It may be getting more flexible now.

But nobody in the industry in either New York or Hollywood had any interest at all in film students. They didn't feel that a student learned anything that would be of any value. So the first job that I got when I finished school was getting coffee for a man who was casting a picture and shooting screen tests and things like that. I worked with him for about two months at sixty dollars a week. The second and third jobs were as an apprentice editor with guys who made industrial films. They were all jobs that I could have gotten just walking in off the street, having absolutely no experience with film whatsoever.

A friend of mine, Chuck Hirsch, and I started showing films at an off Broadway theater called the Gate, once a week, on Monday nights when the theater was ordinarily closed. We ran a sort of film society, except that it was open to the public.

At that time in New York it was practically impossible to see any decent shorts. So we decided we'd show just shorts. We had about twelve weeks at the Gate and we showed all the shorts of directors who had gone on to make important feature films—people like Truffaut, Godard, Antonioni, Richardson, Anderson, Reisz, Resnais.

About ten or twenty years ago in Europe, short films were subsidized by the government, so it was a training ground for new filmmakers. Most of them went that route. I worked at the Gate for about six months until I fell into another job—this time as a fullfledged film editor for a house production unit of a gigantic real estate company that sold land in Florida.

During the year I was at this place, I learned a great deal, in a primitive way. They had a little bit of equipment, including a Bolex with a zoom lens. And there was a film in the back of my mind that I always wanted to make. It was a film about this man who makes a film about himself.

I used to borrow the company's camera on weekends and just sit at my window and film people going by. It was tentatively for my film. And it began to take shape. I didn't shoot very much, and I'd buy dated stock. And I was able to sneak the film in on our order forms, to get it developed for nothing. My boss was very nice about that.

I wasn't really very happy with the footage I had been shooting. A lot of it was shaky and overexposed. I didn't feel competent. As it began to take shape, I figured that I could rent a synchronized Auricon 16-mm camera, a tape recorder, and accessories for sixty dollars for a one-day rental on a Saturday and then get to keep the stuff over the weekend.

G: How did you teach yourself to use a camera?

MC B: I read everything. I went through the whole gamut of trying to educate myself, just as I had paid attention to all those useless courses at school. I was never terribly good at technical things. But

I knew somebody who knew somebody who was an assistant camera-man. He said he would shoot the film for me. Another friend of somebody's was an actor.

It all happened in this very haphazard way. We got together on one weekend and shot all the synched scenes. This was to be about fifty per cent of the film. And I imagined the film was to be about a half hour long. I did everything wrong. I didn't write dialogue. It wasn't at all what I thought I wanted. Half the film was dated stock and there were scratches all through it.

Yet there were still things in it that were salvageable. But I didn't have another sixty dollars to spend in doing it over again. Then I got fired from the editing job. All of a sudden, that was it for the film. But I had shot just about all that I needed to and I was beginning to edit it and do sound recording.

I packed all the footage up into a carton and put it in the trunk of my Volkswagen. And while I was looking around for an editing room I could use at night to finish the film, I left the carton in the car. A few days later I came back and it was all gone.

I had no way of going back to it. No job. No money. Nothing. But, shortly after, I began to work with a couple of guys who were a team. They were a cameraman-sound man team. They did a lot of documentary, hand-held, cinéma vérité kind of shooting for National Educational Television. I began to do editing work with them once in a while. They had some equipment. And one day Mike Wadley, who's a brilliant cameraman, said: "Why don't we do your movie?"

It was about eight months after the original fiasco when we actually started shooting the film again. I think it was April 1967. I found a new David Holzman, a friend of mine named Kit Carson, who seemed to be right for the part. I had a little money then because I'd been married a few months earlier and we'd gotten some presents. We decided to blow our savings, one thousand dollars.

We used a 16-mm Eclair camera with a 9.5 to 95 Mersault zoom lens, a Nagra tape recorder, a shotgun microphone, and one light. We spent some money in the rental of a cop's uniform. But the other costs were basically lab work and footage.

Over a period of three months, including one big four-day weekend when we shot all the footage in the apartment, we filmed *David Holzman's Diary*. Then, over another couple of months, I put it together in the evenings. When it was finished, I didn't know what to make of it. It was a pretty good approximation of what I wanted. But I had no idea of whether that was worth anything to anybody else at all.

What happened from then on is totally mysterious to me. The American representative of the Mannheim Film Festival had heard about the film. He called me to ask if I'd like to submit it. I sent it to Germany. A couple of weeks later the festival director wrote and sent me airplane tickets. So I went. And the film won the grand prize. It went on to a lot of film festivals and has gotten a lot of notoriety. But it's never been released commercially.

The film had cost twenty-five hundred. I didn't get any financing. It was all done on a principle of deficit financing that I didn't even know I was doing, until much later. I spent about a thousand dollars cash and I just didn't pay the rest of the bills. It turned out that the grand prize at Mannheim was twenty-five hundred. So I was able to pay off my debts and come out about even.

G: What has been your experience in trying to get *David Holzman's Diary* distributed?

MCB: I've been exhausted by the whole world of distribution, which is perfidious and corrupt. I didn't know what the hell I was doing. I made a deal with a French distributor and a British distributor, without a lawyer. So I ended up not getting any money at all from either of them. The film still hasn't been released. They're under no obligation to do anything with it, and I can't take it back and negotiate with somebody else.

Then I came back to the United States. I didn't know how you go about selling a film. I was approached by Grove Press. They said they'd like to distribute the film. But we couldn't get together. They wanted to put it directly on college campuses and I wanted a theatrical opening. That took a few months of dickering, before I finally decided not to go through with it.

Next I went to Leacock-Pennebaker, who had expressed interest in the film. I signed a contract with them very quickly. They offered to blow up the film to 35 mm. They offered to give it a New York theatrical opening and to give me a small advance. For three months I sat around doing nothing. They didn't give me an advance. They didn't blow up the film. We fought and finally agreed to dissolve the contract.

Then I went to Paradigm Films, which used to belong to my friends Mike Wadley and John Binder, and is now a subsidiary of a big videotape company. We're still working out details of how to distribute the film.

I've spent a year and a half of my life *not* making movies but just trying to get *David Holzman's Diary* shown. I was twenty-five when I made it. I'm twenty-seven now. It hasn't done me any good. I haven't made a penny out of it. And I hate this whole business of distribution and exhibition. It's awful. It's a disgusting business. And I don't want to have anything to do with it any more. I don't see why anybody should.

Bruce Connor, for instance, who to me is one of the country's really fine filmmakers, has made only ten short films in the past ten years. They're all distributed through the Film-Makers' Cooperative in New York. He makes about three thousand dollars a year out of it. He has to work as a salesman in a head shop in order to make a living.

But at least there's a direct relationship between him and the people in film societies and campuses who see his films. And they're growing in numbers, as he gets more and more exposure. Unlike the perverted commercial distribution system, the Co-op people who distribute those films are only there to provide a service. The Film-Makers' Cooperative is just that, it's a cooperative, a service owned by the filmmakers themselves.

The Film-Makers' Distribution Center, an adjunct of the Co-op which distributes feature films and tries to get them into theaters, is hopelessly inefficient. But it's just a question of the people involved. The system is right in a way that the commercial system is wrong. The problem with it is that it doesn't provide you with a way of continuing to make films, unless you make them very, very cheaply.

If you can make a thousand dollars a year from your films and it only costs you a thousand dollars a year to make them, that's okay. But it would be better if you could make a living from them as well. I would prefer to make films that way. My problem is that the kinds of films I seem to want to make are very ambitious, expensive films. In a very simple, literal way, I want to make long films with synched sound that tell stories. That means you can't go out and make them in 8 mm or with a 16-mm Bolex.

G: How did you happen to decide on a diary form for your first film?

MCB: It's a very mysterious process, how you get a film. It starts out for me as just a need to make a film. And then it comes to images, obsessive images. And because I was so involved in movies, there was always in my mind an image of a guy with a camera on his shoulder filming himself in a mirror. And that image seemed terribly profound to me. I'm not sure I could explain why.

At the same time, I was also very interested in banality—the banal facts of a person's daily life. Another thing that obsessed me was the oppressiveness of the New York environment and how it affects the way you view the world, how it forces you to be what you are. I was living in similar circumstances as David Holzman's, and I suppose the film was partly about me.

But it's just those random images and ideas and obsessions that suddenly come together. If you take the image of a guy filming himself in a mirror and you put that together with the other elements that I mentioned, you come up with a diary as a logical form.

This particular film had about a three-year gestation process, from the time the original idea occurred to me until the film was made. In all that time I was thinking about it. Images were coming to me and it was like fitting a puzzle together. I think you discover a film. There's something there in the original intention, the original idea. Then apparently irrelevant things come to you from somewhere else, and all of a sudden you discover they all fit in.

G: Do you write these ideas and images down as they come to you, or do you write down dialogue as it occurs to you?

MCB: The second time around I wrote ten pages, breaking it down into scenes in which I described what happens. Sometimes I wrote some of the monologues. But it was never intended to be spoken. It was intended to be a direction the language would take.

The way it actually happened was that Kit became very absorbed in the idea and really understood it very well. So we became collaborators. I didn't know it at the time, but he had been an actor and had abandoned it.

He and I spent a week together before the shooting. We sat down in a room with a tape recorder—and I think this is the way Brian (De Palma) got the idea to do *Greetings*. I would say, "This is what happens in this scene. This is what I want you to say." As you know, most of the film's dialogue is in direct confrontation with the camera.

So I would tell him what I wanted and he would do it. He'd put it in his own words and throw in new things of his own. Then we'd listen to the tape together and I'd tell him: "I don't like this. You missed this. I've got an idea; put this in." He would do it again and together we refined each scene. We didn't transcribe it. We just listened to it, again and again, until we both had a fairly clear idea of what was going to happen when we were actually pointing the camera at him.

It never got down to a word by word situation. And when we started shooting it was always better than it had been in the taping sessions. He always threw in a little zinger for me that he hadn't told me about. Kit's great. We only did, at the most, two takes of any scene. As far as the camerawork is concerned, I had an absolutely clear and vivid idea of exactly what I wanted.

G: Do you plan to use that system of creating dialogue and working with actors in other movies?

MC B: I don't know. That's the way I would like to work. I don't believe in *actors*. The kind of people I want in my films are real people who are at ease in front of a camera, and who can project themselves into a role. Maybe that's what an actor is. But I don't think that people who've gone to acting school for three years are any safer or better to use than people off the street.

I'm kind of innocent about this whole business. But the way I imagine myself working is sort of typecasting, finding people who really fit the character. And from that point on it becomes a collaborative process.

G: What is the role of the director, then, if the cameraman is doing the shooting and the actor is creating his own dialogue?

MC B: Traditionally, the director is the guy who tells the cameraman where to put the camera and tells the actors how to say their lines. But that's not what I am. I just don't think that that means anything —to be a "director." I prefer to think of myself as a "filmmaker"—as someone who uses people and equipment as tools to make an expression of himself. You're using all these disparate elements that go into making a movie the way a painter uses his brush and his colors.

Warhol, for example, is a consummate artist. Yet sometimes he's not even in the room where his films are being made. But they're *his* films. And maybe all a director is is someone who chooses people, chooses all these elements and throws them together. I assure you that Mailer's new film, *Maidstone*—which had ten thousand people in it and was shot on a wild orgiastic weekend with twenty cameras and a loose improvised situation—I assure you that it's going to be the epitome of the personal film. It will be a perfect expression of Mailer's sensibilities.

G: How do you feel about spending other people's money on personal films?

MC B: I don't think I would ever ask somebody to give me money to make a film unless I really believed that he could get that money back. Maybe it's just that I don't feel that confident in myself, that everything I do is *de facto* valuable.

I'll give you an example. There's a film that I've been wanting to do for about a year and a half. This is the film that the American Film Institute is interested in. It's a very ambitious film, compared to *David Holzman's Diary*. It has a pretty big cast. It has sets. It has

animals. It's epic in scope and is in color. It'll be hard to make and
it'll cost a lot of money. I know I can make that film for either
$120,000 or $200,000 or $400,000. The AFI wants me to make it for
$400,000. And I feel very chary about that. The reason they want it
made for $400,000 is that they've got all sorts of hook-ups with the
major studios. And they feel they've got to do it with union crews
and in a very conventional manner, in production terms.

But I don't know. The way it works in the American film industry is that a film costs X amount of dollars. Before there's any
profit, it has to make back two and a half times that much. It would
mean that if I made this film for $400,000, it would have to make
$1,000,000 before any money was coming back to the people who
financed it. Well, I don't know whether this film could make a million dollars. I think it could make a half million. We could make
it for $200,000, and that would be fine. But I feel funny about making
it for $400,000.

This is all beside the fact that I don't even like working in so
conventional a production system. But whenever you get to talking
about the problems of making films, it always comes back to this
system—which is so totally outrageous. The way people get paid in the
movie business is just criminal. If I make this film, I'm going to
make about $20,000 salary. I don't deserve that. I would be much
happier making $150 a week over the course of a year, as a regular
wage, and be able to make the films that I want to make. Rather
than wait six months and then make $1,000,000 on one film. That's
all a lot of crap to me. I just want enough money to live on.

G: That sounds like the Czech state studio system. You're on a
retainer all year, enough to survive, and when you start work on a
film you get more money for the duration of the production.

MCB: I don't know much about the Czech system. But I know a
little bit about the Yugoslav system, which sounds more or less similar. One of the things that came out of that Mannheim Festival
was that I got an offer to make this science fiction film—that the
AFI may do—in Yugoslavia. I went there in June of 1968 to talk
about it. The whole thing fell through. But it could have been made
there for $120,000. The same film that's going to cost $400,000 here.

The Yugoslavs operate in the way you described, with retainers
and then higher fees when they're working. And the way they often
do it with films that are called "artistic endeavors" is that it becomes
a kind of cooperative venture. The whole crew gets less than half
salary. When the film is released and makes money, they get their
full salary out of the excess returns and they each get a percentage of

the film. That seems to me like a much more realistic way to make films than we have here.

G: What kind of script do you have right now for the AFI?

MCB: It's not a shooting script. I wrote it with a friend of mine. It describes what happens, has dialogue, and is broken down into sequences. It's about eighty pages and doesn't have any camera directions.

G: That doesn't sound like the method you were describing as your ideal before.

MCB: I don't want to get too rigid about method. This is a film that involves great numbers of people. There's a long shooting schedule. And it's necessarily a more formal way of making a film, just by virtue of what the film is itself. I wrote the script in order to get money to make the film. I probably won't even use the script as it is now, when I make it myself—if I do make it.

There's another thing. You also write a script just to facilitate the pragmatic problem of getting this whole machine of twenty people and all kinds of equipment to function smoothly and together. You need a basis for communication. And that's what the script is.

G: Is one of the problems in making a film like *David Holzman's Diary* that the young, inexperienced filmmaker doesn't know enough to get legal releases for people and songs and places they're shooting?

MCB: Yes. It's a real problem. Everything I've done has been wrong—in economic terms, in legal terms. I don't know what the hell I'm doing. And I'm sure that I wouldn't be in such a screwed-up situation today if I had known about all these peripheral elements of the movie business. Nobody got paid for acting in the film. We had an understanding that if it made any money we would share in the profits. But when our actress heard it had won at Mannheim she sent a lawyer to see me and I'm being sued, though the film still hasn't earned a cent.

G: How much of the film was inspired by your own feelings at that time?

MCB: I guess I was very much like David Holzman about a year before I made the film, which is what got me thinking about his obsession in the first place. But one of the problems of making films is that there's such a distance between the impulse and the act. It probably would have been a truer film if I'd been able to make it right away.

I'm really beginning to worry that the new film I want to do is just getting away from me, that I won't know how to do it when the time comes. The film is about something I was concerned with a year and a half ago. Not now.

G: Why did you make *My Girl Friend's Wedding?*

MCB: It came about because I'd been dying to make a film. I hadn't made a film in a year. I'd been trying unsuccessfully to figure out a way to make the science fiction film. And I'd met this girl and fallen in love with her and was going through a very chaotic time in my life. I'd broken up with my wife. My whole life was changing.

I not only fell in love with Clarissa, but I thought she was one of the most extraordinary people I'd ever met. Coincidentally, it was just at that time I was making my deal with Paradigm for them to distribute *David Holzman's Diary*. And something interesting was happening in Clarissa's life.

She was an English girl who came here and decided she wanted to stay. She figured out that the only way she could stay was to get married to an American. This was right around the time that she and I were falling in love. She was finding herself a husband—who is a Yippie, an activist, who was delighted with the opportunity to do something disrespectful to society.

None of us were really into the idea of marriage, anyway. As an institution, it had lost all meaning for me a long time before that. It never had any meaning for Clarissa. She had never been married. She had two illegitimate children.

So here we were. We were falling in love. She was living with me. And all this time she was planning to get married to someone else. She couldn't marry me. I was already married. Everybody kept saying, "That's a movie. You've got to make a movie about yourselves."

In point of fact, I'd wanted to make a movie about her from the moment I met her. I wanted to make that kind of personal movie, in any case. I just didn't have the wherewithal to do it. I couldn't go to somebody and say, "Look, give me some money, I want to make a movie about my girl friend." But I could go to somebody and say: "Here's this peculiar situation. Let's make a movie about it. I promise you it'll be cheap to make." My idea was to make it all in one day, the day of her wedding. So that it would be very inexpensive to shoot. And that's what we did.

The film is in color, runs about an hour, and is in four sections. The first section takes place in the morning at our apartment. It's just a kind of a long interview in which Clarissa talks about herself. The second section is the wedding ceremony at the Municipal Building, and the lunch we had together—she and I and her husband.

The third section is very short and it takes place at an abortive wedding party that we were having that night up at our place, where a few friends came over. It turned out to be really a drag. The final section is four or five days later, when Clarissa and I took off together by car for the San Francisco Film Festival. And it's just a home movie of our trip as we cross America by car—in three minutes and forty-eight seconds.

G: How have you been supporting yourself?

MCB: I haven't. In 1967, I made $5000. Of that, $2500 was the prize from the Mannheim Festival. The other $2500 was from jobs I picked up. In 1968, I made about $4000. Of that, the AFI gave me a $2000 writing grant to develop the film script. And I got $1500 to cut *My Girl Friend's Wedding*. Clarissa is working as a waitress. She makes sixty dollars a week. I have no money.

G: You've made two films so far, neither of which has been shown in theaters, and you've already got a reputation as a director. Has Hollywood approached you yet?

MCB: Yes, very recently. A few agents got interested. Prints of *David Holzman's Diary* have been shown around. Everybody's looking for young talented directors. But what they all do is: they'll take you, as a young talented director, and take a young talented writer, and a young talented producer and they'll give you a young talented property about young talented people and they'll put you all together and you'll make a young talented film.

So they've called me up and said, "We're interested in you." And I say, "Well, I'm interested in doing this movie. I'll send you a script." And they say, "Well, we've got a famous book," or something like that. So I say, "Forget it."

I'm just not that hard up for work.

BRIAN DE PALMA

"With rare exceptions, the studios
are only interested in filmmakers
who've established track records."

Greetings was one of the most celebrated successes among independent films in 1968–69. The film was shot in two weeks at a cost of $43,100. The distributor has projected a million-dollar gross. And the film's producer and director, both in their twenties, suddenly had money for two more films thrust upon them.

Brian De Palma, the director of Greetings, was born in Philadelphia in September 1940 and majored in science at Columbia University. His first feature, The Wedding Party, a collaborative experiment, was shot in 1964 but did not get a theatrical release until 1969—after the success of Greetings. His second feature, Murder à la Mod, had opened at a revival house in Greenwich Village and died a quiet death after receiving mixed notices.

Charles Hirsch, De Palma's producer and partner, was born in New York December 1942. He attended Penn State, made a couple of shorts, but decided he was no director.

The following interview was held in Manhattan last spring after the first day of shooting on their new film, which was untitled and was being referred to only as Son of Greetings. To make it, they had twice their previous budget ($95,000) and double the shooting time (a month). And, for the summer, they were planning to make a thriller with about a $400,000 budget.

Greetings was an episodic topical satire about evading the draft, computer dating, voyeurism as a life style, and the conspiracy theory of President Kennedy's assassination. Unlike the competition—films about youth by patronizing middle-aged producers—Greetings displayed an understanding of the sensibilities of its heroes that made it popular with draft-age audiences.

Hirsch and De Palma are friends of independent filmmaker Jim McBride. De Palma borrowed from McBride his technique of tape-recording the sessions in which the actors create their own dialogue in rehearsals. And he planned to use in his new film a segment about a housewife filming her memoirs, which he derived from McBride's David Holzman's Diary.

FILMOGRAPHY:

ICARUS (Short: '60)
660124, THE STORY OF AN IBM CARD (Short: '61)
WOTAN'S WAKE (Short: '62)
THE WEDDING PARTY (Shot in '64, edited through '66)
THE RESPONSIVE EYE (Documentary: '66)
MURDER À LA MOD ('67)
GREETINGS ('68)
SON OF GREETINGS ('69)
DIONYSIUS (Cinéma vérité collaboration of a performance of *Dionysus in '69*: '69)

GELMIS: How did you each get involved in making films?

HIRSCH: When I got out of college, Jim McBride and I founded the Huntington Hartford film center at the Gallery of Modern Art. We were there for six months and then got fired because we didn't make any money. After that, I ran the Garrick Cinema, a revival house, for about a year and a half. I was the manager and the booker. And then I made two disastrous shorts. I wrote and produced and directed them. They're both in my closet now, and that's where they belong. Then in January of 1967 I went to Universal Pictures as Director of New Talent. I was Director of New Talent because I knew more young filmmakers around than anyone else.

G: Who did you convince of that?

H: A guy who was head of publicity and who is now the Director of New Talent. I met him at a party. Anyway, at Universal, the idea was to start a short film program to subsidize young filmmakers, have them make shorts, and if the shorts were good, make features. I found seven or eight guys immediately. But it was too fast for the studio. Nothing happened. I was constantly stalled. And there were also a lot of ego problems involved.

One day I was just looking around desperately, trying to get something going. And I discovered that Brian had done two features. Brian and I met and became friendly and started writing things together, on company time and money. He got paid for one treatment they were going to do—and it's still very good, if you know anybody who wants to make a film about a mass murderer.

What finally happened was he said, "Get out from behind your desk. Let's go make a movie." I kept saying no. But I had a vacation coming up by March of 1968. So we did all the pre-production work on our film, and then we shot it during my vacation.

G: What was your background, Brian?

DE PALMA: I started making movies when I was at Columbia University as a sophomore. I was with the Columbia Players, and I had a background in photography. I was obsessed with the idea of directing the Players. But they wouldn't let undergraduates direct them, so I was frustrated. I figured I'd go out and direct movies instead.

I bought a Bolex 16-mm movie camera second hand for about $150. I hocked everything I had and used my allowance over a period of a year and a half to finance a long, forty-minute short called *Icarus*. It was pretentious and disastrous. But it was a beginning.

Then I made another film called *660124, The Story of an IBM Card,* which was pretentious but a little better, technically. Then I finally made a short called *Wotan's Wake,* which won a lot of prizes. It won the Rosenthal Award, and all the awards that were available to short films in 1962–63.

G: What practical good did winning the awards do?

DE P: Not much good. You think, wow, terrific, the world's really ready for you. But you find you haven't gotten anywhere. The third short did go into distribution, through Canyon Cinema, and I got $1000 from the Rosenthal Award.

By then I was going to Sarah Lawrence College on an MCA writing fellowship. And I got involved in making movies. I collaborated with a teacher and a very wealthy girl, who put up $100,000, and together we created a 35-mm black and white feature called *The Wedding Party.*

I wound up producing and directing and editing. I went out on location without a production manager. So I ended up waking everybody in the morning, and getting the guy who got drunk out of jail. Consequently, the weaknesses of the movie are due in part to my not having worked things out very well in advance. I'm not a very good producer.

After we made *The Wedding Party,* we tried to get a distributor interested. We had about eight hundred screenings and people saying, "Well, it's interesting, but . . ." and it went on and on and on. Because the film wasn't strong enough. So we were stuck. Nobody wanted to show it. We're finally opening it now ourselves, since the success of *Greetings.*

Then I started to make documentaries. I made one with another guy in England, and one for the Treasury Department, and then we made one about the Op Art opening at the Museum of Modern Art called *The Responsive Eye,* which is very good and very successful. It's distributed by Pathé Contemporary and makes lots of money. I shot it in four hours, with synched sound. I had two other guys shooting people's reactions to the paintings, and the paintings themselves.

Through the company that we formed, we made enough money from the Treasury movie to go on and make my second feature, *Murder à la Mod.* It was a sophisticated thriller patterned after *Pyscho.* I'm very turned on to Hitchcock and I like that kind of filmmaking, putting all those little pieces of film together.

Murder à la Mod was a film I did completely. It has many weaknesses and strengths. It's both good and bad. The only thing you learn about making features is that you've got to keep doing it and get over those weaknesses. We couldn't get a distributor for that movie, either. We opened it at the Gate Theater in the East Village. The *Times* gave it a nice review. But it died. That was the end of *Murder à la Mod*.

G: How did you talk people into financing *Greetings?*

H: *Greetings* was just an idea. On my part, I was very much influenced by Godard's *Masculin Feminin*. The idea of a kid and contemporary problems. So Brian and I wrote an outline together which evolved into *Greetings*. While we were in pre-production, I was raising money. And I kept on raising money right through the production, whenever Brian said we needed more to film a scene.

What made it possible was my having worked at Universal Pictures. People extend you a lot of credit, because they think that you're the fair-haired young boy at Universal and that they're going to get all of MCA's business. Therefore, they'd better be nice to you. And you don't tell them they're wrong.

So I got $20,000 of credit extended to me at the lab—which is unheard of—for $1000 cash. Then, after an unsuccessful 16-mm version of the film had been shot and abandoned, we started again in 35 mm. It's easier to use 35 mm, because there's only one kind of film—color. Shooting in 35 mm was more theatrical. We only shot three to one, which is unusual. Ordinarily, as in this movie we're shooting now, it's more like six feet of film shot to every foot of film that appears in the final print.

In raising the money, of course I hit my parents. I got a couple of thousand from them. Then I hit myself. I had a Bolex. I sold it. And I sold some stock. So I got another $1500 that way. And then I got two investors for the film, when I thought it was going to be a cheap $20,000 16-mm film. I raised $7000—$5000 from one and $2000 from the other—and gave them large percentages of the film. I hadn't given percentages to myself or my parents. That was just: "Hey, Ma, give me a thousand bucks." But with these bigger investors, I had to be very businesslike. So I convinced them that the film was going to make money. And I didn't even believe it myself at that time.

Greetings was shot for under $15,000 cash and the rest was all deferred. The total cost of the film was $43,100, which includes about $4000 of mistakes made when we started in 16 mm, rentals, and other things. I paid out very little money. I gave away twenty-eight per cent of what's called the producer's share of the profits. Brian and I are taking out a chunk apiece, first. A fair one. But after that, whatever comes in, thirty per cent goes to the two major investors and twenty-eight per cent goes to the cast and crew.

G: What made you switch from 16 mm to 35 mm?

DE P: Two problems. One, the fact that the commercial labs have the attitude about 16 mm that it's for newsreels and junk. That's why our first version in 16 mm was badly scratched—because they just don't take that much care with it. The other reason was that I felt that the weakest part about the film was the way it looked. The performances and the ideas were good. But it looked terrible. We had shot about a week's work, an immense amount of footage—I'd been shooting four and five scenes a day. And it would have meant going back to reshoot it.

So Chuck was already $4000 in debt with this useless footage. And I was saying, "The only thing we can do is go forward and shoot in 35 mm." The fact he did it still amazes me. He was really scared. And so was I.

H: Once you get into debt past a couple of hundred dollars you become a big shot. Technically, *Greetings* is doing very well and has already taken in $130,000 in New York alone. But I'm still $31,000 in debt on it. Now I don't have to worry too much about it, because it looks like I'm going to get it back. But when I went into debt, it was weird. I had a lot of status. People thought, "That Chuck, he owes thirty grand. He's a big deal all right." So what happens is that once you're in debt past a certain point it all becomes unreal and you don't worry about it any more.

G: What sort of preparations were involved in writing and making *Greetings?*

H: It works this way. We start on a general theme. And we get a broad idea. Then we put in all the incidents. Brian puts in most of them. And then I say, "This has to go here, this has to go there." We both like to screw girls, so the girl-chasing part of the three guys' obsession in *Greetings* was easy enough. And I'm a bit of a voyeur. But Brian's the real voyeur—so that element was Brian's contribution. And he's a bit of a Kennedy conspiracy buff. But I'm the nut. So we put those two things in. And then I give an order to it. I say, "Here's a beginning and a middle and an end," and I give it to Brian. Then Brian, when he rehearses with the cast, develops the dialogue.

G: Would you describe the process?

DE P: It's one way to make movies, hardly the only way. But for this kind of situation, where we deal with basically political material, it's all in the casting. If you cast the right people, it's hard to go wrong. I try to use very real people. Like in this new film we're doing, we have a black militant. Not an actor. But a young kid who's radical and who's not play-acting. So once you get the people who really know the material and feel very strongly about it, they can work up scenes like nothing you've ever done.

I constantly shape that material. We tape-record the rehearsals when the actors are working out the dialogue in the scenes. Then we make a transcript. Then I constantly move the material around, shaping it, compressing it, putting in lines that I think are good to point up the scenes. Very seldom do I ever let an actor learn a script, learn the lines. For this movie we're doing now, I'm the only one who has a script. I'm the only one who knows how all the parts and dialogue and scenes fit together.

When you have a script prepared in a conventional way it tends to be organized along a certain set fashion, which looks great on paper. Then you give it back to the actors. And it has an arbitrary shape. I prefer spontaneous confusion which has a central impetus carrying it.

The thing that we do, that others seldom do, is to rehearse our actors intensely. For this new movie, we've been rehearsing nearly eight weeks. They know the shape of the scene. Once I've got that in my head, what the material is, then I go home and think out formal ideas of how I'm going to shoot the material. When the actors get there, I just run them through it a couple of times and then go.

Most of the time I get things on one take. If you have the right elements, and they've built up their own material and you get them on camera and work them up to the right degree, they can carry it right through. It's like they've been through that path and they know where they're going.

G: Where did you get the three lead actors in *Greetings?*

DE P: The assassination buff was a sophomore at Columbia. He handled most of the intellectual material. He's a very bright guy. Most actors aren't that sharp. I have to have actors who can really think on their feet. Usually, since they make up their own material, it has to be very close to them. Like the painter in the zoo who's talking about his "blow up" paintings, he's a real artist. And the guy at the party coming back from Vietnam and talking about his experiences. He was a real GI.

What you have to understand is that I don't write lines for anyone. They create their own material. Of course we create the situations.

But they're cast so close to type that our character who plays an intellectual *is* an intellectual and does have strong feelings about the assassination of President Kennedy. And *all* those guys *are* afraid of being drafted.

Every time we went down to Whitehall Street everybody was scared stiff because next week *he* was going to go down for real, or he had just come back from taking his physical the previous week. All the problems were very close to the cast and the crew. There's nothing in that material that had to be interjected.

G: Those were location shots of the front steps of the Whitehall draft induction center?

DE P: Yes. All the guys standing on the steps the first time you see the place are the whole crew of *Greetings*. We told anybody who asked what we were doing there that we were shooting a documentary about GIs.

G: Where did you get the crew? It was a non-union picture, wasn't it?

DE P: It certainly was. We had a crew of eight, made up of friends and relatives and students from NYU—anyone who wanted the chance to work on a feature film for fifty dollars or a half per cent interest. It took us two weeks to shoot.

There wasn't much material to edit, really, in *Greetings*. It wasn't very interesting to put together. We shot in four-minute takes, mostly. So it was just a matter of stringing together a series of episodes.

G: What was your reason for shooting in complete four-minute takes?

DE P: When you've got to get enough footage for a ninety-minute film and have so little time in which to do it you have to conceive things in very large chunks. So most of the scenes were shot in planes, where two things are going on and playing against each other constantly.

I don't usually make shots unless there's some reason for them. I'm a very strong believer in the fact that the camera always has to reflect the content. I'm very conscious of the attitude of the camera toward the material, always. Godard was into that nearly ten years ago, of course. But we're just getting into it now, and maybe even more intensely.

Every shot should have a justification, a justification relative to the material. For instance, take the scene where the guy is tracing the course of the assassination bullet on the naked girl and the camera is overhead. The strength of that is the fact that you get used to that position—overhead and looking down on them. When he turns around, it's suddenly a shock. Because you never thought that he would look up. He might have been expected to look left or right. But having him turn all the way around and look up at us gave the scene enough structural interest to help me get away with a four-minute take.

Plus the fact you've got a nude girl on the bed anyway, so people will sit there and watch that while he's drawing the angles of entry of the bullet on her back. So that entire action is holding the shot as a whole together. Yet *Greetings* is long and talky. It bothers me. I like films that use cuts to build suspense. There's not much of that in *Greetings*. But that's something we didn't anticipate when we started.

G: Where did you learn the technical aspects of filmmaking?

DE P: I have a very good scientific background. I used to build computers in high school. I know all about sound, optics, and cameras. I never considered myself an artist. I was going to be a physicist. I did all the work on my shorts, all the shooting, all the cutting, put all the sound in.

G: Who are the influences on you as a filmmaker?

DE P: Godard's a terrific influence, of course. If I could be the American Godard, that would be great. I think there are more interesting social and political things going on here in the United States than in France. And if we can have some kind of sounding board through movies, if Chuck and I could develop that material and evolve a structure and a style for it, that's the millennium.

G: Why doesn't anything ever come out of the young talent programs the studios periodically inaugurate?

DE P: With rare exceptions, the studios are only interested in filmmakers who've established track records. I know every up and coming young director there is in this town. The studios do too. There are at least a half dozen young talents who've already shown they know how to make films but couldn't convince a studio to finance or distribute a project. They weren't interested in me until they saw the grosses for *Greetings*, which Universal had refused to handle when we first offered it to them. Nobody takes a chance on you until you've got a film that's earned some money, so you've got to raise the money for that first film yourself.

G: How did you finally get a distributor for *Greetings*?

H: We were getting pretty desperate and even thinking of opening it at Jonas Mekas' basement (the New York Filmmakers' Cinémathèque). Someone knew the son of the guy who runs Sigma III, and we invited him to see the film. He saw it and made an offer. At that point, we thought: "My God, an offer." So we accepted. And it was a big mistake. Because there aren't many guys whose first independent film is successful. But of those guys, nearly all of them make bad distribution deals. They're as innocent as some foreign directors. For instance, *Dear John* was sold in the U.S. for $30,000 and made millions. *A Man and a Woman* was sold for $40,000 and made $8,000,000. So we've joined the ranks of successful filmmakers who dealt themselves out of the major share of the profits of their film. If *Greetings* makes a fortune, Sigma III is going to get nearly eighty per cent of all the profits. I call that giving it away.

G: How has the success of *Greetings* affected your position as filmmakers?

H: Marty Ransohoff, who owns Filmways, the parent company of Sigma III, saw *Greetings* and flipped. He offered us a two-picture deal. We wanted to buy a property. And he said, "Okay, what else do you want to do?" We had this idea for *Son of Greetings*, the as-yet-untitled picture we're doing now. We really wanted to do it. But I didn't feel like going around and raising money again. And I didn't feel like doing it on a shoestring.

So we gave him a twenty-page treatment—which we've already made major changes in—and he gave us $95,000 under the table to go out and make a non-union movie in New York. The deal we have for the second picture is a big one. He said $300,000 and we said $600,000. So we'll compromise. And that's for this summer, or whenever we can get to it.

He wants an option on our services. But we don't want to give him an option. Because it's very possible that not only will Brian and I become wealthy young men as a result of this picture that we're making now and the one we'll make this summer, but that we'll be in a position where it will be more advantageous not to belong to Filmways. In the meantime, so far as I'm concerned, we have a great deal.

G: What is your relationship with the unions on the new film?

DE P: The unions say you can't make a non-union picture. So we work undercover. There's been absolute secrecy in the making of this new movie. No publicity at all, because of how the actors' union almost wrecked Bob Downey's picture *Putney Swope* by scaring off his leading actor.

We hate the pressure of being forced into a bigger budget for the wrong reasons. For this kind of material, we've got to keep down the budget. I don't want to be smart-assed about the unions. But why should I be spending all my money on unions when I'd rather put it into the talent and the other areas like that?

G: Are there enough technicians and actors around to work outside the unions with you?

DE P: Sure. Actors prefer our kind of movie. We give them a chance to do their own thing. And there's another aspect to our kind of production. It's an entity. There's a strong solidarity of purpose. We're all in it together the whole time. There isn't any of the big-budget operation, where some people fly in for four days' work and then fly out.

We can't just hire technicians. Suppose I had a union crew here. All those guys are four hundred years old. I would probably have very little rapport with them on any level. You know, "We come, we do our job, we leave as soon as possible." There can't be that kind of feeling on a movie like this. Everybody's committed, politically, because they like the material, in all ways.

There's virtually no problem with amateurs not being serious enough to keep showing up for work. The fact is, for this kind of movie, kids can handle it. Kids can make features. Kids can do these things. We don't need all this union nonsense. You're looking for content and style. You don't need heavy equipment. I admit our sound isn't going to be perfect, because it's not shot in a studio. But that seems to me less important than the kind of freedom and flexibility in space and time you can have by shooting films this way.

G: What is it that everybody is so committed to in your new film?

DE P: This film is much more radical than *Greetings*. It deals with the obscenity of the white middle class. And we are white middle class, Chuck and I and everybody we know. So we're making a movie about the white middle class. And we're using the blacks to reflect the white culture. Because the blacks stand outside the system and they see what we are.

The film is divided into three parts. There's a housewife's diary, which gives you an interior view of one apartment in a white middle-class housing project. And there's a pseudo cinéma vérité documentary on National Intellectual Television, called *NIT Journal*—and it's the documentary of the revolution, the outside, the black view of the white middle class. And then there's the white voyeur, carried over from *Greetings* and now working on an entire housing project as his *grand opus*. He has the overview of the whole thing.

Within the documentary section we have something called *Be Black Baby*, which is an environmental play in which white middle-class audiences are painted black so they can be put through the black experience. The thing that holds this documentary together is that it's a journal of the day in the life of a black revolutionary. He's part of the troupe putting on the *Be Black Baby* play.

I got the idea for the housewife making a film diary of her life from *David Holzman's Diary*. She starts out with home movies. It gets more and more obsessive. She's very concerned with *things*. She has a scene where she talks about her body the way she talks about chairs and objects. Everything becomes an object for her.

The section with the voyeur is going to be intercut between these other two worlds. The voyeur is like a character in a John Barth novel who takes on whatever happens around him. He's environmental. As soon as the environment changes, like a chameleon, he joins it. A voyeur is always outside. But once he gets in, he becomes revolutionized. And he's in the front ranks when the revolution comes.

The *NIT Journal* is being shot in 16-mm black and white. The woman's diary is being shot in 16-mm color. Because it's all things she could conceivably shoot herself. The rest of the movie, the overview, is all shot in 35-mm color. They're constantly weaving into each other. Finally they all come together in the housing project. It's a film that says that the only way to deal with the white middle class is to blow it up.

G: What's the movie you're hoping to do this summer?

DE P: It's probably going to be a Hitchcockian suspense movie, which I think will be good for us. I'd like to try a change of pace and concentrate on a technical, stylistic exercise. I'm interested in things like split-screen and 3-D. I'd like to work in a different form for a while. I wouldn't mind doing something like *Pyscho* the next time, something that reprieves me from the political and moral dilemmas of our society for a while.

ROBERT DOWNEY

"The first thing you gotta have
if you are going to make movies
this way is a good old lady, or
it's impossible."

*Elsie Downey has faith in her husband. She played a mutt in one of
his plays. She played all thirteen female roles in one of his movies,
Chafed Elbows. She packed the suitcases and the kids when they took
the Super Chief cross country and back so he could be near his film
editor—he's got a phobia about flying. And she just goes to sleep early
when the utility company turns off the electricity several times a year.*

*The odds might appear to be against a high school dropout with a
wife and two children to support breaking into the movies as a director
at age thirty-two (born June 1936). But Robert Downey has been
making sacrifices for seven years so that he could make films. And
now his big chance seems to have arrived in the shape of a $200,000
independent feature financed by an industrialist.*

*As a talented amateur without any formal training, Downey got
enthusiastic notices from most of the New York film critics for
Chafed Elbows. If Putney Swope generates any kind of national
interest, it's likely that he could get studio backing for his next topical
satire. Downey has no objection to making some money with his
movies. He just wants to make movies, any way he can. The interview took place in March 1969, before the film opened.*

FILMOGRAPHY:

BABO 73 ('63)
CHAFED ELBOWS ('65)
NO MORE EXCUSES ('68)
PUTNEY SWOPE ('69)

GELMIS: Does growing up absurd account for the insane humor in your movies?

DOWNEY: Sure.

G: Would you describe what kind of background you had before you started making movies?

D: It was like a bad version of *The Catcher in the Rye*. My mother was groovy-looking and was married four times. I got booted out of three prep schools—St. Paul's, Peddie, and Lawrenceville—and never got past the ninth-and-a-half grade. I was on athletic scholarships, and I never went to classes. When I was in the eighth grade at St. Paul's, on Long Island, I struck out seventeen men in seven innings and set a record. But that was a lame school in a lame league.

I went in the army, under age. My mother signed a waiver saying my birth certificate had been lost and that I was born in Tennessee. I spent most of my time in the army in the stockade, I think. For fuck-ups, you know, which I enjoyed. They took my stripe away the first time, and I never got it back.

In the stockade, they put you in the *black box*, a room with a hole in the door. You sat there in your underwear on a cold cement floor without lights. They sent in bread and water every four hours. You just jerk off in there. That's where it is. And if they caught you jerking off, they'd add time. But there was nothing else to do. You couldn't read. You couldn't talk, make noise, sing.

At 4 A.M. they'd give us our P for prisoner tee shirt and take us out to work. We would go on a truck with rocks. They had us unload the rocks on the ground and then load them back onto the truck again.

When the Yankees made a tour of the Far East, the army took me out of the stockade to pitch against them. I did well for two innings. Then I walked three guys and Yogi Berra came up and hit a triple. So they put me back in the stockade.

One of the times I fucked up was at an early warning radar post on Prince of Wales, near the International Dateline. The lieutenant was asleep. So this other guy, from the Bronx, and I disconnected the phone back to Fairbanks. And we drew on the plotting board all these arrows representing bombers coming from Siberia. I woke up the lieutenant and he panicked. He went out of his skull.

We let him stew awhile, and then we told him it was a joke. He was so happy he laughed and cried and hugged us. Then he testified at our court-martial. I was court-martialed four times altogether in three years in the army. I was finally dishonorably discharged at age nineteen.

After that, I played semi-pro baseball in Pittsburgh and in Georgia. Then I got a job as a waiter. And I got into the theater, acting and writing. I met Elsie, my wife, in an off off Broadway play, *The Comeuppance*, which I wrote and which ran back in '61 or so.

I guess the play paralleled those stockades I'd been in. It was about dogs. Everybody played a dog in a pound, waiting to be adopted, or gassed. I played a greyhound whose legs have worn out. Elsie played a mutt. A German shepherd keeps trying to make it with a French poodle. But the poodle says, "Not after what your country did to mine." And a penguin keeps saying, "What the hell am I doing here? I'm a *penguin*."

G: How did you get into making movies?

D: I was in a play on Broadway, *The Andersonville Trial*, starring George C. Scott. I was an extra and wore this Civil War uniform. And I thought it might be funny to make a film about a Civil War veteran walking through the streets of New York. That was the original segment of *No More Excuses*.

All that film is is five shorts intercut in and out of each other. The Civil War thing, *Ball's Buff*, used to be a separate short, which I made in 1961–62 for $2000. The segment showing the New York singles' bars were made up of the outtakes for a job I'd done for ABC TV. So, *No More Excuses*, when it was finally finished and released in 1968, had cost me about $12,000 to make, altogether.

G: How did you get the money to make your films?

D: I waited tables on weekdays to buy film to shoot on weekends. *No More Excuses* and *Babo 73* were just 16 mm. *Chafed Elbows* was 35 mm. It took two years to make and cost me $25,000. I raised $3500 with an ad in the *Village Voice*: "Walk softly and carry a blank check." I had to dub practically everybody's voice myself in *Babo 73*, and they were talking to each other. It was horrendous. I did a lot of the shooting on those films, too.

I don't like any of them now. To me, they're not funny. They're too sophomoric, except for about seven or eight jokes in *Chafed Elbows*: Like the guy that fired two warning shots into the cop's shoulder. And the idea that the guy's banging his mother and living on welfare. And the guy drawing the line down the middle of the street because "you've got to draw the line somewhere."

G: What's going to be different about your new movie, *Putney Swope?*

D: It has more characterization. The jokes are more honest. I took more time, nearly a year, writing it. And we're taking tremendous care in the editing of it. The editor is as anxious as I am to take the stuff out that doesn't work.

G: Where did you find the backer for a $200,000 movie?

D: He was wandering the halls of William Morris, which was my agent. I hadn't made a penny for them till then, because I didn't want to get involved with some big production as part of a package with a full crew. And this guy wanted to invest in a film. So they put us together. And six months later, he put up the money. He's an American industrialist tycoon, loaded, with silk factories, rubber factories, and so on. Only he doesn't want his name used.

G: Is it true that your salary was supposed to be $18,000 but you cut it to $9000 because of increased costs in making the film?

D: Right. We needed the money for the film itself. Still, that's the most money I've ever made in my life. I've never seen that much money. But I owed it all out. I owed $6000 right off the top. And I promised my wife $1000 to spend any way she wants. She's been putting up with a lot. The first thing you gotta have if you are going to make movies this way is a good old lady, or it's impossible.

G: Does having a bigger budget than you've worked with before make it easier to get a better movie?

D: No. Because I've had enormous problems even with $200,000—with unions and teamsters and pressures and certain actors who couldn't understand what I was trying to do. But we have so much material that really is a variation on the theme that we've *got* our film anyway. It's just a different film than the one we started out to make. We started out to show how a system—like the advertising business—corrupts people, even somebody as anti-system as a black nationalist. We ended up with, I think, a more interesting film about the corruption *in* people that perpetuates a system.

The idea of having been able to do more than one take in *Putney Swope* was a big experience for me. I'm used to working with just one take, or maybe two, on occasion. As we edit, I sometimes can't believe we actually have five or six takes to choose from. But I still blew it. I still blew a lot of it, learning how to make a movie. But I learned enough on *Putney Swope* so that I know I can make a helluva better picture next time.

G: What kind of problems did you have making *Putney Swope* in New York as a non-union picture?

D: We were leaned on by the unions. My original lead was J. Errol Jaye, who I had seen in *The Electronic Nigger* and liked a lot. The day before we were due to start shooting, the Screen Actors Guild intimidated him and he had to pull out of the film. I had to get another guy, Arnold Johnson, in twelve hours. I had seen a picture of him on a wall and I liked his face. He looks like Haile Selassie.

It turned out to be okay, because Johnson was pretty good. And it wasn't too long before Jaye regretted having buckled in to the union, I think. They're trying to keep actors from making deals directly with filmmakers so they can control the wage scale, but there are too many guys who'd rather act in our kind of movie for them to be able to police it.

And we also had hassles with the teamsters and had to agree to have a driver sitting around on call at all times. And the technical unions were upset because we were using non-union guys and college kids and film nuts to make *Putney Swope*.

G: Why didn't you photograph any of *Putney Swope* yourself?

D: Because I don't know anything about a Mitchell camera. The cameraman, Jerry Cotts, who didn't know much more, had at least shot the *Black Journal* for NET (National Educational Television). And he checked himself out on the Mitchell. His footage is steady and clear and sharp. I mean, it's not fantastic photography, but it's serviceable and good and it moves. There's very little hand-held stuff, except when we needed it. It's distracting, unless it's for a documentary. When you hand hold everything, usually, it's just because you don't have time or money to get a tripod or a dolly.

G: How many setups did you do yourself, and how many did you just tell him to improvise?

D: I had so much insanity and so many actors in *Putney Swope* that I only personally set up six shots.

G: Do you regret it now?

D: Yes, because I'm very happy with those six shots. To cover up for some shooting mistakes, we've had to play around with cutting the film and using sound from one take over shots from other takes. I've learned from *Putney Swope* that you've just got to take your time, rehearse more, so when you want to do some improvisation you feel secure about it.

There really wasn't too much improvisation in the film. There was one ten-minute take, which we cut down to six minutes, where a secret service man is trying to tell jokes to the President, who's a midget. The actors were given a premise and they improvised for ten minutes.

G: Why did you make *Putney Swope?*

D: It was an idea that was knocking around in my head for a few years. I was the resident eccentric at an ad agency for a while there, and everybody told me how much they liked me but they never used any of my ideas. So I wanted to make a film that would show how really incredible Madison Avenue is, and to put some of my commercials in it.

The film's about an ad agency that's taken over by black militants. It opens in the board room with this old guy who runs the place coming in and explaining that everybody has a shampoo box inside his head. And he's talking this nonsense and he starts stuttering, trying to get some word out, and he's choking on his own words and all the hired help are yelling, trying to help him by finding the right word as if it's a charade, "Looks like . . . Sounds like . . ."

The old man keels over on the table, dead. And they strip him of his watch, rings, and wallet while the body's still warm. It's a white ad agency. This one black cat is there and he gets nominated because they're all maneuvering each other and he's just a pawn in the office politics. But suddenly he gets enough votes and he's the man. And he assures them not to worry because there's not going to be any changes. In the next shot, the guys at the board meeting are all black —except for a few middle-aged token whites. Then the titles come on and the film starts.

G: What kind of problems with the actors did you have in making the film?

D: We had a cast of two hundred. Most of them were extras. There's about a hundred and twenty speaking roles, and maybe thirty key parts, including the guy who goes all the way through the film. We used a lot of non-actors right off the street. At one point, we just rounded up all the Negroes we could find for a scene.

I liked the non-actors, because they came as themselves. We had this wino who did a part for ten dollars and a bottle of wine. The worst problems we had were the method actors who were looking for their motivations and their inner life, and meanwhile the jokes were being blown.

We had a ten-week schedule and, on our budget, no studio work. We shot on location, which meant using offices and corridors at nights or on weekends when they weren't open for business. Most places didn't want to get involved with us when they peeked at the script. But four or five out of the fifty we asked agreed to do it.

And our backer knew David Rockefeller, so that's how we got into the Chase Manhattan Bank. We were shooting nights and sleeping days, so there was no time for rehearsals. To shoot the big opening scene, we camped in the board room of the Chase Manhattan for thirty-six straight hours one weekend. Everybody was stumbling around over each other, grabbing a nap on the rug, getting up to do a scene.

It was just the right groggy atmosphere we needed. People are nodding and dozing off with all this talk—"We've got to get this account" and "We've got to get that account." And the old man is trying to explain his philosophy of what advertising is all about, when he conks out. The guy was actually eighty-three and he sat there for thirty-six hours, never got up except to go to the bathroom and to eat.

When he finally did flop over dead on the table, he was so tired he really just lay there looking like a stiff while everybody went berserk and robbed him and voted for a new chairman. We got a great four-teen-minute scene, so it was worth the thirty-six hours it took. Anyway, we had to finish before the bank opened because we knew we wouldn't be able to get back in there again. In falling forward again and again, the old guy scratched this fifty-foot green marble conference table with a little plastic box he was holding. Our insurance company got a $15,000 claim on that table.

G: How are you going to get *Putney Swope* distributed?

D: I have a handshake from Don Rugoff to open the film (at a Rugoff theater in New York), and Haskell Wexler (the Oscar-winning cinematographer) saw a rough cut and liked it enough to urge some people he knows at Grove Press to distribute it. It's not really an underground film, of course. It's an outrageous film—you know, the black ad agency whose commercials hypnotize the whole country so nobody wants to move from in front of the television set—that's well made, which is a breakthrough of sorts.

The film is shot in black and white and the commercials are in color. It would have cost us another $100,000 to shoot the whole film in color. And, oh yes, we don't mention the color of the people in the film—blacks or whites. I think the film shows that no matter what your color you're in trouble with the power structure. And, so, I guess that, in a way, it's the story of my life.

G: What's the best way for someone to learn to make movies?

D: To just go out and do it. If he can get money from relatives, to make the films completely his own way. Otherwise, to go to film school and make films there the best he can with what they give him. And I think he should write it himself. For me, writing and editing is the best part of making a movie. Everything in between is insanity.

G: You're thirty-two and you've got a wife and two kids. How do you plan on surviving in the months between now and the time your movie comes out and, hopefully, you get more job offers?

D: Borrow again. Then get a salary on the next one and pay back all my debts again.

G: How long can you continue doing that before you get emotionally exhausted?

D: Well, I've got a wife who's in complete sympathy—even when they turned off the electricity and we could only get incoming telephone calls. I'm lucky. She knows that right now if it was a choice between films and her—she'd go. Because I really feel that I want to do it. I love it. If this film doesn't open at a theater and at least make some racket, I'll be back working as a waiter until I can come up with something else and raise more money.

THEIR OWN MONEY, THEIR OWN SCENE

NORMAN MAILER

"Making a film is a cross between
a circus, a military campaign, a
nightmare, an orgy, and a high."

*Movies were the logical extension of the irrepressible personality of
Norman Mailer. How else could he be a Mafia chieftain* (Wild 90), *an Irish homicide squad detective lieutenant* (Beyond the Law), *or
a serious candidate for the Presidency* (Maidstone), *except by bank-
rolling, directing, and starring in his own movies?*

*The most garrulous, stimulating gadfly of his generation, Mailer
became a filmmaker at forty-five with the release of his first film on
the twentieth anniversary of the publication of his first novel,* The
Naked and the Dead. *The film critics mugged him on the way to the
box office.*

He suggests that the flaw in Wild 90 *was that the sound was bad—
which does pose problems for a film that is nothing but three men
playing thugs sitting and talking in one room for two hours. He spent
six months editing his next film,* Beyond the Law, *with a young filmmaker named Jan Welt. The film, a kind of staged documentary
about a night in a police station, was shot in four nights and was cut
from 11 hours of footage to 105 minutes. It impressed a number of
critics with its wit and vigor, but it didn't make any money.*

Mailer's third film, Maidstone, *was shot in the summer of 1968
and he was still editing it when we talked in early 1969. It was shot
in four working days in the Hamptons on Long Island, with as many
as five and six cameras filming at once. In it, Mailer plays a film
director running for President during a campaign in which all of the
leading political figures have been assassinated and most of the fifty
contenders remaining are from show business.*

*Shooting without a script and from the vortex of the activity,
Mailer's unorthodox approach polarizes critics into those who love
him and those who hate him. His casts are chosen from among his
friends who reflect facets of his persona. His filmmaking could be
described by the title of his 1959 collection of short works:* Advertise-
ments for Myself.

*Born January 1923 in Long Branch, New Jersey, Mailer grew up
in Brooklyn. He has a house in Brooklyn Heights overlooking Wall
Street across the river ("So I can keep my eye on the enemy"). He
lives with his wife, Beverly Bentley, an actress, and their two sons.*

He has four daughters by three previous marriages. When he isn't performing the Public Mailer role, he is a generous, gracious, warm human being.

Between the first novel and first movie, Mailer has lived a Faustian public life as novelist, pamphleteer, mayoral candidate, para-journalist and participant in events he was covering (Gore Vidal says Mailer "intervenes in history"), and neo-Hemingway tough guy who patronizes boxing and bullfighting and bars.

FILMOGRAPHY:

WILD 90 ('68)
BEYOND THE LAW ('68)
MAIDSTONE ('69)

GELMIS: Why, on the twentieth anniversary of your becoming a published novelist, did you embark on a filmmaking career?

MAILER: I didn't. I got into it bit by bit. I got into it, I think, the way some of those old Jewish businessmen became moguls of studios. Which is, they owned a little theater somewhere that they had taken over because they tried to put their nephew in business and the nephew had turned out to be a no-good and a bum. So to keep from losing a few thousand bucks, they had to take over the movie theater.

And when they took over the theater, they began to see what people liked. And lo and behold, before they knew it, they owned twenty movie theaters, because they were very good businessmen. The next thing was they looked at the product that was coming from Hollywood and realized it was all wrong for what they needed. So when they owned enough theaters to command money and influence, they started making movies in New York to supply product for their theaters. Then they moved to Hollywood for the sunshine. And they ended up being tycoons and geniuses.

But they didn't start out with the idea of being tycoons or even being in the movies. They started out with the idea that they were going to give their nephew a job, they were going to buy a little business for him. And at the other end, they changed the history of the western world. I'm not saying that's going to happen to me at all. It's a useful metaphor, though. What I'm saying is that I got into the movies just as inadvertently.

What happened, in brief, was that *Deer Park* was running as a play and my wife (Beverly Bentley) was in it. And, like any stage-door Johnny, I picked her up every night after the show. Actors, of course, are all wound up. So about six or eight of us would sit around and drink every night. I got very bored with that. You know, it's very boring to discuss your own play with actors every night for three months. Because actors, particularly stage actors, are extraordinarily literal people.

It's very important to them whether the salt shaker is here or there. After all, a stage actor is a man or woman who is, if you will, the president of an emotional factory which has to produce the same product at the same minute every night. And so they attach all sorts of conditioned reflexes in the gearing of their emotions to the placement of objects.

They may pretend that they want motivation, a reason to pick up a salt shaker. But the fact of the matter is that the only way you can produce a certain emotion a certain hour every night and do it without killing yourself is to set up a whole series of conditioned reflexes. Therefore, just as the dog salivates when he hears the bell ring, so the actor begins to weep as he reaches for the salt shaker.

But the thing is, a guy or woman who works that way and lives that way is not the most interesting person to talk to at night about their work. They're just very concerned with that salt shaker. You know, what happened was that the salt shaker wasn't in place. The prop man left the salt shaker over *there*. And they're having a hemorrhage. So you get into these problems night after night after night. And what you end up doing finally is saying: "Sorry, I'll look into it." And you become some sort of stage manager rather than a playwright, all because your wife is in the play.

Anyway, it was getting pretty desperate. So two of the guys in the play—Mickey Knox, an actor of twenty years and one of my best and oldest buddies, and Buzz Farber, a pal who had a part in *Deer Park* as a kind of gag—would go off to the side of this bar where we drank every night. And we began playing this game. We began improvising, to take on parts. I was like the head of a gang, very Mafia. These guys were like my hoods and I was lecturing them all the time.

We had absolutely fantastic stuff going as we were drinking, stuff that was far better than anything we ever came close to in the movie that grew out of those evenings (*Wild 90*). It got so good at a certain point I said, "Jesus, isn't it a shame that we can't film it? All we'd need is a cameraman and a sound track. Warhol is doing this very interesting stuff with his kind of people. And I think it'd be fun to try something altogether different. Instead of being ourselves, let's see what we're like as movie actors."

So Farber looked around. He was working at CBS at the time. And he happened to run into Don Pennebaker. I didn't know anything about him at the time. We met for a drink. And Pennebaker was sort of intrigued with the idea. He's not only a marvelously gifted photographer but he has an odd, very private aesthetic about film-making. He's an innovator and a discoverer. He loves anything that's new, any new way of approaching the idea of a film. Film is almost an object of religious veneration for him. He'd made a number of documentaries over the years and had just finished his Bob Dylan film (*Don't Look Back*), and our project seemed curious to him. So he said, "All right, we'll film for a couple of nights."

We figured out that what we'd do was he'd contribute his services for part of the film and give us the editing equipment and we'd pay for the raw stock, which was supposed to cost about $1000—it turned out to be $1500. At the time I had quite a bit of money, and I thought: "Gee, that's a good way to blow a thousand dollars. Better than going to Vegas for a week." So we blew it. We made the movie.

Originally the film cost $1500. Before I was finished, *Wild 90* cost about $50,000—and *Beyond the Law* has cost about $60,000 to $70,000 by now. Part of it was just waste motion on *Wild 90*. I didn't know what I was doing. It should have cost about $20,000 to make. What happened was that I got fascinated by the film as I saw the rushes. But the sound track is awful. There's not much going on.

So, finally, it can't be a successful movie because you've got three guys sitting in a room for forty-five minutes before anybody else comes in. And if you can't hear what they're saying very well, what kind of movie have you got? But at that time, I didn't know how bad the sound track was going to be, because we had it in double system. We had a magnetic track. And when you go from double system to optical, you lose something like twenty to thirty per cent of your sound. I almost cried when I heard the sound track of *Wild 90* optically. I didn't know that. People kept warning me. But I didn't really listen. You know, you get in a funny daze when you're making a movie.

G: How serious a limitation are the sound recording techniques involved in low-budget filmmaking?

M: Well, our sound's been getting better and better. We work on it and concentrate on it as we're filming now. Also, I'm beginning to change the way I cut a picture. For instance, often I won't use a scene now if the sound isn't good. I've come to recognize it. You just can't get away with it. You see, my feeling at the beginning was that there's too much attention paid to good sound. You give up a lot to get really good sound. One of the things you give up is the possibility of using people who are not actors. And that's a terrible thing to give up.

What happens is that an actor has a certain kind of psychological structure. Maybe one person in fifty is potentially a good professional actor. But half the people alive are good actors. We spend our lives acting.

Anyway, I spent about six months cutting *Wild 90*. It became my hobby. I'd been without a hobby for a couple of years. I'd put on some weight. I hadn't been skiing for a few years. And I was doing nothing but write, drink, and have a life, more or less. This was really the first new thing I'd become interested in. I just loved cutting. I loved the sort of—if you will—the metaphysical problems involved. The ethical problems. The moral problems.

G: What are the metaphysics of cutting?

M: It's the extraordinary reality. When you cut from one piece of film to another, you are creating a truth. And this truth is intangible, because it's images. By putting images together in one way, you have one truth, and by putting them together in another way you have another truth. I realize that, in a way, it's very much like writing. Getting toward the statement is like writing, in that the same sort of taste could be used. One of the things that's been said about *Beyond the Law* that I think is true in a funny way is they say: "The amazing thing about it is it's as if you *wrote* the screenplay. It's all you." Well the reason it's *all* me, despite the fact that everyone improvised his own lines and there was no script, is that I cut it to my taste.

Granted, I chose people who represented part of my vision. But finally it was in the cutting. Because when I saw the rushes of *Beyond the Law* there was a lot I liked and a lot I detested. Obviously what I liked was the part that fit the particular vision I had of what this reality was. What I was trying to do in *Beyond the Law* was to create the reality, if you will, below the reality, beneath the reality, within the reality of an evening in the police station.

I think that cops and criminals are incredible people. No one's ever begun to deal with how fantastic they are in their love-hate relation. It's like the relation between two linemen in professional football. What goes on between them in the course of a game is closer than a marriage. They know each other in ways that are incommunicable.

G: In the *Armies of the Night* you spoke of them as cops and crooks and then qualified it to "actually detectives and suspects." Why the fine distinction?

M: It's rude and inaccurate to say "cops and criminals." These people are suspects. We don't know whether they're criminals or not. But finally it comes down to cops and crooks anyway. And that's the relation. Because whether you're innocent or guilty, when you're in a police station you're treated as if you're a crook. So existentially you are a crook. At that moment, everything in you is reacting as a crook. You're in trouble. You're now beyond the law.

G: I've heard that you shoot twenty scenes and discard nineteen, rather than shoot twenty takes of the same scene and just pick the one you like.

M: That's true. I don't like to go back. In *Maidstone*, I shot a couple of things twice, just to see. Because you know I feel that if the vocabulary of filmmaking goes from A to Z and people like Bergman and Godard and Antonioni are somewhere between T and W, X, Y, or Z, I've gone from A to C. I mean, it's not a matter of being modest, just a matter of recognizing the simple truth that I know very little about making films. I got interested. They caught me, entrapped me.

G: *Wild 90* was an expensive experiment and unpopular with the critics. Why did you make your second film, *Beyond the Law?*

M: I had already shot *Beyond the Law* before the reviews came out on *Wild 90*. And a lot of people had loved *Wild 90* before it opened in a theater, when they saw it privately and could hear the soundtrack. So when I shot *Beyond the Law* I didn't shoot it as a loser. I shot it as a guy who had found an interesting way to make a film.

G: Was there a particular part of the experience that made you want to continue and to commit months of your life and energies and more of your bankroll to filmmaking?

M: Something in the experience had turned me on. You know this so well, we're writers. So we spend our lives working with words. And once in a while we catch our hand in the act of writing and we're overcome with the mystery of it. It's a mystery. The peculiar power that we have, or the lack of power. The ability to alter reality in other people's minds by the way we use words, by the insertion of one adjective or another, bears such an odd relation to the truth—and what we mean by the truth is just the sort of *feel* of our perceptions. I think it was this mystery that drove Hemingway insane, or partially mad. Dealing with words is a mysterious matter. It's very insubstantial because they're just little pieces of dark curly pigment on a white page.

   Well, working with movies, on *Wild 90*, I think I got back to the freshness of it as a kid. I felt the same sort of interest that I felt when I was eighteen and starting to write stories. It was wonderful when I was eighteen and writing. To be corny about it, it was first love. And that's gone. It's been gone for a long time. I'm a professional writer now. I can do a job. And I'm very much like a prizefighter who packs a suitcase and gets on a train or a plane and goes out to fight an opponent in some town. It doesn't matter what the conditions are particularly. I still have reverence for writing. But you can have reverence for something and at the same time not necessarily get much immediate pleasure out of it. I still get pleasure out of writing. But the *act* is not pleasurable. It's hard work. But making a film is a cross between a circus, a military campaign, a nightmare, an orgy, and a high.

G: That sounds like chaos.

M: That's the way I make films. If there isn't chaos in the making of it, then you can't get anything because everybody gets uptight. Because there's no script you've almost got to have a sort of chaos. It's the only way to get people relaxed enough so you can get something out of them.

G: Yet it seems to me that if one doesn't have good footage the best editor in the world can't do too much with it.

M: If you don't have the material at *all*, then you're dead. But the art of cutting is to find material where no one else can find it. It's a little like a detective story. You can cut something out of nothing, almost. In *Maidstone*, we have twelve-minute reels, and these are a unit in a way, because that's what a cameraman sticks in his Arriflex magazine. We shoot until the reel is empty. We look at the reel in the projection room and we all groan. There isn't a thing in it that has any life. It's dead, it's horrible.

Suddenly you take out the sound in a place and then you look at it and it's not a bad piece of film without sound. And then you see another piece five minutes later on which has a relation to this piece. Or you might get thirty really good seconds out of that twelve-minute reel if it's hopeless, and it'll have an artistry and elegance to it. So that afterwards, you'll say: "How the hell did you ever get that?" Where you get it is that you try to create a curious maelstrom in which marvelous facets of people will reveal themselves.

G: To make your cast loosen up, you create a *Mailerstrom?*

M: Oh, wow, stop! I'm not doing it as a manipulator. Because I'm not in command of it, don't forget. I'm no more in command of it than a general is, in the middle of a battle, where he's fighting for his life. The way I make the film, I have to act in it. It's the only way I can direct it. Because there's no script, something has to be going on in scenes. And so there has to be somebody in the scene who really has some conception of what he's driving toward. It's equivalent to— you can't have a party without a host or a hostess. And the host has to be in his own party. He can't send orders down from upstairs. He can, but it'd be a very bizarre affair.

G: How have directors managed until now to make films without acting in them?

M: They have a script. They have professional actors. They have extraordinarily skillful technicians who work generally with fixed cameras. That is, the camera lens may zoom or dolly, but finally the one thing they're obsessed with is: no vibration, no jar. The film image must be rock steady. They spent forty years developing techniques to give them a rock steady image. It's the most important single thing to a distributor. You get some of those distributors, they come to see a movie and the one thing they say is: "I like it so it doesn't shake." We're dead with our movies with the average movie distributor in a small town. He says, "You call this a movie? It shakes all over the place."

That's what we're up against. That's why there are certain respected film critics who detest my films. Because what I'm doing is going into the church. And we have to face up to the drear eye of the movie critic. And the movie critic is a religious man. Movies are his church. What I'm getting at is that a good film made without vibration has a magnificent quality to it, has the magnificence of a dream. You see, in a dream things don't shake. But the commercial movie, beautifully made, is an abstraction. It doesn't pretend to be life. It says that "we are some weird creature from the netherworld and we are perfect." And that's why it's not a light matter when there are imperfections in films.

It's a sacrilege. I'm committing a sacrilege when I put out a film which pretends to be a major film, a good film, a marvelous film and yet has certain crudities in it that are forty, fifty, sixty years old. For instance, my backgrounds will not be evenly lighted throughout. My camera will not be rock steady. Not every word of my films can be heard. The camera work will be spotty, brilliant at one moment and somewhat disappointing the next. I'll be in and out of focus more than is permissible. These are all terrible imperfections.

It's like that scene in Faulkner, you remember, in one of his short stories where the hired hand comes up to the plantation mansion and walks in over the white carpet with his boots and they're filled with cow manure. And as he walks across the carpet the owner of the plantation is so horrified he can hardly move and he gasps: "See what you've done to my carpet." And there Faulkner symbolized the absolute horror of one part of the south as it saw another part of the south rising.

You know, I've got enormous respect for the beautiful movie as a creature of the netherworld. I grew up with it, as everyone else did. And I love it. But I think there are other kinds of movies possible. And I think they could even transcend this.

G: On this question of imperfect films, don't you think that much of it isn't aesthetic choice at all but a simple case of insufficient funds that makes attention to technical polish impossible? Isn't it a rationalization of the underground to say that anything slick is bad *per se* and thus to institutionalize its shortcomings?

M: Yes, they have institutionalized it. Jonas Mekas, for instance, has certainly tried to legitimize it. And Mekas I find a marvelously interesting critic because he's so passionate. I rarely agree with him on particular things. But while we're on Mekas, I must mention that I have love for him because he's one of the people who introduced me to movies, in a funny way.

I happened to see him on the street once and he said: "Why don't you ever come to see any of our underground films? Do you realize we're a lot of serious people? We're working very hard to make these films. And you ought to see them." A year went by. But I remembered that conversation. So finally I said to my wife, "Let's go over to the Filmmakers' Cinémathèque." And so I started going to the underground's showcase. And I saw about twelve or fifteen underground films in that period. *Scorpio Rising* was far and away the star of all the films I saw. Technically, it was exquisite. I saw one Warhol film, *Kitchen*. It was horrible. But it had the horror of the twentieth century in it. The refrigerator is making too much noise. The beautiful heroine, Edie Sedgwick, has the sniffles. She keeps blowing her nose while the hero keeps trying to rustle a sandwich together out of wax paper. It really had the horror.

G: What was your reaction to the films?

M: Something was going on, but I couldn't dominate it with my mind. The greatest intellectual pleasure I have is carrying an experience I can't dominate with my mind. Because I come out of a tradition of people who are born to dominate life with their minds. The Jews are the greatest intellectual machines of any species of man on earth. I think that's really the reason, beyond any other, why the Jews are next to universally detested by people who don't understand their fine, warm, tender, loving, and forgiving sides.

The reason why every farmer alive, why every redneck, instinctively distrusts the Jew is because the Jews are intellectual machines. And they are, you know, more than anyone else. I grew up in that tradition. And I had a mind, when I was younger, which was like an intellectual machine. It wasn't that *good* a machine. In comparison with certain other machines, it was second rate. But it was a machine. It had that habit of dominating every experience it encountered. This went on for years.

And I remember that there were certain experiences I had—I mean, one of the reasons I've always been, in the view of critics, obsessed with sex is that sex is an experience you can never dominate. You have to approach it with—dare I use the word again?—veneration. Bull-fighting was something I couldn't dominate with my mind. It took me about three or four fights to get to like bullfighting. Once I got to like it, it was a passion. I lived with bullfights for a year. And the reason was, I encountered an experience that was larger than my mind. Something was going on that I couldn't dominate. I couldn't sit down and write a piece, which, as far as I was concerned, was a definitive piece about it. And I had to live with it and learn it and recognize that I'd never be able to dominate it. Boxing is easier to dominate because of the limitations of it. Boxing you can dominate to a degree with your mind, whereas a street fight you can never dominate with your mind. The greatest professional fight in the world is probably not as great a spectacle as the greatest street fight in the world.

G: Why? Because of spontaneity or improvisation or no rules?

M: Terror. The terror of the audience. What if one of the guys starts to kill the other guy? Are you going to get in and stop it? Why do you think that big men always stop other big men from a fight? It's because nobody wants to face the ultimate chickening-out point. What do you do if the thing gets out of control? The stronger the man, the more it worries him. The less he can afford to discover at any given moment that he's chicken. There are endless codes about this.

G: Even though I grew up in Brooklyn too, I managed to talk my way out of most fights.

M: Well, most men do. Who doesn't? You think I don't intellec-tualize my way out of most fights? You think I pick up every fight that comes my way in a day?

G: I think so, but I'll have to find out for myself.

M: Oh come on, come on. I'd have to stay in the shape of a professional fighter to pick up every small sort of subtle offer of a gauntlet.

G: Well, now, you've thrown the gauntlet down, because you ask if I think you accept every challenge. So let me ask you: why do so many people have the impression that your masculine ego, your image of yourself as a virile man, is somehow involved in almost every story you cover as a reporter-writer, as a para-journalist? And why do some of your projects, like your last film, *Maidstone*, turn into a brawl, by all accounts, where you and your buddy Rip Torn almost took each other apart and in another incident a young actor ended up in a hospital bed? What has that got to do with the artistic process, the journalistic process?

M: On *Maidstone*, I'm just going to say: "Wait until you see the movie." I can't defend the movie before you see it. You're going to see that film one of these days. And when you do, you're going to walk out to the street and ask yourself the same question in a way that I think will be like a turn of the spiral. In other words, you'll be at the same point you are now but you'll have had an experience which will have you somewhat higher in that blue netherworld of questions. You see, there's the black netherworld of answers and the blue netherworld of questions.

c: And you're concerned with the blue netherworld of questions in your movies?

M: I think *Maidstone* is concerned with the resonance of questions. A beautiful movie is an experience that you cannot dominate with your mind. That's why you film critics love a perfectly made movie. Because it gives you no opportunity to start ripping the thing apart. When you see a movie that is flawless, one of the wonderful things about it is that you can't get in there and start taking something that was done sloppily and from there make an attack on a picture. Like, you guys are lovers. Everytime a movie critic goes to see a movie . . .

c: What's wrong with beautiful movies, or beautiful women for that matter? Why should we like a movie with problems or blemishes which might have been avoided if the director had $500,000 instead of $50,000?

M: I adore beautiful women. There's nothing wrong with beautiful movies. Every time a beautiful movie is made by commercial processes, it's a miracle. But how many beautiful movies are there? There's *Belle du Jour*. Let's think of another beautiful movie at the moment. I can't think of one.

c: What about *2001: A Space Odyssey?*

M: I thought that was a bold, beautiful, extraordinary effort in a way. But I'm going to tell you something. I slept through half of it. And the reason I slept through half of it was that I hadn't had any sleep the night before. I went there with my children.

c: Now you understand the critic's problem.

M: Yes. But I still liked it. I got involved. But the pace was so slow, it was exactly the pace you would have on one of those interplanetary trips. And what would you do? You would sleep, so I did. I had regard for the film because it was an experience. And I thought it was bold of Kubrick to spend $10,000,000 giving us an experience that was not on the face of it box office, and then getting away with it. I think that was splendid.

G: But you thought it was boring.

M: Boredom has an aesthetic, also, in the commercial film.

G: Antonioni proved that.

M: Yes. But I don't think Antonioni's films belong in the dream factory. I think Antonioni oppresses the critic to the point where you lose the feeling of splendor and living in another world that exists nowhere but in the movie. There's a boredom in Antonioni that's almost physical. It's like dealing with sort of a foreign personality; there's almost a physical impression there.
Seeing an Antonioni film, I wanted to punch people. I didn't want to punch Antonioni. I didn't want to punch the actors. I didn't want to punch the person next to me. I just wanted to take the chair in front of me and start breaking it because the movie was doing something to my nervous system that wasn't nice. I'd almost put the blame on Antonioni. It's half his fault and half mine. The only film of his I've seen was *L'Avventura*. And I saw it again in the last year or so and found I just wasn't prepared to accept it.

G: Where does what you are doing fit into the film scene?

M: The way I look at the movie business is that the commercial directors are mining one end of the tunnel and I'm mining the other. What they're saying is that I'm crazy and that I'm digging holes like an earthworm and I'm going to drown in my own stuff. And what I'm saying is I'm digging in from the other end and we're going to meet in the center of the tunnel and we're going to come in so close that we won't be an inch apart. Now if not me, another. What I do know, and they don't know, is that a movie can be made this way, which is interesting.

G: How do you feel about the people who had violent reactions and walked out of Philharmonic Hall when *Beyond the Law* had its première there during the New York Film Festival?

M: Novels are supposed to hit people where they live. You're supposed to read a novel and change your life. A movie is supposed to

keep you living. That's why one serious critic said in his review of
Beyond the Law, "Norman, you don't understand the movies. The
movies are not there to hit people where they live. The movies are
there to keep people alive." You go to a movie and you pay your
money and you're supposed to have a good time. The horror of life
should be alleviated for a little while. That's what most critics feel
movies are supposed to do. But what I'm saying is that the horror of
life has become so completely pervasive that movies no longer enable
sensible and sensitive people to survive. It sickens them. The most
beautiful movie in the world will sicken you, if you can conceive of
a better movie than the one that was there.

G: You were telling me earlier how nebulous your plans were and
how you might give up filmmaking if *Maidstone* didn't get a favorable
reception.

M: I don't want to load it that way. For one simple reason: I
don't trust critics. I think every critic is schizophrenic. On one hand
he's a count who's taking care of a mysterious surrealistic estate.
And on the other hand he's nothing but a gang bully and a thug
who's waiting for the first victim to come down the alley. So if you
think I'm going to say for the record that *Maidstone* is going to be the
one that proves whether pictures can be made this way or not, you're
crazy.
I'll say that *Maidstone* is going to influence my mind to a great
degree. I will be either vastly more optimistic or vastly more pessi-
mistic about what can be done by this method of working after *Maidstone* is finished and I see how it's received than I am now. I will
be confirmed or denied in my present vision. *Maidstone* is not
necessarily it. But it is possible that when I finish it, I may say:
"This is it." I may say, "Gang, if you don't like this film we have
come to the parting of the ways. And I'm going to stop making movies
and you'll be the guys who'll be crying in twenty years because nobody
makes movies like Mailer any more."

G: Would you make another film before *Maidstone* comes out?

M: I don't think so, for one simple reason. Everything is going
into it: money, resources, time. It's going to take six months more to
finish it.

G: Let me pursue the matter of cost, which has to be a serious
problem in personal filmmaking. You said before that initially $1500
went into *Wild 90* and yet it ended up costing $50,000. Why?

M: Because of overhead. It didn't have to cost anything like that.

The fundamental error I made was that I thought it was going to be box office. I knew nothing about the movie business. Never did more of a country simpleton come down the pike than your humble interviewee. To use the army expression we once had, I didn't know a-hole from appetite about the movie business. I still don't, by the way. All I know now is that I don't know a-hole from appetite.

In those days I thought that was the way to make a quick buck, believe it or not. So I thought, "Well, we've got to distribute this thing. We've got something that nobody's ever come across. I mean, this is magical, this is fantastic. We're going to knock the movie business on its ass." So not only were we making a movie, but we were trying to set up a distribution business. We had overhead. It took us six months to make the movie. And all the while it was costing us at least $1000 a week. It was a luxury operation at that time, compared to the small staff we've got working now.

G: How were you financing the operation? From the magazine articles and book sales and the movie rights from *An American Dream?*

M: Right. All that ignoble money I got for *An American Dream*, which I understand, because I haven't seen it, is one of the worst movies ever made . . .

G: Why haven't you seen it?

M: Because I'm close enough to the violent not to want to see it. *American Dream* happens to be my favorite novel. I think it's my best novel. Most people I know don't agree. They think it's my worst novel. But, either I'm right or they're right. It would be awful if neither of us is right. At any rate, it's not only my favorite novel but also I think it's the only novel I ever wrote that would have made a transcendently splendid movie. So if I go see it and see what they did to it, I'm likely to get violent. And I just stay away from it. It's like an Italian saying, "Don't insult my mudder." Friends of mine said, "Don't go see it." It's the first time in my life I've listened to friends' advice.

G: Would you make a movie of *Deer Park?*

M: I might. If I did, I'd do it with a script. Because the dialogue is so good.

G: Why make movies which are improvised without scripts, without dialogue written in advance, in that case? Since you're a writer, it would seem a natural thing for you to write dialogue.

M: Well, this is what we're really talking about. The moment you know what you're going to do, you make a preparation. The moment you make a preparation, you're a step removed from the *moment* in life. You see, I'm an existentialist, through and through and through. And I have a certain amount of respect for the moment, because I think the moment is a mystery. The moment that there is not a moment, then you merely have programs. You're bureaucrats. You're bureaucrats of the mind, speaking to one another. You know what you're going to do and I know what I'm going to do and we're no longer talking as men across the table. We're talking as bureaucrats. Then you're concerned with your interests and I'm concerned with my interests. What's been agreeable about this interview up to now is that neither of us has been thinking particularly about where this is all going to go.

Every time I hear questions I feel like a kid who's in the study hall answering exam questions and I get flat and nervous. So, my feeling is that the amount of talent that exists but that's not approached is incredible. One of the experiences that I had in *Beyond the Law* was to see how good my friends were as actors. You know I really think *Beyond the Law* is a tremendous movie. I think in twenty years people are going to go to that movie and say, "But why didn't we see how fantastic it was?" I don't take that kind of credit for it. I didn't conceive it. I didn't direct it that way. I didn't dominate it. This wasn't my plaything. What happened was that these friends of mine suddenly absolutely amazed the hell out of me.

G: Why did you put the dozen newspaper and magazine photographers assigned to cover the making of *Maidstone* in the film as participants?

M: If the movie was the kind of movie that shouldn't have had cameramen there, I would have barred every still photographer from the set. The reason I let all those guys hang around was that this was a movie about a man running for president. So you'd have still photographers in every corner, wouldn't you? Part of the idiom of *Maidstone* is the still photographers clicking away, clicking away, clicking away. We have scenes in *Maidstone* where there are ten photographers visible in panorama.

For instance, we have the candidate throw a big party, a rather mysterious party. All sorts of documentary photographers are making a picture of this man's activities. Everyone says he's presidential material. So what we have is an absolutely wild party with movie cameramen all over the place. Now if it was another kind of party, a quiet tea, I've gotten to the point as a filmmaker where I wouldn't want cameramen all over the set.

I don't want a false myth to start that what I do is to get fifty people together, pull down my pants, do A or B, here or there, and then say: "Let's have some fun." It isn't like that at all. There's an extraordinary amount of work involved. What we were like was a commando team. I had brilliant technicians working with me. The thing is, they may not look like great technicians because they're working under conditions that no Hollywood cameraman would ever go near.

We used hand-held cameras, little hand booms or directional mikes, Nagra tape recorders, and whatever light was available. We worked fast, fast, fast. Each cameraman photographed an average of an hour and fifteen minutes a day during the seven days we were shooting *Maidstone*. That's a hell of a lot of attention to demand of a cameraman. It's the equivalent of a writer, I'd say, writing for ten hours a day.

G: Do you think there's any validity to the nonlinear, nonverbal, nonintellectual aesthetic of movies?

M: Yes. I think movies are in a different place entirely than novels or plays. In fact, my idea for a proper audience for *Beyond the Law* is not intellectual at all, because I don't think it's an intellectual film. I'd love to see *Beyond the Law* played in every slum neighborhood in America. A slum kid would feel about *Beyond the Law* the way I felt about *Studs Lonigan*. I read that and I suddenly realized, "My God, you can write about those things. They're part of art too."

And I wanted to be a writer. Reading James T. Farrell gave me the desire to be a writer. I think that you might get some slum kid who's about ready to blow up something, one way or another—if nothing else, he's going to blow up his own mind, by taking too much of this or too much of that. Maybe he'll see the movie and he'll say, "I've got to make movies." And he's going to want to learn how to read and write and add and measure because of his profound desire to make movies.

These kids should not only make movies but they should cut them themselves. Because as you see yourself in film over and over and over again, you lose all the worst aspects of narcissism. It's really like having psychoanalysis.

G: Do you speak from experience, in terms of self-image?

M: Yes. You come to recognize your relation to others. You recognize that it's not what you thought it was. It's subtly different. In other words, you're not as terrific as you thought you were. It's wonderful that way.

G: What did you think of your performance in *Beyond the Law?*

M: I thought it was good here and not so good there. I thought it was just good enough to create a character that a really good actor like, let's say, Richard Burton, could do fantastic things with. If you took that script that we've transcribed from the screen now and had Richard Burton act as Lieutenant Francis X. Pope, you'd have a memorable performance.

G: What did you think of Raoul Walsh's film version of *The Naked and the Dead?*

M: Considering what they could have had, I think it is the worst movie I've ever seen.

G: Would you like to have directed it?

M: I wouldn't have been able to. Someday, maybe. Someday maybe I'd remake it.

G: If you could write and direct your own scripts, would you work in Hollywood today?

M: I'm not interested in getting a job in Hollywood. I have no desire in the world to write a movie script. Why the hell should I write a movie script? Scriptwriting has nothing to do with writing. The best scriptwriter in the world, ideally, would be a film editor with a novelistic gift. And those are qualities that don't usually go together. But the way things are happening these days, we're going to find some film editor who'll come along and be a born novelist and he'll write movie scripts.

I learned something from the bad review in the *Village Voice* of *Beyond the Law.* I don't have to agree with it. But the fundamental complaint was that I don't go deep enough into the art, that I'm not really willing to give myself to it utterly. What I have learned is that there's no way to get around it, making movies is a religious act. I haven't been a dilettante. But I've just been having an affair with the movies up to now. And if you ask me whether I'm going to be in the film business for the rest of my life or am I not, I'd have to say that sooner or later I'm going to have to make a decision. I'm not giving up writing in a hurry, I can tell you that. Writing may give me up.

G: Would you describe your method of filmmaking?

M: Most moviemakers work off a blueprint. They have a plan, a master plan. They bring in technicians and talent. And whether they're working on a $500,000 budget or a $22,000,000 budget, it works in a corporate fashion. Everything is geared into the blueprint. It's an assembly line. And they can do marvelous work or abominable work, but they work off the plan.

What we do is to work like a military operation. We get a lot of interesting people. Very often we don't know if they're talented or not, but they are interesting. And we get the best technicians we can get who can work in this method, which is very demanding on the technicians because they're terribly orderly people and have to live in disorder. And then we make a raid. We attack a terrain. All right, in *Beyond the Law* what I was attacking was the old terrain of the Warner Bros. gangster and cop movies. I loved that kind of film and I wanted to see what you could do if you shot them in a more realistic vein.

G: Godard said that when he made *Breathless* he was trying to make *Scarface* but that it turned out to be *Alice in Wonderland*.

M: In a funny way, I think Godard approaches films in the same way that I do. Which is, he loves these myths. He grew up with these myths. They formed him. So he sets out to make one film and makes another. *Weekend*, which is one of the best films I've seen in years, I think started out to be *Bonnie and Clyde*. Remember, Godard was supposed to do *Bonnie and Clyde* at one point and they wouldn't let him do it. And I think there was a profound fury in his veins which found outlet in *Weekend*. He made an altogether different film, of course.

I think it was a tremendous theme. In a way, what he was talking about was the death of the twentieth century. And he was talking about the fact that we may all perish, that our salvation may be cannibalism. And I would have almost liked a more thoroughgoing treatment of the matter. The only fault I have to find with *Weekend* is that it isn't pretentious enough, isn't grandiloquent enough. The man has a vision. There are parts of that film that to me are like Hieronymus Bosch. I'd never been a Godard lover until I saw that film. It converted me. But I still think there are terrible things in it. I think Godard is tiresome. He delights in boring the very people he attracts.

G: Are you referring to the two men by the garbage truck in *Weekend* who make long Marxist speeches?

M: Yes, one of the worst moments in the history of film. He does it in every film. That's his trademark. It's like he's saying, "You're *happy*. You're *enjoying* yourselves. You're really *enjoying* my movie. This must come to an end. Now you'll be bored for a while. You have to pay your price for my movie." I'm against that.

G: During your own filming, do you use any kind of outline or notes or script at all?

M: No, none at all.

G: Is it all in your head? Do you know exactly where you are going from beginning to end?

M: Yes. I know where I'm going, more or less. That doesn't mean I'm going to get there. I have a precise idea of where I'm going. To continue that earlier military metaphor: I'm leaving from point A and I'm trying to get to point B, which is two hundred miles away, let's say, across enemy territory. I'm leading a commando raid on fixed positions in certain commercial-aesthetic territory. So I don't get to B. The bridges are blown up. B is no longer there. So I decide, all right, we'll take C, which is fifty miles from there. That's what a commando raid is. A commando raid is not measured by its aesthetic perfection. It's measured by the amount of life it generates, by the amount of stimulation it gives in military history and the amount of time professional soldiers will spend in discussing it afterwards. What I'm getting at is, supposing I make movies that are only half successful but which stimulate moviemakers who are absolutely dedicated to making movies? What if people who are far better suited to be film directors than I am see *Beyond the Law* and get ideas from it they would not necessarily have had? For instance, I think Andy Warhol is the world's worst moviemaker. But he's enormously stimulating to other moviemakers. He made every director brave enough to shoot a slow scene without trying to speed it up. I think what people will say in a hundred years is: "Warhol made the worst movies in the twentieth century and influenced more people than any other director around."

G: Is there anything in your experience in making three movies that is relevant to young people who'd like to make movies but have been discouraged by the idea that they can't break into the system or raise the money?

M: I think there's at least one thing that's relevant. The less money they have, the more they have to know technically about their subject. If they're serious about making films, then obviously the first thing they've got to do is get their camera one way or another. And they've got to get a good tape recorder, a Nagra, and generally they shouldn't try to do their own sound while they're filming. I think just as a technical matter they should get a good sound man. They've got to get married to a sound man who's terrific. Because that's an art, it's a separate art. Audio is separate from filming. It demands a different kind of athlete, if you will. A different kind of aesthetician. But they've got to find a reliable sound man because sound can make or break their film, as I learned with *Wild 90*.

c: But you found out that there's no viable way to distribute low-budget films commercially even after you've managed to make them.

m: That's a separate problem. That's not really for them to worry about, in a basic way. The only thing they should worry about is making an extraordinary film. If the picture is fantastic enough, they'll find a way to distribute it. If it isn't, then they have a very expensive hobby. And they might eventually get to the point where they work at it and work at it and fail and fail. They're like poets, if you will. How does a poet make a living? The point is not to make a living making films. The point is to participate in the experience, which is an extraordinary experience—filming a movie and then editing it afterwards. Moviemaking is like sex. You start doing it, and then you get interested in getting better at it. I believe that if somebody really wants to make movies, he'll make them.

ANDY WARHOL

"We haven't made a *movie* yet."

It's problematic whether Andy Warhol operates a freak show or is making documentaries about the horror of modern life. He is a phenomenon whose influence, or at least whose reputation, had an impact on moviemakers in the 1960s.

Norman Mailer says of Warhol: "He made every director brave enough to shoot a slow scene without trying to speed it up." Warhol himself suggests that the biggest influence he's had has been on nudie movies—giving the sexploitation filmmakers the courage to go beyond previous standards of what was acceptable for the screen.

Since so few people have actually seen Warhol movies, his reputation is an index of his gifts as a self-publicist. He is plugged into the mass media in a curious symbiotic relationship so he almost always knows as if by instinct what to do next to keep his name in the public consciousness.

From his silk screenings of Marilyn Monroe pictures and his Campbell Soup cans he moved into filmmaking. As the painter turned director, he used minimal technique—"just photographing what happens." He might, as admiring young filmmakers point out, leave the room and just let the cameras keep going. It would still be his film.

His contribution to film aesthetics has been in his use of passivity— a passive camera and a passive audience. His camera was simply set in one position. Occasionally it zoomed in arbitrarily. He rarely edited, preferring to splice reels together.

There was that illuminating moment in Chelsea Girls when "Ondine," a transvestite who played the Pope, got bored and wanted to stop talking. But the camera kept filming. And Ondine petulantly talked to it and then kept up his monologue until the reel ran out.

Warhol's earlier films were supposed to be continuous in time and space, like paintings. In his exhibit at the 1964 New York Film Festival, four of his short films were played continuously on machines that had TV-sized screens.

As an ex-painter, Warhol says he doesn't expect his audience to just sit and watch eight-hour movies like Sleep or Empire (the camera was simply pointed at the Empire State Building). He expects them to react as they would to a painting in a gallery or museum— to watch it, leave for a while, come back, look some more.

For months after he was shot in 1968 by Valerie Solanas, the lady from SCUM (Society for Cutting Up Men), Warhol hadn't made a film himself. His retinue and associates, led by Paul Morrissey, had been turning out films, like Flesh, *in his name. He had made one TV commercial and was talking about going to Japan when this interview took place in the spring of 1969.*

Warhol is evasive about his background. His parents were Czech immigrants who settled around McKeesport, Pennsylvania. According to one source, he was born in 1929 but others say he is older. He studied art at the Carnegie Institute of Technology and was designing ads for women's shoes as late as 1961 before he became one of the country's best-known pop artists.

The banality of his statements and films leads some people to assume that Warhol is really putting everything and everybody on, that he's really critically detached and cynical and superior to what he's saying and doing. He is, in fact, precisely what he seems to be.

He is a listener and observer who absorbs and absorbs and absorbs. Ordinarily, he is like a somnambulist, with very gentle, doe-like eyes, slack, melancholy mouth, straight, platinum-dyed hair, soft, courteous voice. He is a listless conversationalist, totally passive.

In the following interview, which was conducted at his "factory" in a Union Square loft, the only time that Warhol became at all animated was when he started to discuss the "beavers" he had seen earlier in the day. In talking to others who came and went during the afternoon, he spoke in the same monotone and drifted around in a kind of vague torpor.

It has been estimated that Warhol's factory has produced as many as 150 films of varying sizes. He says he doesn't know their names. He hasn't made a movie yet, he says. Where technical ineptitude ends and style begins for Warhol is impossible to determine, since his film primitivism may really be the natural expression of his vision of life.

GELMIS: Why are you making movies? Why did you give up painting?

WARHOL: Because movies are easier to do.

G: Easier than signing Campbell Soup cans?

W: Yeah. Well, because you just turn the camera on. And then, if you go into commercial filming, it's even easier because people do it all for you. They really do. The camera person is really the person that usually makes the movie.

G: Do you really think that Lester and Penn and Kubrick and Nichols let their cameramen do all the work?

W: Yeah.

G: There's an element of confession and of autobiography in almost everything you film. The people who act for you seem to be constantly confessing. What's your fascination with the confessional?

W: They're just people who talk a lot.

G: Where do you get your actors? Where did Ingrid Superstar and Viva and Ultra Violet and Mario Montez come from?

W: Just around, I guess. They were just the ones who wanted to be in a movie. So that's how we used them.

G: Have you since gotten many more people interested?

W: No. It's very hard. Those people just sort of happen. You can't look for them.

G: How much of your films is fiction and how much of it is real? Is this what they'd be doing whether you had the camera turned on them or not? Would Ondine do what he did and said in *Chelsea Girls*?

W: Yes. He does better things now. I wish I were filming it now.

G: How do you see your role in getting him to do what he does?

W: I don't do anything. That's what I don't understand.

G: What's your role, your function, in directing a Warhol film?

W: I don't know. I'm trying to figure it out.

G: It's been suggested that your stars are all compulsive exhibitionists and that your films are therapy. What do you think?

W: Have you seen any *beavers?* They're where girls take off their clothes completely. And they're always alone on a bed. Every girl is always on a bed. And then they sort of fuck the camera.

G: They wriggle around and exhibit themselves?

W: Yeah. You can see them in theaters in New York. The girls are completely nude and you can see everything. They're really great.

G: If they aren't prohibited by the state obscenity law, what's preventing other filmmakers from doing the same thing?

W: Nothing.

G: So why haven't you done it? Or have you?

W: We're getting there. *Lonesome Cowboys* has two fucking scenes. There's hard-ons and the actors go down on each other in *Fuck.* That's a movie we made when I got out of the hospital after I was shot. It's been shown at the Museum of Modern Art.

G: Have you actually made a beaver yet?

W: Not really. We go in for artier films for popular consumption, but we're getting there. Like, sometimes people say we've influenced so many other filmmakers. But the only people we've really influenced is that beaver crowd.
The beavers are so great. They don't even have to make prints. They have so many girls showing up to act in them. It's cheaper just to make originals than to have prints made. It's always on a bed. It's really terrific.

G: How did you learn to make movies?

W: I bought a 16-mm camera and took a trip to California four or five years ago. We were going to Hollywood, so that's what made me think of buying a camera.

G: Did you bring along a tape recorder or shoot silent first?

W: Silent. I was just learning how to use a camera. I'm still learning how to use a camera. We haven't made a *movie* yet.

G: What have you been doing until now?

W: Just photographing what happens.

G: Is it preparation for something you're planning in the back of your mind?

w: No. Things always happen, so you never know what's going to happen. You can't really prepare for anything.

G: When did you make your first movie, or non-movie? How do you refer to them, incidentally, if you don't call them movies?

w: Depending on the time, we have short ones and long ones.

G: But are they called movies, or what? You say you haven't made any movies up until now.

w: I think movies are the kind of things Hollywood does. We haven't been able to do that. Because you need a lot of money to do that. So we're working it out our way.

G: Why was *Chelsea Girls* half in color and half in black and white?

w: I don't know. We got a little more money, I guess.

G: Is money still the chief consideration for why things are done the way they are in your movies?

w: Yeah. We have to make our movies look the way they do because if you can make them look better bad, at least they have a *look* to them. But as soon as you try to make a better movie look good without money, you just can't do it.

G: It looks shoddy?

w: Yeah.

G: When people went to see *Faces* many were disappointed because they thought it would be a slick Hollywood movie but it was grainy 16 mm enlarged to 35 mm and it wasn't carefully lit.

w: It was very slick when I looked at it. I saw it in *Life* magazine and it was cropped. If it were shown in a square it would have been awful. But it was shown in a nice super-oblong.

G: Do you experiment much with various projection shapes yourself?

w: Well, you get used to cutting off things. It makes the movie more mysterious and glamorous.

G: Why did you make a movie like *Sleep* about a guy who sleeps for eight hours?

w: This person I knew slept a lot.

g: During the day?

w: No, at night.

g: Doesn't everybody? Don't you?

w: Not when you turn the camera and the lights on and everybody's making noise.

g: You just set the camera on a tripod and had operators spelling each other behind the camera for eight hours?

w: Yeah. Well, it didn't turn out the way we wanted it to because I did it in three-minute things. So now we do it in thirty-five-minute things.

g: Were you using a simpler camera then?

w: Yeah. We use an Arriflex and a Nagra tape thing now.

g: Have you made a 35-mm film yet?

w: No. I guess we'll do that someday. It's expensive.

g: *Sleep* was shown silent, wasn't it?

w: Yeah. The first time we showed it, we had a radio on in the theater. Instead of recording a sound track, we just put a radio next to it and every day put on a new station. And if a person were bored with the movie, he could just listen to the radio. People listen to radios.

g: You've said you like television a lot, too. Any special programs?

w: I like it all.

g: Why?

w: There's just so much to see. You can change all the stations. As soon as it gets a big picture, it'll be even more exciting. Everybody should have two television sets. So you can watch two at a time. Every time you see the President, he has three.

g: Can you really pay attention to two sets at once? Or is it just images and sensations, anyway?

w: I put two things on the screen in *Chelsea Girls* so you could look at one picture if you were bored with the other.

g: How do you feel about the interruptions of the commercials on television?

w: I like them cutting in every few minutes because it really makes everything more entertaining. I can't figure out what's happening in those shows anyway. They're so abstract. I can't understand how ordinary people like them. They don't have many plots. They don't do anything. It's just a lot of pictures, cowboys, cops, cigarettes, kids, war, all cutting in and out of each other without stopping. Like the pictures we make.

g: How many pictures have you made so far?

w: I dunno. It depends on how you count. We have small ones and big ones and sometimes we make two from one or one out of two older pictures. We stopped making so many now. We thought we'd wait a while to see what happens.

g: You recently made a one-minute television commercial for Schrafft's.

w: Yeah, well, that just took a minute to do.

g: But it took more than a minute to put that minute together, didn't it?

w: No, it just took a minute.

g: What about the use of videotape? You've said you're enthusiastic about using tape. Why?

w: Oh, it's like instant pictures. You can see it right back. You can combine things together that you can't do in films. You have to send films out to be processed.

g: Can you imagine yourself making a full script sometime, written out in advance?

w: Yeah, if anybody asked us to do it, we'd do it.

g: You did make a western, or at least you made a movie, *Lonesome Cowboys*, on location in Arizona.

w: Yeah, that was with Viva. We asked them to make up something, but they were still themselves. They were in cowboy hats.

g: You were supposed to go on a tour of colleges last year and you sent someone else in a wig who pretended to be you on the stage introducing the films.

w: We went to about fifty colleges last year.

G: Is it true that you sent a stand-in to the college lectures?

w: I only did it because I thought it was what they wanted. It was more entertaining.

G: You're really anxious to entertain?

w: Oh, sure. That's what we're trying to do now. The cowboy movie is more entertaining than the early ones.

G: Is there a market for your films in colleges?

w: Yeah, that's where we get most of our films shown. I think movies are becoming novels and it's terrific that people like Norman Mailer and Susan Sontag are doing movies now too. That's the new novel. Nobody's going to read anymore. It's easier to make movies. The kind of movies that we're doing are like paperbacks. They're cheaper than big books. The kids at college don't have to read anymore. They can look at movies, or make them.

G: What was the reaction of the college audiences to your films last year?

w: We showed them so much they didn't know whether they liked them or not.

G: Is that the reaction of most people?

w: When people go to a show today they're never involved anymore. A movie like *Sleep* gets them involved again. They get involved with themselves and they create their own entertainment.

G: Your audience is forced to do the work themselves?

w: It becomes fun.

G: Do you mean people who don't like your films or are bored by them just aren't working hard enough?

w: I don't know. But it's a lot of fun.

G: Most of your films have little or no editing. You keep the camera in one spot and keep shooting until the reels run out. Your characters enter and leave the frame. But there's no cutting, just reels spliced together. Why?

w: The reason we did that was because whatever anybody did was always good. So you can't say one was better than the other. You get more involved and time goes by quicker if you stay with one scene.

c: Have you changed your opinions about the need for editing?

w: Well, now we really believe in entertainment, and that's a different scene.

c: You've said, "I like boring things." How can entertainment be boring?

w: When you just sit and look out of a window, that's enjoyable.

c: Why? Because you can't figure out what's going to happen, what's going to be passing in front of you?

w: It takes up time.

c: Are you serious?

w: Yeah. Really. You see people looking out of their windows all the time. I do.

c: Mostly it's people who are stuck where they have to be, like an old person or a housewife waiting for the kid to get out of school or the husband to come home from work. And they're usually bored.

w: No. I don't think so. If you're not looking out of a window, you're sitting in a shop looking at the street.

c: Your films are just a way of taking up time?

w: Yeah.

JOHN CASSAVETES

"It's really no fun to work with sane
people, people who have a set way of
doing things."

Faces *is a classic case of an independently made film that found its
audience. It is a Hollywood home movie made outside the system in
private houses and borrowed offices over an eight-month period.
Faces cost John Cassavetes about $50,000 and had to be edited in
his garage on and off during a three-year interval between jobs until
he found a distributor, Walter Reade-Continental. Cassavetes got
$250,000 outright and a deal that could eventually earn a couple of
million dollars for him and his friends.*

Cassavetes made Faces *as a deliberate attempt to recapture the
experience of directing his semi-improvised* Shadows (1960), *which he
has said "was one of the happiest experiences of my life." His actors,
as in* Shadows, *were friends between jobs. His wife, Gena Rowlands,
who played the prostitute, was three months pregnant with their
second child when filming began. No one was paid a salary. Each
got a share of the film, instead.*

*The film was paid for with money Cassavetes earned as an actor
on* The Dirty Dozen *and* Rosemary's Baby *and with whatever, in
his words, "I had to beg, borrow, and steal. I conned my friends. I
got bank loans without collateral." The film was shot in 16 mm and
enlarged to 35 mm. The first version ran six hours. It was cut to 129
minutes.*

*The film was sold to the public, and then to the industry, with a
high-pressure campaign by Cassavetes. He got it talked about by taking
it to festivals like the one in Venice, where serious films about
American social and family problems are given special consideration.
His star, John Marley, won the acting prize there.* Shadows *had won
a prize in Venice in 1961.*

An influential American critic saw Faces *in Venice—having missed
the first half hour or so—and wrote a rave review that was instrumental
in getting the film noticed and, ultimately, a distributor. Then Cassavetes, who had an edge over most directors, as a popular actor,
made an exhaustive one-man tour of major cities in which he got
unprecedented saturation coverage in every media for his passionate
promotion of the picture.*

Yet, obviously, if Faces *hadn't evoked emotional responses in its audiences, Cassavetes could have sold his soul to the devil as he did in Rosemary's Baby and it wouldn't have helped. The object lesson of Faces was that dedicated people could make and sell to a mass audience a low-budget 16-mm feature film that made up in visceral involvement for what it lacked in technical polish.*

In his direction of Faces, Cassavetes made it a vehicle for his actors and let the form take care of itself. His gestalt theory of film-making is, like Mailer's, that he and his friends are making pictures to learn something they don't already know about themselves.

Cassavetes describes himself as "a forty-year-old kid." He was born in 1929 in New York. The following interview took place in January 1969 at a hotel in Manhattan. Cassavetes is a formless talker who rambles in ten-minute takes, like his films, until the reel runs out. He smiles easily, though his closed-mouth grin becomes menacing when he is interrupted. He lost the habit of smiling as a youngster after his teeth were chipped in a fight, and it was only later when he became an actor and had his teeth capped that he learned to smile again. Faces has given him a lot of practice in smiling.

FILMOGRAPHY:

SHADOWS ('60)
TOO LATE BLUES ('62)
A CHILD IS WAITING ('63)
FACES ('68)
HUSBANDS ('69)

GELMIS: Why have you directed just four films in almost ten years?

CASSAVETES: Basically, because I'm not a director. I came into this business as an actor to express myself and to express things that I thought might be of value to other people. When I first started to make a picture, which was *Shadows*, it was because I was predominantly an actor who was frustrated in expressing human qualities rather than in expressing qualities that were more *thing* oriented or concerned with plot. I've been concerned from the beginning with the problems confronting real people rather than emphasizing dramatic structure or bending characters to the plot.

G: Yet you didn't act in *Shadows* yourself. If you felt you were getting Hollywood scripts that lacked this human dimension, why wouldn't you be anxious to act in a film that did have such a quality?

C: I really think that acting and directing are two separate things. At the time, I was only concerned with having people express themselves as I would have liked to express myself. And it's very important that they express themselves individually. Somebody had to stand there and see that that happened. If I was involved in it as an actor, I wouldn't care about their expression very much.

As you know, a director gets so terribly concentrated on what he has to do that it becomes impossible to live anything but a hermetically sealed existence. All your energies and all your interests are centered around one thing. And that is the script at hand, the story you're telling, the people's interrelation with each other. The task is to do it as honestly as you possibly can and to have those people really express something, not just stand there and repeat dialogue.

G: Do you think you can do two things well at once, be part of the scene and also be an observer to the scene?

C: I don't know that yet. I'm going to try it in the next film. In my second film, *Too Late Blues*, I was working under a studio system which I find just doesn't suit me. It's a system based on departments and department heads and chiefs. I'm not very good at dealing with department heads. So I find that I really can't get anywhere that way, simply because I'm not concerned with their problems. I'm only concerned with mine. That might be a selfish attitude. But there it is. I don't want to hear about nine other pictures when I'm working on mine. All I want to talk about, all I want to think about, is getting my picture made.

When *Too Late Blues* was over I thought I would be over too. And then the studio, Paramount, asked me if I'd like to sign a contract. At that point I realized that success and failure weren't necessarily success and failure. I had heard so much about people who fail and then get enormous contracts. I never could quite believe it, until it happened to me.

I think that *Too Late Blues* was potentially a hell of a lot better picture than I made it. I'm not copping any pleas. I just didn't know how to work under that system at that time. But I learned a few things in the course of that film. For instance, there is no such thing as a low budget picture at a major studio. At least not from a director's point of view. Once you say it's a low budget picture it's like being a man with no credit in a rich neighborhood.

So I decided that the third picture, *A Child Is Waiting*, would be done in a certain way and that I'd spend as much money as I had to and make absolutely no compromises, and not associate myself with the money end of it. Well, I worked with Stanley Kramer as my producer for about four months on *A Child Is Waiting*. Kramer had me replaced and the picture re-edited to suit himself. I didn't think his film—and that's what I consider *A Child Is Waiting* to be, *his* film—was so bad, just a lot more sentimental than mine.

The philosophy of his film was that retarded children are separate and alone and therefore should be in institutions with others of their kind. My film said that retarded children could be anywhere, anytime, and that the problem is that we're a bunch of dopes, that it's our problem more than the kids'.

g: How did Kramer sentimentalize your film?

c: If you double-cut on closeups you can make the thing seem a great deal more sentimental. In other words, if I look at you and you look at me and then I look back at you and you look back at me there's a feeling there of sentimentality. It's automatic, like pushing a button. I have nothing against it, when it's not based on an important idea. An editorial doesn't *do* anything. An editorial only makes you feel guilty. And I don't think that's what a film is about. I don't think there's any reason to bring any people into a theater to be told that retarded children are sad, or whose fault it is. The point of the original picture we made was that there was no fault, that there was nothing wrong with these children except that their mentality was lower.

To tell the truth as you see it, incidentally, is not necessarily the truth. To tell the truth as someone else sees it is, to me, much more important and enlightening. Some documentaries are fantastic. Like

Lionel Rogosin's pictures, for instance; like *On the Bowery*. This is a guy who's probably the greatest documentary filmmaker of all time, in my opinion. He doesn't care about what anyone thinks, the *Cahiers du Cinéma* crowd, the underground, or anyone else. He's interested in the films that he makes. Another person like that is Shirley Clarke. Outside of those two in this country, you can have all the independent filmmakers. Shirley and Rogosin are really interested in their subjects, and in finding out about what they think and feel.

G: Do you consider yourself an "independent" filmmaker, in the sense that you had to make *Faces* outside the studio system?

C: I'm not part of anything. I never joined anything. I could work anywhere. Some of the greatest pictures I've ever seen came from the studio system. I have nothing against it at all. I'm an individual. Intellectual bullshit doesn't interest me. I'm only interested in working with people who like to work and finding out about something that they don't already know. When we work on a film like *Faces*, we work for nothing. Everyone will share in the profits, if there are any. I wouldn't want anyone to work for me ever, ever, not a soul. If anyone has to work for me, then there's something wrong with them. The hardest thing for a filmmaker, or a person like me, is to find people—actors and crew—who really want to do something. If people want to work on a project, they've got to work on a project that's theirs. It's not mine and it's not theirs. It's only yours if you make it yours. With actors, as well as technicians, the biggest problem is to get people who really want to do the job and let them do it their own way.

In a sense, I feel that a director is an administrator. He has to be able to make a great many people feel that they're working on something important constantly, no matter what the disappointments are. If, at the critical point, I show disappointment, they're going to be disappointed. What we're working on is not a house, or anything tangible. It's just something that you see up on a screen. And it disappears in a second. And it's only an opinion if you think it's good or not. My job is to look at that stuff and see what people are trying to say and see if it's clear enough—to be close enough to the people to allow them to say of their *own* work, "Gee that wasn't good enough. My work wasn't good enough."

G: Why did it take four years to make *Faces*?

C: How long have we been fighting the Vietnam War? If it takes that long to do something that destructive, why can't we be allowed to take four years to do something constructive? I think basically we were trying to find out the answer to the story. I don't know anything about marriage at all. I've been married a long time. But I don't know anything about marriage. I don't know anyone who does.

The simple problem we had in this film was to try to create a situation for people which allowed them to be themselves and to say things without feeling they were going to be electrocuted for saying them. To let them put themselves in a position where they may make asses of themselves, without feeling they're revealing things that will eventually be used against them.

I am who I am and I don't know why. It's a disappointment to me, sometimes when I see myself behave in a way I'm not proud of. I mean, for instance, I can't sit in a situation where I'm with a bunch of polite people talking bullshit. I just can't. It's not a question of wanting to or not wanting to. It makes me terribly uncomfortable, and I just can't do it.

G: Were those characters we saw on the screen in *Faces* really playing themselves in some way?

C: I don't know that. For instance, there are a million things that you think you are going to do if you walk in and find your wife in bed with another man. Some guys say, "I'll kill that son of a gun" or maybe "I'd shoot 'em both" or "I'd walk out; I'd never see her again" and so on. You can sit and discuss it, but I don't think anyone really knows until it happens how he will react. John Marley was so close to his character we almost all became neurotic with him worrying about how it was going to happen for him, how he'd react to the situation when he finally had to face it. And as a man, it shocked me that Lynn Carlin's character, a woman who had been faithful to her husband all her married life, would suddenly have an affair this way . . .

G: But you wrote the script. How could it shock you?

C: The first part of the script was structured very carefully to set up a whole new pattern of thinking so that the audience could not get ahead of the film. Most people think, "Oh yes, this is what's going to happen in the next moment." What happens with *Faces*, though, is that the first half of the film really bugs people because it doesn't fit an easy pattern of behavior. Well, I don't know anyone who has an easy pattern of behavior. I know people who are just sensational one minute, and absolute bastards the next. Terribly funny one minute, and morose the next. And these moods come from specific things that I can't put my finger on because I don't know their whole life. And in two hours and nine minutes, we can't put their whole life on the screen. So I've got to depend on that person to identify with his role enough that he can express those things. And to get it on the screen is something miraculous. I can't say that anyone was acting in that picture. There was no stopping those people once they began.

c: Didn't you do retakes of each scene?

c: Sure, many, many takes on almost every scene. But from the beginning of straight acting to where they arrived was a long time in between. I would say that practically the whole first month of the filming was thrown out. The terrible part was that they were very good actors to begin with and their performances were very good. And I'm not the most articulate man in the world, but I kept telling them, "Listen, we've got to go further and we've got to go underneath." I was giving these absolutely amateurish directions. I would stand there like some tyrant—to the point where everyone would want to quit—waiting with great faith and apprehension for this miracle to take place.

It doesn't take a genius to recognize it when it's brilliant. It takes somebody who's stupid to compromise on something when it's not brilliant. A lot of directors say, "Well, let's work freely." And they get to a certain point where it's failing. At that point, it's a crisis. Because it may be a day or two away. It may not be quite ready. The oil may not be right on the surface. But it's there. If you believe it's there, it'll always be there for you.

When I told you before that I'm not really a director, I'm really not. I'm a man who believes in the validity of a person's inner desires. And I think those inner desires, whether they're ugly or beautiful, are pertinent to each of us and are probably the only things worth a damn. I want to put those inner desires on the screen so we can all look and think and feel and marvel at them.

c: The kind of filmmaking you're doing takes a lot of time. Are you prepared to work continuously as a director, or do you see yourself calling it off after a while?

c: At times I do. You always feel like calling it off when you really have no ideas. When you're dry, you feel like running away and doing something else. But I don't think you can any more turn off what's inside of you than you can die before you're ready to die. I have an edge, you see. Directing really is a full-time hobby with me. I consider myself an amateur filmmaker and a professional actor. I'm a professional actor out of defense. I'd prefer to be an amateur actor.

But I've got to have money to make films. Unfortunately, it's an extremely expensive hobby.

I paid for *Faces* out of my own pocket, $50,000. I worked in films—*Rosemary's Baby* and *The Dirty Dozen*—to pay for it. Luckily, I liked the films. That's why I have the edge. I like acting.

Whereas, you might ask, "Why don't directors go out and make the films that they like?" One, it's terribly expensive and they have no other source of income. Usually a director is strictly a director. And, two, maybe they haven't had some of the benefits I've had—having so many talented friends out of work. My friends haven't grown bitter or disillusioned. Beautiful.

And like I began to suggest before, it seems to me that if I ask someone to do something for my gain I shouldn't be disappointed if they don't want to do it with the same eagerness that I bring to it. But if I ask somebody to do something with me for our mutual benefit absolutely straight down the line, and that is the making of a film we can all care about, I think there's a good chance that we will do something worth while.

In the commercial world, I drive a pretty hard bargain as an actor. I drive people crazy with the same things that any other actor drives people crazy with. But when I'm working on a film that's for nothing, there is no other goal except to do the picture the best way that we can. So the minute I feel that way and someone else feels that way, it mounts and grows and if some jerk comes in and thinks he's going to work in a commercial system I don't even have to say anything. The hope always is that that's the way that it can be in a commercial film project too. But it just doesn't work that way. Once you set up an employer-employee relationship, you divide people. It's only when there's nothing or everything to gain that each gives completely with faith in the film.

G: What approach did you and your cameraman take in shooting *Faces?*

C: I feel we have to move beyond the current obsession with technique or camera angles. It's a waste of time. How you shoot a film is a diversion. I think anybody can shoot a film. Look at the most commercial things in the world—television commercials. They're magnificently photographed. What are we wasting our time doing that for? It has nothing to do with life. Now we're making that a value. Pretty photography is part of our culture.

In *Faces*, Al Ruban did the lighting and I had a great operator who worked the camera. They had individual pride in their work. But they also realized that they were a part of an overall thing. It wasn't decisively important how beautiful their photography was, except to them personally. The question was: "What are we working for?" And the obvious answer was that we were working for these *people*—we're not dealing with objects and walls—to look better. Now it doesn't really make any difference whether the wall behind them is white, dark, black. I don't think it means anything to anybody. It's what these people are thinking, what they're feeling. And that's the drama of the piece.

So when we did the film, the operating was handled by following the people. It's as simple as that. It was absolutely hand held. No harness. And I think we used only about three set shots in the picture. But the idea was, "How do we get to these people the fastest, quickest, most expedient way before that little feeling that they have disappears?" That's the important thing. So sometimes we'd shoot when the lights weren't ready. We'd shoot whenever the actors were ready. We were slaves to them. All we were there to do was record what they were doing. Much like an interview. You really want me to say something. So you've got to help me the best way you can to say something that will be interesting. And if I want to talk on and on and on and on, that's my way. And you've got to sacrifice your style.

G: There's always the editing room.

C: Ah, good, you can get me later, right? That's the way we feel about the actors. We'll get them later, if they make a mistake. But it's got to be there to begin with . . . Working on a limited budget, I find that half of the creative things I do technically are accidents or unforeseen necessities. You have no real equipment to do the things with, so you take a chance. And in taking a chance you ofttimes are much more creative than if you had all the equipment and all the time and all the futzing and painting you could do to make a set letter-perfect.

G: What parts of the film were improvised and what parts were written and memorized by the actors?

C: The emotion was improvisation. The lines were written. The attitudes were improvised, as they always are, but I think a little more deeply in this case. The reactions to leading performers were not modulated. In other words, if somebody had a smaller part he didn't have to bend to the film's superstar role and didn't have to listen to the hero's sad story. He could do what his character would really do, without fear of offending the main actor—who keeps a tight rein, in commercial filmmaking, on everything happening in his scenes.

In that sense, it was improvised. I really didn't care if they stuck to their lines. But they did stick close to the dialogue, anyway. I didn't know this while we were shooting, because I don't look at a script during the actual filming. I'm not really listening to dialogue. I'm watching to see if they're communicating something and expressing something. I don't know if they're stumbling or carrying on or over-lapping or anything. I'm just watching a conversation. You're not aware of exactly what people are saying. You're aware of what they're intending and what kind of feeling is going on in that scene. So in that sense I guess it was improvised.

G: How many pages of script did you have to start out with?

C: We had about 270 pages, and that was about three quarters of the film. We wrote it from that point, as we went along. I think the whole script, when it was done, was something like 320 pages. A normal script today runs about 140 pages. Our first cut of *Faces* ran six hours. The version we ended up with runs two hours and nine minutes.

It was stupid of me to allow myself that kind of indulgence. But I believe that if somebody has a large part they work harder. And if their part is complete, they'll express a complete person. When they come to a small scene, they will do it much better. Commercial pressures don't allow you to do this.

What people usually do is to trim a long film. But Al Ruban and I and Maurice MacKendry, who edited *Faces*, all sat there and dis-cussed what would happen if we did make certain trims. We went through the same things that everyone else would do in a more pro-fessional way. And we came to the conclusion that each cut we made hurt the film. We looked at each other and thought, "Jesus, are we getting so close to it that we're becoming punchy?" The timings of the people were real. And so, in altering their timings, we were altering the truth. So we were forced to make extremely large block trims.

There was a sequence where the women come to this woman's house after her husband leaves her. And they find her talking on the phone with her mother, arguing with her mother in her husband's defense. The idea of the scene was: Here was a wife whose husband left her and, for once, instead of her getting sentimental, or crying or carrying on, she was furious with the son of a bitch for leaving her. But here were a bunch of women trying to calm this woman down. And all their personalities were working on her to make her more bugged. By the time the scene was through, her only alternative was to become silly and happy and cover up her emotions.

I loved that scene and the interference of those women. But we found that the whole half hour scene wasn't really necessary. It just wasn't necessary to explain why all of a sudden we find this woman going out with a bunch of broads we've never seen before. We just decided, "We understand who these women are. They're friends. We don't need that other scene." It was a shock to us to make that discovery and to see how idiotic we really are. We were able to shorten the film and at the same time make the audience do a little work, make the jump, the connection, themselves. We realized that originally we had been talking down to the audience.

G: How do you feel about the criticism that *Faces* doesn't really begin until halfway through when those predatory women take the gigolo home?

C: I don't think life has a beginning, a middle, and an end. The form is in the content. We've taken the climax of a relationship, a changing point in a marriage, picked it up at the moment where it's accelerating. The whole film is just one day and a little bit of a morning in two people's lives.

G: When you're dealing with the tempo of reality, don't you risk boredom by imitating its dull pauses?

C: I didn't find *Faces* boring in any sense. As a matter of fact, I found it extremely fast-moving. Sometimes when it slowed down from extreme speed it was like stepping off a fast train. I think that, more than the picture slowing down, or reality slowing down, what happens in our picture is that you're getting so many vibrations from people and you're seeing people behave so honestly, when they stop you get irritated. It's more than boredom. It's antagonism. You identify with a character and then he does something you don't want him to do. It becomes personal. You can't stand for it not to have the answers every moment. You don't want to waste your time going through their self-exploration. You want them to get right down to it and give you the answers.

G: In filming *Faces*, did you shoot long takes? Did you keep shooting a scene until a reel was used up?

C: Yes. We didn't do it as much in *Shadows* because it had far less dialogue. *Faces* was loaded with dialogue and we had to let the actors play the long scenes through. If we'd filmed short takes, we'd probably still be shooting *Faces*.

G: Did you use 16 mm in shooting both *Shadows* and *Faces*?

C: Yes. It's much cheaper. And much more difficult to edit. One of the reasons I wouldn't do any more films that way is because I can't think of 16 mm over a long, extended period of time again. The film breaks, tears, gets old. And the sprockets tear and you spend half of your cutting time repairing sprockets. You have to be almost like in the army, where you have no mentality of your own. You have to just divorce yourself from all that and think: "Sprockets. All right, I've got eight thousand sprockets to repair."

g: In that case, I take it the next film will be in 35 mm?

c: Right. The next one is a commercial film, actually. It's called *Husbands* and Peter Falk and Ben Gazzara and I will cavort in it. I've written the script and it's my first crack at directing a film I'm acting in. Peter and Ben and I get along so well I think I won't have to prove anything to them about directing.

These three men are forty-year-old kids. They're happy. They just do whatever they want to do. It's our night out, the way we'd like to take our night out. We'd like to take people on our trip with us, to break all the conventions that bug us, without being moralists about anything. It's not a comedy, either. I can't tell you what *Faces* is, and I can't tell you what this will be.

I've had to make some concessions on this picture. The minute you accept money you have to make concessions. And the minute people want to do it in a professional way, it's already a concession because you've got to work with people who are in a professional market. We'll be shooting in New York and London and the film will cost a million. I'm not looking forward to some of the hassles I may have in store for me with the guys with the money.

Husbands has to do with three men whose best friend dies and we go out on a three-day wake without going to sleep. Then one of us takes a shower. It's that simple. He goes home and changes his clothes. We get so angry with the son of a bitch for changing his clothes that we have to play a joke on him. And the result of the joke is what the picture is about.

g: What kind of movies do you want to make next?

c: Peter Falk and I will be making a movie with Elaine May called *Mickey and Nicky,* which we're in love with. The hope of course is that people stay crazy. It's really no fun to work with sane people, people who have a set way of doing things. There's no doubt, for instance, that Fred Zinnemann is one of the best directors around. Yet as an actor I would never want to work with him, even though I know he's a genius in his area. He's just not my kind of a guy.

A lot of it is chemistry. I mean, I'd want to work with Orson

Welles. I don't care what the problems are, because he's an exciting man. That's also the reason I'm looking forward to playing with Peter Falk and Ben Gazzara. We don't care what the problems will be. As long as we stay crazy. If we became all nice people who are very polite, we'd never get along together. Because basically we're bums. I mean, I'm basically a bum. I know a lot of my enemies would agree with that too. But I don't think that's such a bad thing. I think it's more fun. I think I probably have the philosophy of a poor man. You know, like maybe I'd steal the pennies off a dead man's eyes.

PART TWO:

THE EUROPEAN EXPERIENCE

THE UNDEREMPLOYED INDEPENDENT

LINDSAY ANDERSON

"My films are handmade."

Britain's mini-New Wave, the Free Cinema (1956–58), produced three directors of consequence: Tony Richardson, Karel Reisz, and Lindsay Anderson. Free Cinema, a series of programs of short films, was dedicated, in Anderson's words, to the proposition that "If you're going to get attention, you've got to get together and make a row."

Besides their knack for getting publicity, the young filmmakers knew how to help each other. Richardson succeeded first as an independent director, with Look Back in Anger in 1958 and The Entertainer in 1959. The following year he produced Saturday Night and Sunday Morning, which Reisz directed. Then, in 1962–63, Reisz produced Anderson's first feature, This Sporting Life.

They began as reformers, angry young men making naturalistic films about working-class characters. Richardson moved on to alternate between satire and the baroque. Reisz veered off into modish films, like Morgan and Isadora. They mellowed enough to make the traditional accommodation to the "realities" of the film business—box office, banks, and the seductiveness of big budgets.

Anderson, at forty-six, is still a rebel, impatient with compromise and other people's ideas. He has remained on the periphery of the film industry as a vigorous individualist who would rather hand-craft a small film his way or not make it at all. "I'm not a careerist," he explains.

In the six years between his two features, he directed in the theater, made two short films, and did commercials for TV. He says he would rather make commercials than bad movies because of the larger investment of time, boredom, and shame involved in feature films.

Born in 1923 in Bangalore, India, of Scottish ancestry, Anderson studied literature at Oxford after serving in the army. A founder of a disputatious film magazine, Sequence, he drifted by chance into making industrial documentaries. He made some shorts, and finally made This Sporting Life—a naturalistic yet poetic story of a professional football player who is incapable of sustained tenderness in his relationship with a woman.

Anderson is becoming more overtly anarchistic as he gets older. His latest film, If . . . , is set at a British public school (the equivalent of an American prep school). It is a blend of documentary naturalism *and adolescent fantasy about the violent overthrow of authority. "My sympathies," says Anderson, "are always with the revolutionaries." He was interviewed in February 1969 in New York. The co-producer of If . . . , Michael Medwin, was present.*

FILMOGRAPHY:

O DREAMLAND (Short: '54)
THURSDAY'S CHILDREN (Short: '54; Academy Award, '55)
EVERY DAY EXCEPT CHRISTMAS (Short: '57)
THIS SPORTING LIFE (released '63 in U.S.)
MARCH TO ALDERMASTON (Short: '63)
THE WHITE BUS (episode in trilogy, *Red, White and Zero*: '66)
THE SINGING LESSON (Short: '67)
IF . . . ('69)

GELMIS: Before you became a filmmaker, you were a critic for a magazine?

ANDERSON: Yes. It was called *Sequence*. It started at Oxford, immediately after the war. For some time I wrote criticism. Gavin Lambert, who's now in Hollywood, and Karel Reisz were on the staff. It had a small circulation, but a great penetrating power. It was one of those magazines for which nobody got paid for their writing.

G: How did you become a filmmaker?

A: When I left Oxford after the war, I simply was given, quite by chance, the opportunity to make an industrial documentary for a firm in the north of England. It was through a personal contact. And they were mad enough to ask me to make it, because I had talked about being a director. They really were mad, because I had no experience. All I had done since coming back from the war was to read English. So I started making these industrial documentaries, advertising films for a rather broad-minded company. My first film ran for about forty minutes and was about this factory and the men and the tradition.

G: How did you handle the technical part of it?

A: I don't know. I just did. We had an amateur, a local schoolmaster, as our cameraman and a chap to help me who was an assistant director in features. He didn't know very much but was quite a nice chap. I just did it, that's all.

G: Does that imply that anyone with good intelligence and instincts can come in and direct a film without prior training?

A: And talent.

G: What kind?

A: You're born with it.

G: What were your strong points that gave you the ability to direct a film without the training as an apprentice or an assistant director first?

A: You don't learn how to be a director by being an assistant director. You only learn by doing it, really. It's a different kind of job, being an assistant director. It's an organizing job. It doesn't have much to do with actual directing. As for the director, I always felt that a sense of rhythm is very important. And a visual sense, a sense of how to fit things together into a dramatic and rhythmic whole. It's something forgotten and not talked about today.

A lot of modern filmmakers tend to make films shot-by-shot or scene-by-scene. Yet the sense of form is fundamental to art. This thing of seeing every element of every shot in a film somehow as part of a whole pattern or a melody which starts at the beginning and inevitably arrives at the end. I think I have a strong musical instinct, although I don't play an instrument. Music is very important in this work.

I think that, as Walter Pater said, "All art aspires to the condition of music." That is to say, music is the purest of the arts. And it is where this rhythmic quality that's so essential is most apparent. It's very important in film. But it applies in theater direction as well, and in painting a picture.

G: Some directors say they see the film in their head before they even edit it. Others say they discover the film during the editing.

A: No. You don't see it, but you must have an intuition. And the editing comes out of the shooting. The idea of an editor as somebody who puts shape and rhythm on incoherent material comes from good editors working on badly shot documentary material.

But for a good film, the rhythm of the editing must be implicit in the construction of the script. A really good film is an organic growth from the very beginning through the stage of scripting, the shooting that follows out of the scripting, the editing that follows out of the shooting.

G: At what point in your life were you when you developed the radical social attitudes which are so much a part of *If?*

A: I've never been, for instance, a politician. I've never belonged to a political front. When I was in the army during the war, and I was about twenty, I think I became politically conscious in a fairly naïve and simplistic way. So that at the end of the war, when Labor won the election, I was very pleased and had high youthful hopes of Socialism.

In the middle of the 1950s, when the New Left began in Britain simultaneously with the time when we started Free Cinema and the theater was having its renovation with John Osborne at the Royal Court in 1956, that was a period when I think I probably *hoped* for more support in a political way and thought there could be an alliance of sympathies between oneself as a progressive artist and actual progressive political movements.

Those hopes and ideals didn't last very long. I soon saw the New

Left petering out and becoming very like the Old Left. I realized that, in fact, any alliance between an artist and a political movement can only be very temporary.

G: You've described yourself and some of your short films, like *Every Day Except Christmas,* as idealistic in the 1950s. What state of mind are you in now?

A: I've always alternated. A film like *Every Day Except Christmas* is a kind of idealized, poetic, romanticized view of work. But another short film I made earlier, *O Dreamland,* is a rather satirical and fairly harsh kind of human comment about an amusement park. If one is a humanistic artist, and I suppose my work is humanistic, you have to be very careful not to become sentimental. There's too strong a tendency to equate humanism with sentimentality. If you're not capable of a fairly satirical viewpoint, your work may get soft. I think *If* is both idealistic about human nature and satirical about it, which is another reason why it may be regarded as ambiguous at times or why people who expect a film to be utterly simple or to say only one thing may find it confusing if they can't get the point.

My films are subjective, both the features and the shorts. Subjective to me. In a certain way, an artist's films are all about himself. And my films are really about myself. So when I make a film about Covent Garden market and those workers and it is idealized, this is actually a part of myself and the way I look at life, the way that I look at my fellow human beings. I'm trying to make other people share that way of looking at life. It doesn't mean that I'm not capable of being cynical or satirical about them, which I can also be in a different context.

Every Day Except Christmas was attacked in Britain by some of the more traditional documentary filmmakers of the '30s because it didn't have any information about the pay of the porters in Covent Garden market or the frequencies of strikes. I simply said: "Okay, I have no objection to anyone making that kind of a film. But this just doesn't happen to be that kind of a picture, just as Robert Burns can write 'My love is like a red, red rose' without talking about green fly."

G: What was the Free Cinema?

A: It was the name given to a series of programs which ran at the National Film Theater from 1956 to 1958. The first of these programs was really the result of Karel Reisz and Tony Richardson having made a 16-mm film about a jazz club called *Momma Don't Allow.*

It was made with money from the British Film Institute and shot by Walter Lassally.

At the time Karel was finishing editing it, I was finishing up editing a film also made with money from the Film Institute called *Together*, which had been directed by an Italian girl, Lorenza Matzeti. This was an ambitious 35-mm picture of about fifty minutes shot by Lorenza for practically nothing.

I'd had experience in editing my own films. I was largely responsible for the editing for *Thursday's Children*, which I had made with Guy Brenton. So I agreed to edit Lorenza's film. Walter Lassally came in and shot a few more scenes for *Together* and we ended up with this fifty-minute picture. And I'd also made a film of my own, *O Dreamland*, two or three years before on 16 mm. It was only a ten-minute film about a fun fair, which of course had never been shown at all. Nobody was interested. Even one's friends who were film critics couldn't be bothered to come and look at it.

So we got together and we thought that the thing to do was to put all our films together in a program. We made a program of *Momma Don't Allow*, *Together*, and *O Dreamland*. And we decided to try to get the National Film Theater to show them. And we thought that to do this we must call the program something. We hit on the title of Free Cinema.

Then we formulated a kind of manifesto, propaganda, which was a sort of declaration of freedom for the film artists, an attack on the British cinema of that particular time—which was completely middle-class-bound. Ealing Studio comedies—for example, *Kind Hearts and Coronets*—and the like. Emotionally quite frozen.

It was thought of originally as only one program. Then what happened was that, maybe three or four months later, Lionel Rogosin arrived in London with a copy of *On the Bowery*. We met him and saw the film. He didn't know what to do with it, couldn't get a booking. So I had the idea to put on a second Free Cinema program, with *On the Bowery*. We got a couple of other shorts to go with it.

Then later, after that, Karel had got me to make *Every Day Except Christmas* for the Ford Motor Company, and we made it the center for a third Free Cinema program. The programs only ran at the National Film Theater for about four days each. But it was a means of attracting critical attention. Which indeed we did get. And in that way Free Cinema was very important for us. And then it spread abroad. There were showings of our films in New York and on the Continent.

G: Was it the novelty of your movement that got you attention?

A: Certainly. The New Wave in France, which came a few years later, was really a loose journalistic catchword for a whole renaissance in the arts in that country. Britain has never had a genuine underground cinema such as has grown up in New York. We were the first and the last such phenomenon. What we learned was that if you're going to get attention you've got to get together and make a row.

You've got to give journalists something to write about—and even give them a catchword, if possible. It's no good expecting journalists simply to write about a single film. I've often said to young filmmakers in Britain since those days, "Why don't you try to get together and make a movement out of it? Whether you're a movement or not, at least pretend to be one."

G: But filmmakers are generally strong personalities and egotists who don't want to be part of a movement.

A: Yes. But they're also bloody fools. We were strong personalities too. But at least we managed to cooperate *that* much. We couldn't any more now, of course. We've all gone our separate ways since then. My development from those days has been, to me, a fairly straight line, actually.

Karel Reisz has changed quite a bit. I think he has rather abjured the social elements in cinema (from *Saturday Night and Sunday Morning* to *Morgan* to *Isadora*) to a greater degree than I have. Tony always has been, shall I say, a creature of infinite variety. His personality expresses itself in its variety of responses and styles.

G: As you saw your peers—Richardson and Reisz—making an accommodation and joining the film industry, wasn't there ever a time when you said to yourself: "I can just as easily make an entertainment kind of film. I'll get an agent and have him package it. I'll beat the system from within"?

A: No. Probably because I'm born to do the other thing. I don't go naturally to that whole horrid business of getting an agent and packaging and all that. I'm not a very good careerist. It's infinitely boring. It would involve me in a way of life in which I would be ill at ease, which I would feel to be totally unreal, and which I would be very, very bored and frustrated by. I mean, I can't bear being with people whom I don't like to be with. It's as simple as that. It's been said, and I forget by whom, that the secret of being a success is an infinite capacity for being bored.

G: And yet isn't the job of a director, whether he's an artist or a hack, to *make* films? And if through principle he doesn't make the films—that six years pass between films—how can he continue to function as an artist?

A: I should have felt more uneasy about your question if I hadn't made *If*.

G: Do you feel you were right to wait and make *If* on your own terms?

A: So much of this is really dependent on chance and on character. It's quite speculative, whether I could or should have made more films. I don't know. I just haven't.

G: Is it just a question of pride, or of boredom?

A: I think boredom, neurosis, and laziness. There is certainly laziness, of course. When you know that you're going to make a film and it's going to be absolute murder for two years, then you hesitate before taking it on.

G: Why did you stop working with films in the period from 1958 to 1962—after those Free Cinema shows?

A: I was a documentary filmmaker. And I'm really not a pusher or organizer of my career, unfortunately. Nobody was running after me asking me to direct a film. And though I could have made documentaries, they would have been commissioned films. And I didn't want to make films for oil companies, or films about aero engines.

And generally when I did get the opportunity to make a film there seemed to be a row because what I wanted to do was too individual. I happened to be offered a play to direct. So I did it, and I enjoyed doing it. It was at the Royal Court Theatre—which is not quite off Broadway, and not quite Broadway. It's a respectable middle ground.

G: Was it an experimental play?

A: No it wasn't. It was about the most commercial play I've ever directed, except for *Billy Liar*. It was called *The Long and the Short and the Tall*. They made a dreadful movie of it, later. And though I'd done a certain amount of filmmaking, and had directed the play, at that point they wouldn't let me direct the film. They chose some conventional hack, who really made nothing out of it.

G: What happened after *This Sporting Life* opened in 1962–63?

A: I did some work in the theater and I got money by making television commercials. Not a great many. But they're quite well paid.

G: How did you feel about making commercials?

A: I don't like doing them terribly much, but I can't pretend that it's very painful.

G: Is there anything that makes a filmmaker feel like he's lost all self-respect?

A: Yes, much worse than making commercials is to undertake feature films that you don't respect. Much worse. I'd far rather make commercials where you know what you're doing. You're working within certain limitations. They needn't be disgraceful and they're over quite quickly. They're quite modest. Not like making a feature film where you're committing yourself much more fully on the basis of compromise. I wouldn't do that.

G: Before you made *If* you were in Poland for a time?

A: Yes. I presented my stage production of *Inadmissible Evidence* there and I made a short documentary film and I also made *The White Bus*. It's a forty-five-minute film that was meant to be part of a trilogy of stories by Shelagh Delaney. The other segments, by Tony Richardson and Peter Brook, were never joined to this one. When Tony and Peter saw my film, they rejected the related stories and said: "We're going to find new stories." They made their films. The result was that the trio were never combined.

G: Does it seem likely to you that student filmmakers, with their low-budget films and nonprofessional actors and location shooting, must ultimately influence the more traditional films?

A: I suppose that will happen. But I must admit that I myself have always been strongly biased in the direction of form, of artistic form and discipline. In fact, of course, these principles apply whatever your means. So when I was making a film simply with a 16-mm camera and no direct sound, I still always tried to shape the film, to give it a form and a rhythm which would make it a work of art. And that is what is missing in the work of a lot of young people today. Direct cinema, or *cinéma vérité*, has resulted in a lack of artistic form and discipline. It's become very loose and self-indulgent often.

G: What do you think is the impulse to make a film?

A: Part of the impulse to make any work of art is to *make* something—an object. That's part of making a film, aside from communicating ideas. There's the actual impulse that operates in carving a statue or painting a picture, which is to make something. The artist or the poet is a *maker*, isn't he? To make something that exists in terms of that medium, in terms of images, in terms of rhythm, in terms of shape, that is in itself an object. Another reason why I haven't made so many films is because my films are handmade.

G: In a mass-production consumer society, what kind of market for such a costly handmade product is there?

A: Fortunately one can occasionally turn around and discover that it isn't necessarily unprofitable to make the handmade film. In point of fact, *If* has made more money thus far in London than another Paramount film, *The Brotherhood*, which has Kirk Douglas and a big budget.

Yet, I don't mean to emphasize the financial aspect. I am surprised by this. Because I have that feeling that something which is handmade in that way in a system dedicated to the machine-made object is at a certain disadvantage.

G: What was the origin of *If*?

A: Two boys, David Sherwin and John Howlett had just left school and gone up to Oxford. They began writing a script, *Crusaders*, based on their feelings about the British public school experience. The script was in existence for about five or six years before getting to my hands.

It was shown to various filmmakers. They sent it to Nicholas Ray, who liked it very much. But he said this would have to be made by a British director. Then they were working with a friend of mine, Seth Holt. And Seth sent me the script. He also liked it, but felt it couldn't be directed by anyone who hadn't been to a public school.

Finally, I started working with David Sherwin. And we took their script as a starting off point. *If* is a complete transformation of the original script. It's a sort of new work, but that was its inspiration. Most of the dialogue, about ninety per cent of it, is David's writing.

MICHAEL MEDWIN (Anderson's co-producer): The script was turned down by the major companies we took it to in London. They said they couldn't identify with it. "How will somebody in America identify with a British public school?" they asked. Yet it obviously isn't just about a British school at all. But until it was made, we couldn't show that clearly.

A: There was another factor, maybe. Because the script had been written by a writer working with a director, it was a very workmanlike script. It wasn't a *selling* script. It was a very direct script for shooting, very economically written, with no descriptive stuff. It didn't have all that bullshit that makes scripts so boring to read.

Most scripts are written like bad novels, because the scriptwriter is constantly putting in all those adjectives which never get on the screen anyway. But I think that unless they're written like that most distributors feel: "Well, this isn't a script. Where are all those adjectives?"

M: We tried Universal, Columbia, everybody. CBS had just started a film division in London. They decided they would do it. The picture was then set up

A: We shook hands on it. (He laughed.)

M: Yes, that's right. Then we got a crew together and everything started going forward. We were six weeks from our first day of shooting. I was in New York for the Broadway opening of A *Day in the Death of Joe Egg,* which was being produced by the company that Albert Finney and I own. And my first phone call was informing me that CBS had canceled.

That was a beautiful beginning. I think somebody in New York had finally read the script. The poor bloke who ran the office in London obviously didn't know the extent of his authority. So we were faced with a crew and literally fifty-six hours in order to get the picture set up. Otherwise, I think it would have been canceled, and perhaps never have happened again. An abortive start often kills a project entirely.

A: Quite right. It would have been impossible to stop and then get under way again another time. We had to shoot at the end of a school term in which they hadn't a heavy examination schedule. It had to be the end of the Easter term. We had ten days with the boys, who would appear as extras, and then we went to another school. It was quite a quickly made film.

G: How did you go on, knowing you had the momentum but no money at that point?

M: I had one script here, which was xeroxed so that we had plenty of copies. I just went to every major company here, cap in hand. It seemed an impossible task. Who's going to say in fifty-six hours with a script like that, "Yes, you can proceed"? I had heard of Charles Bluhdorn (president of Gulf & Western, which runs Paramount Pictures). I knew he was in New York. In extremis, because I knew it's no good going through channels, I realized I had to go directly to see him. But I knew it was no good Michael Medwin trying to see

Charlie Bluhdorn. So I rang Mr. Bluhdorn's secretary and said that Mr. Albert Finney and Mr. Medwin would like an appointment with him and it was very urgent.

Of course that got our foot in the door. We went to see him and we said, "We are in desperate trouble." We had the script and the budget and he asked a few questions, gave the script to the story department and said: "I'll let you know within forty-eight hours." And in forty-eight hours, he said yes. It was fantastic.

G: Was this film made with deferred payments in order to shoot it on a modest budget?

M: The payments were so minimal, deferment would have been absurd. How can you defer next to nothing? The first question Mr. Bluhdorn asked was, "What is the director getting and what is the production company getting?" The moment he heard the ridiculous fees, he said: "Oh, it's a labor of love." If he had heard that Lindsay wanted, say, $100,000 to direct and I wanted perhaps $200,000 for producing it, he would probably have been more cautious. But he realized there was a lot of emotional enthusiasm behind it, so he agreed to do it.

G: Why did you change the name of the script to *If*?

A: It was related to the Rudyard Kipling poem, *If*, which expresses the good side of the public school ethos. It begins, "If you can keep your head when all others around you are losing theirs" and ends with "What's more, you'll be a man, my son." I think these boys, particularly Mick, are traditional heroes. They become men. They stand up for their convictions and for themselves against odds that may be overwhelming. The hero of *If* is a very responsible man. He finds the right solution. Now, because the film is *not* literal, the end is plainly a metaphor.

G: For revolution? "One man can change the world with a bullet in the right place." Are your sympathies always with revolutionaries, whoever they happen to be?

A: Yes. Always. They make mistakes, of course, but my sympathies are always with the revolutionaries. But then, you must define what revolution is because you can make a revolution by making a film, just as much as by shooting somebody. Maybe better.

G: What was the intention of the dreamlike sequence with the housemaster's wife walking naked in slow motion down the empty halls and the homosexual flirtations and the rest of the sexuality, in the context of revolution?

A: I think that the sexual side of the film is important as another comment on this kind of society. That is, it frustrates the natural sexual instincts in the boys just as much as in the housemaster's wife. The scene where they break loose from this society and go out into the world and have this adventure with the stolen motorcycle and the girl, this is—in the good sense—a pure, violent expression of sex. It's part of the anarchic feeling of the film. The relationship between sex and violence. In a way, it's a very anarchistic film.

G: Why is that?

A: Because I'm an anarchist. That's my temperament.

G: In the sense that no authority is good authority?

A: That no authority is necessary. That the real sense of responsibility is up to the individual. Anarchism is always regarded by the representatives of entrenched authority as an irresponsible creed. But actually it's quite responsible. Because it is the creed according to which we don't do what we're told. We do what we know to be right. So the responsibility is up to the individual. That's implicit in anarchism.

G: In *If*, the three boys know what they're rebelling from, but they don't have a program or know what they want.

A: No, they don't. Events actually lead them, through their good instincts, to the right conclusion.

G: The right conclusion meaning wiping out the oppressor?

A: Yes.

G: Why do you want to influence public opinion with your films?

A: Just because I'm made like that. I think that all art is propaganda. I don't like propagandist art. You see what I mean? In a way, all art is, and must be, seen in a social perspective. I still believe in a moral commitment, though the artist may move in mysterious ways his wonders to perform.
Moral influence can't be measured. The artist does contribute to the moral climate of his time. That's what one is aiming to do. Is there a film equivalent of *Uncle Tom's Cabin*? In Britain, I would doubt it. The pressures on the artist in the cinema to be entertaining are stronger than somebody writing a book who is freer that way.
Did a film like *The Grapes of Wrath* play any part in arousing a social conscience in America? Or was it the *result* of the social awareness arising out of New Deal politics? Which is cause and which is effect? We are a part of history and we also make history. Nobody

can ever say how far we are a part and how far we are making history. To me, these are articles of faith.

G: Is the artist someone with antennae who's attuned to the social milieu around him and responding unconsciously? Or is it concious?

A: Both, I think. For instance, I am rather struck by *If* in this context. *If* was not created in any way with a conscious knowledge or analysis of student movements in France, Berlin, Tokyo, London, and Columbia University. None were heard of in that way when the script was being written. The fact that when we were shooting the scenes of student revolt and massacre for *If*, the events of May (1968) in Paris and Berlin and New York actually were happening is a very extraordinary coincidence. In that sense, the film is in a way prophetic. But it was a sort of personal myth that was being worked out in the film.

G: Why did you choose not to make the usual clear distinctions between the reality and the fantasy in *If*?

A: Because I don't like those words. The key to this is that I think film can and should operate with exactly the same kind of freedom that we already grant to literature, painting, theater, or any other form of art. I think the cinema is still trying to recover from the impact of sound. Oddly enough, the silent cinema, which we're accustomed to patronizing as primitive, was actually freer and artistically more mature than the sound cinema.

In returning to a kind of basic realism which can accommodate both naturalism *and* fantasy or poetry or whatever you like, we're only getting back to a tradition which silent filmmakers enjoyed quite freely. I wouldn't like to say, "Now it's *fantasy*. Now it's *real*." Because the whole point of fantasy is that it *is* real. And that there aren't in life any rigid distinctions between what is real and what is fantasy. Our fantasies are *part* of our reality.

Now, you may take a distinction between naturalism and fantasy. But if you start making these very clear distinctions, I think you make what you're doing crude and obvious and you lose suggestiveness. Because the whole point of this use of the poetic is that you should operate suggestively on people so that you let their imagination run free. Then they can get the most surprising things out of a film. And if they can just accustom themselves to looking at films this way, they'll be imaginatively stimulated rather than when you tell them how they are to take each moment of the picture.

Ambiguity is extremely important. Much of *If* is ambiguous, in the sense that people can take bits of it in very different ways. You find certain people in an audience responding very differently to certain things that happen. I don't quarrel with that. I don't want to tell them exactly what they are to think of each moment.

An interesting thing about, shall we say, this "imaginative freedom"—let's use that instead of "reality" and "fantasy"—is that today the younger the audience the more capable they are of taking this opportunity to be imaginatively freed without question. Understanding it instinctively. Whereas, there is much more resistance from the middle-aged and from the so-called "professionals."

Now, by professionals I mean not the filmmakers themselves but the executives whose business it is not to have feelings about films, but to have an idea of what other people's feelings are going to be. So that they are never able to really *look* at a film. They sit there all the time thinking, "What will they think about this film in the middle west?" And since it's probably about twenty-five years since they've been in the middle west, they haven't got the slightest idea. They usually end up by grossly underestimating their public.

This is particularly true of youth. We're constantly told to make films for a young audience. But the people who tell us to make films for young audiences haven't spoken to anybody under the age of thirty-five for a quarter of a century, except to say good morning and good night. So their idea for a film for young people is one that has the Beach Boys in it. The young people are way ahead.

Q: To be specific about the use of "suggestiveness" in *If*. There's just one point in the film when we are able to distinguish one of Mick's subjective fantasies from what is really "happening." The chaplain lying in the headmaster's tallboy drawer after he was—or wasn't—shot and bayoneted by the boys seems particularly fantastic.

A: If you say to me that "You didn't create a style where that moment is totally inevitable and assimilated," I'd say you might well be right. It's a question of style, really. Maybe you might criticize it symbolically, because perhaps it's too easy to interpret. There's a perfectly clear symbolic interpretation for the act, which is: This is where the establishment keeps religion, isn't it? It depends on how much of a sense of humor people have. If people don't have one, they can sit for the next twenty minutes mumbling: "Gee, I don't know . . ." I think it's a memorable image. Now whether the transition to that image is perfectly achieved, I will leave to others to tell me. I don't know.

Q: After seeing the film a second time, I had the feeling you could have ended it after the first act of open rebellion—when Mick bayonets the chaplain—but that the metaphoric climax of the film was the all-out attack, the rebels burning the house down while the general is making speeches. So you in effect had two endings, or climaxes.

A: This is true. But the first one is carried out much more on an impulse or a sudden burst of anger, therefore it's just personal and doesn't have the total power and significance of what happens at the end. It is their use of real bullets and the bayoneting of the chaplain that opens up the whole film because it brings the issue of these boys against tradition into the open. It's stated in the scene with the headmaster and then in the scene where they're carrying out all the junk.

The headmaster says he has a job for them. On the naturalistic basis I feel this is a place that's simply gone through years of clutter and they're sent to clean it up. That's all. Beyond that I guess you can say it has a significance as a symbol. Because plainly they're trying to clean out the dust of centuries of traditions that have just gone moldy and been forgotten or neglected, however much lip service has been paid to them.

G: Why did you switch from color to sepia to black and white to color again? I couldn't find a motif or pattern.

A: There were no patterns. To shoot the picture entirely in color would have meant another week on the schedule or more money on electrics. When we got to the chapel set, Miroslav Ondricek, my cameraman, said: "We won't be able to do this in our schedule and within our budget. We can't shoot this in color." So I said, "All right, we'll shoot it in black and white." And we did the same on other sequences.

G: Why shoot in color in the first place?

A: The initial reason is because you can't get financing anymore for a black and white picture. This is based on the idea that films must now be made with eventual television sales in mind. That in two or three years all television will be in color. Therefore, *all* films must be made in color. It isn't sensible. There may be films that needn't be made for television or which will never be shown because of subject matter or treatment. But the artist has no recourse.

I would have preferred not to shoot in color originally, partly because I'm a bit frightened of color. I'm not very skilled at it. It adds a great deal to the difficulty of shooting a film. It's slower. You want to start repainting walls, as indeed we did. All our passageways shot in one school we had to paint in order to give the picture a color continuity. If you're working in the way we made this film, in which finance is tight, you're not really given the money to balance the extra time necessary to shooting color.

Yet, I must admit, I'm glad we shot it in color. I think the color is an attractive and an expressive element in the film. And I'm especially glad we have these black and white or monochromed sequences which give the color texture of the picture an interest. Another aspect of using the black and white, if you like, was its applicability to our chapter headings. I rather resent it when I'm told I was influenced by Godard because I used chapter headings. Fashionable rubbish. One might more legitimately call it Brechtian. Or call it the influence of D. W. Griffith, for Christ's sake.

c: Was there anything different in the way you had made your first feature film, *This Sporting Life?*

a: Yes. There was more orthodoxy in the way we shot it than the way we made *If.* The interiors of *This Sporting Life* were shot in a regular studio with a studio crew. We did some shooting on location. But *If* was shot entirely on location. Even the scenes that were shot in a studio were done in a temporary studio we had to build on location. It wasn't like going to a regular studio with all the facilities and technocracy.

c: *This Sporting Life* has been described as the story of an animalistic man looking for one scrap of humanity or human relationship.

a: There are many ways of looking at that relationship in *Sporting Life.* That's one way to look at it. Another way is as a fatal attraction between two temperaments that could never understand or accommodate each other. Neither of them is sufficiently understanding or mature enough to make allowances for the difference in the other. So they were doomed to destroy each other.

c: What was the point of the spider Richard Harris squashes with his fist in the hospital death room at the end?

a: The spider at the end was like the chaplain in the drawer. It's another element of the poetic rather than the literal. The spider was an element in the novel. It was an impotent gesture of violence. You could say that at the end, the violence of the man continued, that he could never really learn from his experience, although this indulgence in violence leads him to disaster. It kills the woman. He never gets beyond it. He himself is completely destroyed, desolated.

G: From the vicissitudes of your own career, what kind of advice do you give those coming into films?

A: The great difficulty about filmmaking anywhere is the nature of the system of distribution and exhibition of films, which *most* contributes to holding back the development of the cinema. The best preparation for making films is the documentary, I think. If you can get documentaries to direct, that's better than, for instance, television. Television is almost a remote control method for a director. He sits up in a control box directing people down below.

I feel that for filmmaking it's very important to handle the actual material of film. And this you do on documentary where you shoot your film and then go into a cutting room and cut it yourself and run it through a Movieola. You get to know about the possibilities of cutting, the rhythmic basis of filmmaking, by actually doing it. In TV, you never get this. My own preparation for making feature films, by having documentary and theater experience, was a valuable double and a rather rare one. They weren't at the same time. They followed each other. All my career has proceeded by a sort of luck.

BERNARDO BERTOLUCCI

"The robins sing always the
same song."

Bernardo Bertolucci was a prize-winning poet who gave up written
poetry to make movies because "cinema is the true poetic language."
He was twenty-one when he made his first feature film, The Grim
Reaper. In the seven years since then, he has been able to get financing for only two more films.

During the 1960s, Italian filmmaking has been dominated by a few
maestros like Fellini and Antonioni and Visconti and De Sica on
one hand, and on the other by a mass production system equaled only
by the old Hollywood studios in its output of standard westerns and
gangster films.

There is an age gulf among Italian filmmakers of talent which
is comparable to the one that existed in France at the advent of the
New Wave. Gillo Pontecorvo (The Battle of Algiers) and Ermanno
Olmi (The Job; The Fiancés) are in their late thirties. Pasolini is
forty-seven, Fellini forty-nine, Antonioni fifty-seven, Visconti sixty-
three, and De Sica sixty-seven.

Few Italian directors, therefore, have aroused as much interest and
excitement at festivals as Bertolucci and Marco Bellocchio, both in
their twenties and both able to use film with the sort of fluency that is
the mark of the natural.

Bertolucci's romanticism struggles in his films with his Marxism.
It's a constant battle between his heart and his head. The heroes of
Before the Revolution and Partner are middle-class Italian youths
who enjoy life as it is, but who talk like revolutionaries. Bertolucci
says his films are exorcism for his own ambivalent feelings.

Like many young filmmakers, Bertolucci's inspiration is Godard.
The heady mixture of lyricism and polemics and ribald humor are
part of the Godardian legacy. There is a slapstick horror scene in
Partner in which a girl discusses soapsuds ad nauseam until the hero
drowns her in the washing machine. It could have been lifted—in
terms of its spirit—from a Godard film like Pierrot le Fou or Two or
Three Things I Know About Her.

Bertolucci, born March 1941, is an international filmmaker. The
influences on his work are as much French and American as they are
Italian. He calls the Paris Cinémathèque his film school. There is
a feedback between young filmmakers in every country now. They

are aware of each other's work, even if the public at large is unfamiliar with their names. Festivals, museum screenings, and cheap air travel have made it possible for the new generation of filmmakers to share ideas more easily than ever before.

This interview was held in Bertolucci's hotel suite with the assistance of Michele Barbieri, an interpreter, in the fall of 1968 at the sixth annual New York Film Festival. Partner, which was shown at Lincoln Center, had still not been released in the United States when Bertolucci returned in the spring of 1969 for a retrospective of his films at the Museum of Modern Art.

FILMOGRAPHY:

THE GRIM REAPER ('62)
BEFORE THE REVOLUTION ('64)
AGONY (Episode in *Love and Rage*, with Julian Beck and the Living Theater: '67)
PARTNER ('68)
GOSPEL 17 (Episode with Godard, Pasolini, Bellocchio: '68)

GELMIS: Why did you decide to make films?

BERTOLUCCI: My father was a film critic. I went to screenings with him when I was small, two or three films every day. And when I was fifteen I was visiting in the mountains and someone gave me a 16-mm camera. I made a ten-minute film about kids that was called *The Cable Car*. I wrote it and shot it and edited it. I showed it to the farmers in the little place where we were staying. They were interested, since it was only the second film they had every seen—the other being a United States Information Agency film about agriculture in Vermont.

It was a home movie and did not seem terribly important. But I started to become a film lover. I did another film when I was sixteen about the way farmers slaughter pigs around Christmas time. I never studied filmmaking. The only school for the cinema is to go to the cinema, and not to waste time studying theory in film school. The best school of cinema in the world is the Cinémathèque of Paris. And the best professor is Henri Langlois (curator of the Cinémathèque).

I had gone to a small country school until I was eleven. After that we moved to Rome, and I went to classical high school. I started college. But I stopped because I preferred to make films. When I was twenty, I had an exciting opportunity to be the assistant director of Pier Paolo Pasolini's first film, *Accattone!*.

G: How did you get your job with Pasolini?

B: I knew him. I had read his poetry. Pasolini had read some of my poems. I met him for the first time when I was twelve. My father introduced us. Working with Pasolini was a very important experience. He was just as virgin to the cinema as I was. So I didn't watch a director at work; I watched a director being born.

G: What did you learn about filmmaking from *Accattone!*?

B: Nothing about technique, really. But I probably learned something about human relations. What I did on *Accattone!* was to work with the actors. I had to teach them the dialogue. They were all non-professionals and didn't know how to read or write very well.

As for style, it was very moving because every time Pasolini did a tracking shot it was like assisting the first tracking shot that had ever been made in the world. Even the closeup. It was like the first closeup that had ever been made. It was like the birth of language.

For me, it was like assisting at the birth of the cimema. *Accattone!* showed me that cinema is the true poetic language. It's much closer to poetry than to theater.

G: Did the experience directly help your career as a director?

B: Not really. I've only made three films in seven years. That's about a film every three and a half years. Indirectly, the success of Pasolini was good for me. The film went very well in Italy. And then because the Italian producers are very sensitive to fashion they decided that many films had to be made with the type of scenario in the Pasolini style. That is, dealing with the lower depths, the subproletariat. So a producer asked me to make a script out of three pages that Pasolini had written. The film had to be made by another director. But when the producer read my script, he asked me to direct the film. That was *The Grim Reaper*, my first feature. I made it in 1962.

Like most sons of gifted fathers, I imitated my father up to a certain age. I wrote poetry, perhaps to imitate my father. And maybe I stopped writing poetry to consciously stop imitating him. I had worked on *Accattone!* in 1961. I published a book of poetry in 1962 which won a prize in Italy. And there I finished with poetry written on paper.

G: Who worked with you on *The Grim Reaper?*

B: I had the same script collaborator that Pasolini used on *Accattone!* and whom he calls his "living lexicon." His name is Sergio Citti. He helped Pasolini write the Roman dialect, the slang of Rome. He is the brother of Franco Citti, who played Accattone.

G: Why didn't you get the chance to make a second film right after *The Grim Reaper?*

B: The film cost $90,000. It was not a commercial success. No one rushed to give me more money to make another film. It took nearly two years between the finish of *The Grim Reaper* and the start of *Before the Revolution* in October of 1963.

G: On the script of *Before the Revolution* you collaborated with your friend Gianni Amico. How long a process for you is scriptwriting? How complete a script do you write?

B: I write very fast because it bores me to write a script. It's very dangerous for me to write a script for two reasons. First, having been a literary man I can't write a script in just a functional sense. It comes more naturally to me to find literary stylistic solutions. So this literary approach interferes with my finding direct cinematic solutions. Once I have found the literary solution, I am finished, tired of the idea. Then the script is no good anymore. It's no longer useful. So when I go to make the film, I don't even open the script anymore. Because I cannot think of the cinema as illustrating a written thing. And secondly, one wastes time. These scripts are really three-hundred-page books, but without camera directions. They have just narrative and dialogue and are amphibious in nature. They are neither cinema nor literature.

G: Why do you go through that whole process of adapting, rather than just writing the usual hundred-page shooting script?

B: To charm producers. They are impressed.

G: But *The Double* was a book already, Dostoievsky's book, before you wrote it and filmed it as *Partner*.

B: Yes, but I rewrote it. In *Partner*, I made two major changes. First, the change from the book to the script. Second, the change from the script to the film. The film has little resemblance to *The Double*.

G: How close did either *Before the Revolution* or *Partner* as finished films come to the books you wrote?

B: They're both very different. You must understand that the producer realizes the film will not really be what I have written in these scripts. I write very fast. I wrote *Partner* in just fifteen days.

G: What's the significance of the title *Before the Revolution* for you?

B: At the beginning of the film, there is the quote from Talleyrand: "Who has not known the life before the revolution doesn't know the sweetness of living."

G: Is the film autobiographical?

B: More than just being autobiographical, it was a way to exorcise my own fears. Because to be like that character is almost a destiny for all bourgeois young Europeans.

G: In fact, did you exorcise it? It seems in *Partner* that you're back to the same dilemma. It's basically about a boy who's unable to dissociate himself from his bourgeois background so he can become the revolutionary he secretly wants to be.

B: I think it's the same story. I'm still exorcising.

G: Have you been influenced by Pasolini's Marxism, since your films are socially conscious, radical, even polemical?

B: No, I was always like this. Marxism in Italy is very common.

G: Do you consider yourself a Marxist theoretician, like Pasolini?

B: Yes, like the character in *Before the Revolution*.

G: And do you really believe that anyone who has laughed and been entertained and dazzled by *Partner* is going to take seriously the end of the film in which Pierre Clementi suddenly tells us that the film is actually a parable about American imperialism and syphilitic marines? Can you really hope to tack on such a Marxist sermon?

B: It's because it comes so suddenly that it has an impact, because it isn't expected. If we had spoken about American imperialism during the whole film, people wouldn't have remembered the film so clearly. In the first scenes of the film there is a North Vietnamese flag. The titles are on a North Vietnamese flag, red and blue and a white star in the middle. So from the very beginning, whoever is receptive enough and wants to understand it, it's clear that it's about imperialism.

G: Since *The Double* is so different from *Partner*, why did you bother to use Dostoievsky as your inspiration in the first place?

B: Because I had written several scripts of three hundred pages each after I made *Before the Revolution*. And they were refused by everyone. So when a producer asked for a new idea for a film, I turned to the first book I found on my night table. It was *The Double*. I handed it to the producer because I just didn't have the energy to write one more word of my own. And the name of Dostoievsky sold the material.

Before the Revolution had not been a commercial success, except in France. It cost $300,000 and did not return its money. That meant I had to wait four years, until October of 1967 to make *Partner*. It cost about $250,000. If it doesn't make money, I don't know how long I will have to wait this time.

G: Is it difficult for young Italian filmmakers to get financing because the Italian film industry is in trouble?

B: No, it's just the opposite. It's because the Italian industry doesn't have any problems. They won't risk any money. It's very established. "Ah, now we go western." We make a hundred westerns every year.

G: Isn't it possible for young filmmakers to work within that system and turn out an interesting western or gangster film, to make a few action films well and make a success so they can get the money for more personal films? It would still take less than four years, in any case.

B: Yes, I can, I can. All the time the producers are asking me, "Why don't you make a western?" But I don't want to. Because I love westerns very much. The western means Howard Hawks and John Ford. It would be like asking John Ford to make a Pasolini film. The Italian westerns are not very good.

G: Even the Sergio Leone films?

B: Ah, Sergio Leone I like. But they are not westerns. They are something else. He is a very genial man. I wrote the first draft for the latest Leone film, *Once Upon a Time . . . in the West*.

G: The plot for that film sounds like a remake of *Union Pacific*.

B: I was thinking of *Johnny Guitar*, actually. Anyway, you know, that was a curious experience. My serious friends in Italy have accused me of selling out because I wrote for Sergio Leone, who is considered just a commercial moviemaker. But I worked for Leone because I admired him and thought it would be a good experience. And it was very educational. If Leone reads this, he will have to blush because the film had a $5,500,000 budget. I was paid $700 for a hundred-page treatment, or $7 a page.

G: You came into filmmaking with a background as a writer. How much is it necessary for a director to know about the technical part of filmmaking, lighting, focal lengths, sound? Had you studied photography?

B: No. I've never even been able to make a still photograph. To make a film it is not necessary to know anything technical at all. It will come with time. You will learn. The cinema is not an exceptional moment of life. I would like the cinema to parallel life. I am making always just one film. The filmmakers I love have made only one film.

Godard started with *Breathless* and continued with the same film that proceeds along with his life. It's one film, even if it has many titles or many chapters. It's the same film and it walks along with him. To make film is a way of life. If we take out the title of the film and THE END and put the films all together we will have the figure of one man, of an auteur, the life of an auteur, transferred in many different characters naturally. But the film is one film. It proceeds parallel to what you're doing, as long as one has control of what one is doing. Freedom is the absolute necessity. From the beginning, I've had total control over my films.

Do you know the Italian painter Giorgio Morandi? He painted bottles all the time. Always the same subject. And there are some directors who make always the same film. And poets who write always the same poem. This to me is very beautiful. Because the robins sing always the same song.

G: You've said you'd like to make a film in New York (Raymond Chandler's *The Long Goodbye*). You might not find quite the same freedom you've enjoyed previously.

B: Freedom we have inside. It is not an external condition. Not only that, freedom is a state of being. I can be very free even if I am surrounded by ten gorillas or one producer. And if I cannot feel free enough, then I will simply leave without making the film.

G: For a director who believes that you don't have to know much about technical matters, you undertook a film, *Partner*, dependent on special effects, on one actor playing two roles on the screen. Wasn't that a problem?

B: I swear to you that I absolutely don't even know how this split screen was done technically. I have this technique in my imagination. I don't know how to use the camera. But I know what I want. I want each take to be a film in itself. I am against editing. I would like to make a film of one long take. I feel that editing renders films all alike, gives them a brushing of conventionality. I want to do as many long takes within a single film as possible. I prefer to do an interior editing inside my head.

This forces me to find solutions that are not the usual solutions of editing—of, you know, making the establishing shot and then the closeup and so forth. It forces me to find unconventional solutions. For each shot I must have a new idea. For example, in *Partner*, in the shot of Pierre Clementi and the double in front of the mirror, this for me in my mind was a little thing. Because in the interior of my mind I had three dissolves of light fading on first one and then the other character. I am forced to invent continuously because I don't want to use cutting and editing and the usual conventions.

G: How much footage did you shoot in *Partner*, compared to how much you finally used in the film?

B: Ten to one. Not in the classic sense of shooting ten takes and choosing one as the best. I shot many other things I wanted to do. Then I wasn't able to use them, but they are completely different from the sequences you see in the film. I use ten per cent of the *mass* of material I shoot.

G: How much of the creative job of moviemaking for you is done in the editing room?

B: I make up my mind watching the rushes which scenes to eliminate. I create my film in the shot, not in the editing room. What comes later is arranging the scenes. I am not re-creating a reduced original vision. I am just creating order out of the chaos of my selections. And I must be objective enough to eliminate scenes that don't work, as I did with several very long takes in *Partner*.

G: Hitchcock tried it in *Rope* and wasn't satisfied. Godard used very long takes in *Contempt*, where he panned back and forth in dialogue scenes between Brigitte Bardot and Michel Piccoli. It was disconcerting. Warhol tests our endurance with uncut takes. What is its ultimate purpose?

B: The establishment director cuts when he feels that the emotion becomes too strong or when he feels that there is a near possibility of boredom. He cuts at the moment in which the film could become for the people something more than just ghosts.

G: Since you disregarded your three-hundred-page script, or book, that you wrote for *Partner*, what did you use as a guideline on the first day of shooting?

B: I work on the memory of the script. There is a shooting schedule for the actors. Pierre Clementi was given the three-hundred-page script to read before we started filming. He is an actor who has a theatrical background and he feels he must learn some lines in advance. But we seldom used the dialogue. We improvised or wrote new dialogue as we made the film.

This is one of the first Italian films using direct sound recording on location. It's another way to make a revolution in the cinema. I like very much the sound of the voice of Clementi at eight o'clock in the morning, as if he hasn't slept all night, the way his voice sounds at that particular moment. I don't want to try later to re-create that particular sound with post-synchronization at the studio. It's impossible. I prefer to make movies completely on location.

G: How do you deal with your actors?

B: I make documentaries on actors. All my films are documentaries on my actors. I follow them. I let them do what they want. I don't want them to become something that they're not. I want the character that was in the three hundred pages to become what *they* are. I want the character Jacob to become the actor Clementi, not for Clementi to become Jacob. It's the discovery of a man.

c: What are you trying to do with your films: entertain, educate, propagandize?

b: To know. I want to know.

THE SOCIALIST FILM SCHOOLS

MILOS FORMAN

"To laugh at their own tragedy has
been in this century the only way
for such a little nation placed in
such a dangerous spot in Europe to
survive."

*Czechoslovakian filmmakers were in the forefront of the reform move-
ment that flourished briefly under Alexander Dubcek in 1968. The
renaissance of Czech movies dates back at least three years earlier
than the final liberalization of the government, press, and television.*

*The films had satirized bureaucracy; placed the individual ahead of
society; expressed disillusion with slogans, promises, and platitudes;
and had reasserted man's dignity, his uncertainty, and his need to
doubt all dogma.*

*In the socialist community, movies are a state-regulated industry.
Movies reflect—and influence, through a complex feedback—social
and official attitudes. The government pays the bills, so the assumption is that a socialist country's movies have official sanction.*

*The most consistently admired movies from Czechoslovakia have
been tragicomedies like* Loves of a Blonde, The Firemen's Ball,
Closely Watched Trains, The Shop on Main Street, Josef Killian,
Report on the Party and the Guests, *and* Intimate Lighting. *They
vigorously espoused humanism, rejected ideologies.*

*Even before Antonin Novotny was ousted by liberals in January
1968, the coming democratization could have been predicted from the
increasing boldness of the Czech filmmakers. How had the tiny
Czechoslovakian nation of fourteen million persons evolved a world-
respected movie industry and protected it until the occupation from
neo-Stalinist power brokers within and hostile criticism from Russia
and monolithic East Germany before the invasion?*

*The Czechs have a tradition of civilized self-rule and democratic
institutions which had sustained them through two previous totali-
tarian takeovers. In addition, the intellectual élite rallied to the
support of the film industry. They worked within the Communist
Party to keep Russia placated. Furthermore, their superb film school,
established in 1945, introduced its students to the best contemporary
movies in a context of respect for the past achievements of mankind.*

*Virtually every Czech filmmaker is a graduate of the film school in
Prague, a branch of the Academy of Fine Arts. The school has a
four-year curriculum, accepts ten per cent of its applicants and*

offers free instruction and a modest living allowance. The students are teamed up to write and shoot as many as thirteen movies apiece during their training. All this is in addition to the regular university courses in the humanities.

During the general euphoria just before the Warsaw Pact nations occupied Czechoslovakia in the fall of 1968, I visited the school and talked to the dean, Frantisek Daniel, a genial, keen-witted man. "We were never out of touch with the best minds of world cinema," he said. "On Fridays, our students see two films from the archives and one or two of the latest films from abroad. All the films are discussed. And this is one of the reasons the students are constantly stimulated and kept up to date on what is happening in advanced centers of the world."

The main features of the Czech cinema, compared to other world movie production, Daniel felt, were: "Humanism, even in experimentation; poetry in humor and incongruity, and modern art in the means of expression."

"What school can give to the students," he said, "is art, and that art can be an answer in life, and that if you believe in art you must believe in people. There is a profound influence on the student filmmaker in working with a professor for four years. There is a continuity and the filmmaker is rooted in a continuing tradition of art. Our attitude is connected with the role of art and culture in our lives. We are now celebrating the seventieth anniversary of the Czech cinema."

Once they are graduated from the film school, the young filmmakers are employed by the Barrandov State Studio and earn a minimal basic salary, or retainer. When they are working on a production, they earn more money. Before the takeover, Barrandov Studio information officer Vladimir Bystrov told me: "Once a director starts to make a movie, there is absolutely nobody, nobody at all, who can talk to him, to persuade him to change his film."

What happens now to the Czech film industry is uncertain. In the aftermath of the invasion, newspapers and television broadcasts were being heavily censored and advisors remained in key positions for consultations on what was to be communicated to the public and how. The effect on filmmaking will take longer to ascertain, because of the time involved in preparing, shooting, editing, and releasing pictures.

The film school was, then, for a time, the training ground for a number of talented young directors, the best known of whom in the West are Jiri Menzel (Closely Watched Trains, winner of an Academy Award), Jan Nemec (Diamonds of the Night and Report on the

Party and the Guests), *Ivan Passer* (Intimate Lighting), *and Milos Forman. Forman was born in 1932. The following interview took place in the fall of 1968, when Forman's film,* The Firemen's Ball, *was the final offering of the sixth annual New York Film Festival.*

FILMOGRAPHY:

COMPETITION ('62)
BLACK PETER ('63)
LOVES OF A BLONDE ('65)
THE FIREMEN'S BALL ('68)

GELMIS: As a graduate of the Czechoslovakian film school, would you say that a director can be taught how to make movies at school?

FORMAN: I suppose that the school in Prague is not a bad idea. But everybody can learn things theoretically. It doesn't mean very much, unless you are involved in all phases of filmmaking. And there is another thing. For me, for example, as I see it today, school was not so valuable for the concrete facts I learned there. The most valuable thing was that I had four years relatively free to see films in company with my friends, to talk with my friends, to spend my free time living always in this milieu of people who love films. This, finally, I found the most rewarding part of going to film school. I studied film writing for four years. There were five students in each specialty. Those who were studying directing had the chance to make their own films. While one was the director, the other students in his class would take turns as the assistant, the producer, and so on. And this way they get experience doing each job. What's very important is that after finishing school you have something to show. In the first year, you make an 8-mm film. And then a 16-mm sketch or a small documentary, just to practice, to work with the actors.

As a screenwriter, my program was different. In the first year we just wrote two short stories, without any connection to films, and one outline based on a book. The second year we wrote a treatment from the outline, and we also wrote an outline from an original idea. In the third year, we made a whole script based on the treatment from the book, and a treatment of the original idea. In the fourth year, we wrote a script based on our own original idea.

G: What experience in practical filmmaking did you have at school?

F: None.

G: Wouldn't it have been more useful to you as a future director if you had actually been making films during those four years at school?

F: Yes, but this is difficult you know, because of the bureaucracy at school. Once you are in the branch of study, they don't like to see you transfer.

G: Filmmakers aren't exactly overpaid in Czechoslovakia. Do you recall why you chose to go to film school?

F: I always wanted to work in the theater, from the time that I was eight years old. I played in the school theater and amateur theater, when I was thirteen, fifteen, sixteen years old. And I tried to enter the theatrical school but was refused. It has an older tradition than the film school. So by chance I chose the milieu closest to the theater, which was the cinema. And I was accepted as a screenwriter. That's how I became involved with film. I was rejected by the theater.

G: Does anybody outside the school and state studio bureaucracy make films at all in Czechoslovakia?

F: There are some people who started to make their films as assistants to the filmmakers, rather than going to school. Or they may have come from the short or documentary films. But now it's almost impossible to start at Studio Barrandov, even as an assistant, without having gone to the school. The school only started in 1945 and it wasn't producing enough filmmakers. Now they have enough people from the school to fill all the vacancies every year.

G: Frantisek Daniel, the dean of the film school, says that the students and faculty were never out of touch with the best minds of world filmmaking. Where did they get the films that the school showed two or three times a week?

F: The Czech film library, the cinémathèque, is quite rich in older films. And new films are always available because the foreign companies are proposing to Czech Film Export to buy new films. So practically every interesting film comes for two or three days to Prague to be seen by official people, for them to decide if they want to buy it or not. And on these occasions they generally lend the film to the school.

G: Is there an advantage in learning about filmmaking at school, rather than being an apprentice at a studio?

F: Yes, yes, I'll tell you what a great difference there is. If you start immediately in the film business, whether it's in the United States or in the Studio Barrandov, Prague, you accept responsibility too soon for the commercial results. If you start as assistant, you are immediately working for someone else's thinking. And you have not the time to develop your own personality. Because you are always serving somebody else's style, sombody else's thinking, as assistant. I think that today, as film and television are so hungry for new people, a school which prepares new individualities is a necessity.
You need a place to make your mistakes and to fail. You don't want to take the chances later you can take in the privacy of school. There is a big danger if you have not the possibility to try all your

crazy things, foolish things, stupid things, when you are young. Because, if you have not, later you are always afraid. Maybe it's not such a good comparison, but it's like a young man for the first time making love with his wife, when he's twenty-five. Everybody celebrates him how he is, puritan, clean, proper boy. Yes, but problems start after. A certain schizophrenia starts.

G: What happened to you after leaving the film school?

F: I finished the film school in 1955, when I was twenty-three. I didn't make my first feature until '62, when I was thirty. In between, I did many things connected with the performing arts—television, Laterna Magika, a night club theater. I wrote two film scripts for other directors. The first one was a very bad film and a very bad script, *Leave It to Me*. Martin Frisch made the film. He's a Czechoslovakian John Ford and has made about a hundred films in his lifetime. The other film, which Eva Novack made, would be called in English *Youngsters*.

G: How did you get to direct your first movie?

F: It is not easy to start as a film director if you went through school as a scriptwriter. I wanted to direct my own scripts. I had not felt that way in school. But every scriptwriter eventually wants to direct his own scripts. I started in an amateur way. I bought my own 16-mm camera and Ivan Passer and I started to amuse ourselves with it, as friends do.

I started to make a simple documentary for my friends, who were then running a small theater in Prague. When I had about half the material I showed it to the studio and happily they liked it. And they proposed that I finish the film under professional conditions—still shooting it in 16 mm, but having a good sound man and lighting man and so forth.

The film was called *Competition* and dealt with open auditions for rock 'n' roll singers. The first part, the rehearsal in the theater and the beginning of the competition, was shot before I had the expert help. I was practically writing a script during shooting. I had some material, and now I had a possibility to make a film. But they wanted just a short documentary of about fifteen minutes.

I felt that this could be my chance. Without telling them anything and with a little money which I received from the studio, I started to think about a light feature story. During shooting, Ivan Passer, my friend, and I would discuss the story. You know, about two girls One who is singing with an amateur rock group. And the other who is singing not at all yet going into the competition.

When I finished the film, the studio officials were a little bit angry with me because I had made a forty-five-minute film and they only wanted fifteen minutes. And forty-five minutes is a very unhappy length because it's not short and it's not long. But finally I profited, because since they didn't know what to do they proposed to me that I make another forty-five-minute film and combine them into a single program.

So I made a film about brass bands. And I think I found myself in these two films. I became sure that what I was dreaming was attainable. I learned that the only thing which you must be sure of is that you have something to tell—everything else you can learn during the shooting. I don't mean a message. For me, film is pleasure, a desire to tell stories. Everybody likes to tell stories. People work and in the evening they meet in the cafe and tell what happened to them. And that's what we are doing. We are telling stories with pictures.

G: Was *Competition* a success?

F: The film was very successful with critics but not a big success commercially. Just middling. But the enthusiasm of the critics encouraged the studio to let me make my first feature film. They immediately started to propose scripts I should do. But I am not capable of making a film which I didn't write myself. At that time, I met one of my friends who had just finished a novel. I read the manuscript. I liked it very much. So together we wrote the script for *Black Peter*.

The novel takes place in 1947 and describes the life problems of a young boy just after the war. The boy in the book is an apprentice in a store. The book is autobiographical. By chance, during the war I had been living with the family of my uncle who had a small shop. And I worked in the shop. So I found that the book was also my autobiography.

At first, we wrote a script set in 1947. The script was accepted by the production group at the studio. We started making preparations. I chose my young actors. And I shot the screen tests, the auditions. During the tests, I realized that the young people of today are fantastic when they can talk their own today language, when they can wear their own today clothes, when they can behave like they are.

And I noticed that I was destroying their spontaneity, their freshness, in forcing them to play somebody living in 1947. So we decided to rewrite the script and transplant the story to the present time. It was not liked by the officials of the sudio, because of bureaucratic reasons. They told me, "We approved *this* script. We want you to make *this* script. If you so easily can change twenty years, it means that you are not serious enough." But thanks to the bosses of the production group who were backing me, I managed to shoot with the new script. I even managed to complete the film for only $80,000, though they thought it would cost about $130,000.

G: *Black Peter* was a film about a boy who didn't know what he wanted. He wasn't a Socialist hero. Did you have trouble with the bureaucrats over ideology?

F: No, no. Because it was a comedy. And comedy just wasn't considered a serious art. They didn't worry about it. People laughed. "Oh, it's not serious. It's such a little comedy."

G: In the same year that they showed *Black Peter* at the New York Film Festival (1964), I saw the Polish director Jerzy Skolimowski's *Walk Over* and *Identification Marks, None*. For us, it was the first clear evidence of an anarchistic spirit among Socialist youth.

F: You know, in that period there were suddenly about five so-called controversial films in Czechoslovakia. And before the officials realized that these films didn't correspond to the official ideology, the films had reached international success. And it was not popular to prohibit them in the time in which the Novotny regime announced that we were finished with Stalinism. All circumstances were favorable at that moment.

G: What happened to *Black Peter* in Czechoslovakia?

F: It received the Czechoslovakian critics' prize that year. And also the commercial success was not bad. It was not a big hit like *Loves of a Blonde*. But it was not a flop. And the film was shown all over the world and brought in foreign currency. This made the government happy.

G: What specific things, if any, did you learn from making *Black Peter* that you hadn't come up against making the 16-mm shorts?

F: Each film is bringing you always one problem: that once you achieve something you were dreaming to do you don't have the enthusiasm any longer. Once you finish, you are tired of what you did. For example, in *Competition* I was still enormously fascinated by *cinéma vérité* shots, just observation for observation. When I finished it and when we started to write *Black Peter,* I finally felt that I'm a little tired by this and I prefer to elaborate a script more.

So in *Black Peter* we worked much harder on the construction of the script and the story. There are far fewer sequences than in *Competition* of observation for its own sake. Since that first film, I have worked with a complete script before I begin shooting. But always I try to improvise. When the improvisation is successful, I keep the improvisation. But mostly the results are not good, so I go back to the script. That's why I need to have always an exact script.

G: What kind of schedule do you follow when you write a script?

F: What I need is just to be absolutely free from all other problems, just to be hidden somewhere with my co-writers and friends. Very often we go away from home, to the mountains perhaps, and we stay there for a month or two. We work when we want to work, not following a precise schedule. Sometimes we are working until four o'clock in the morning and sleeping until one o'clock in the afternoon. What I need is not to be disturbed from outside, by family problems, for example. Once I am on the set arranging shots and preparing work, there are so many unimportant things going on you have a fog in front of your eyes. And I like having my co-writer on the set to see with fresh eyes something I may have missed.

G: Are you a one-take director, or a ten-take director?

F: Very rarely one. Mostly two and three and sometimes four, five, and six. I always know what I want from an actor. But when I start to rehearse, I'll give the actor relatively big freedom. And sometimes what he's doing is much better and more interesting than anything I had imagined in advance. In this case, I'll keep what the actor does. When I'm not satisfied, I continue until he's doing what I visualized.

G: How do you feel about actors, and what's the best way to use them in your overall landscape?

F: For me, an actor is a part of nature. First I make a rehearsal. You know, you are sitting here and I need you to go to the telephone and talk to someone. First I ask you to do it. Then I make a composition. I am always looking in the camera and choosing the composition. But the camera must serve the actor and not vice versa. I'm always creating and seeing compositions. But it's in me. Just as I don't move the skyscrapers, so I don't move the actors merely because of composition. I look for the composition respecting what the reality is that I'm filming, including the actors.

G: Why is it you've used so few professional actors in your films? I've heard that you don't like stage actors.

F: I have nothing against them. I'm just tired of the routine. I am not all that excited with the routine that very often professional actors, theater actors, are bringing on the screen. For example, the pianist in *Loves of a Blonde* and the tall mason in *Black Peter* were professional theater actors, and they were the only ones. There were no professionals in *The Firemen's Ball*. But there I was using several actors who had already been in my earlier films.

Competition was very important for me, vis-à-vis the nonprofessional actor. Because before I never considered working with anyone but theatrical professionals. It's a very strong convention, you know: actors are actors, and that's that. But during my work on this documentary, I discovered some surprising qualities in these nonprofessionals and I began to admire them. Seeing them on the screen, I was amazed. The big advantage is that these people can be themselves in front of a camera. That's what fascinates me. That you can see on the screen real, fresh personalities which are not repeatable. Nobody can replace them. You can't replace them by an actor.

G: Yet after the first time acting in a film, don't some of these original personalities become self-conscious and turn into professional amateurs? You can only be a virgin once.

F: Oh yes, you're right. Some people you can use just once. They are destroyed by knowing, by learning the rudiments of technique. But if you look at these people as I do during work, you find that maybe it's only by chance that these people are not actors already. They have certain qualities of professional actors. They have certain talent. Maybe just because destiny was not kind to them they became a butcher or a mason and not an actor.

G: Where do you find your actors?

F: I'm always trying to find them among people whom I know already, my friends. In *Loves of a Blonde*, the main girl is the sister of my first wife. I had known her since she was nine. The principal soldiers in that film are friends from my school days. The father in *Loves of a Blonde* is the uncle of my cameraman's girl friend. The rest you must be lucky to find. If you find the right person, you've solved your problem.

G: Could you be specific about your objections to using stage actors in movies?

F: I admire enormously the transformation capability of actors on the stage. But on the screen I admire real personalities. Because I think that there is a difference between theater and film. Film is photography, finally, and everything surrounding the actor is real. The sky is real. The trees are real. The earth is real. Everything is real. So I want real people too. On the stage, everything is stylized. Everything is artificial. So I admire somebody who can transform his personality to suit the situation and character in that artificial setting. It's difficult for me in English to say this as well as I would like to. But, you know, in the theater you don't pretend that what you see on the stage is reality. But in films—not historical films, but in realistic films—automatically the photography enables you to pretend what you see on the screen is reality. So I am disturbed when in that reality I see theater.

G: What did you learn from making your first films, aside from this introduction to working with nonprofessionals?

F: I knew almost nothing about film technique when I started. And I discovered that in film almost everything is possible. Everything I did in using angles, the lenses, the cutting, and so on, I had no previous experience at. If I had been working several years as an assistant before that, certainly my film would have been more similar to films of directors with whom I might have worked and I would have accepted the same restrictions and conventions which governed them.

G: What were the greatest influences on you as a moviegoer? What, for instance, was the first film you ever saw?

F: My first film, when I was a child, was Walt Disney's *Snow White*. The first filmmaker who really touched me was Charlie Chaplin. All of his films. I don't know if I started liking films because Chaplin was so good or if he touched something which was already in me that I didn't know about before. I was very moved by his mixture of laughter and tears.

G: How do you account for so many of the best Czech films and books having that Chaplinesque quality of laughter and tears? Is it something in the Czech character?

F: The tradition of Czech culture is always humor based on the serious things, like *The Brave Soldier Schweik*. Kafka is a humorous author, but a bitter humorist. It is in the Czech people. You know, to laugh at their own tragedy has been in this century the only way for such a little nation placed in such a dangerous spot in Europe to survive. So humor was always the source of a certain self-defense. If you don't know how to laugh, the only solution is to commit suicide.

G: *Loves of a Blonde* seemed like the story of a female Don Quixote. What was the origin of the film?

F: The inspiration was a girl whom I met by chance in Prague in the street. She told me her life story. From this, I developed the idea of the film. The blonde in the film, my former wife's sister, is like the character she plays in many ways. She is warm and a bit naïve.

G: How did you happen to bring the soldiers to the factory town for the girls? Was there ever such a preposterous situation or did you invent it?

F: There are about seven towns with this problem in Czechoslovakia, where industry in which a majority of women are working developed and not enough men were available. So this problem exists. And I visited all seven towns. In one town I heard that they actually had tried to solve this crisis by stationing soldiers nearby. It was not successful, even though they were young soldiers. But it's not very difficult to imagine that the army bureaucracy would send them old reservists.

G: How much of the slapstick byplay—the middle-aged soldiers sending the wine to the wrong table of young girls, and the wedding ring the soldier was trying to hide rattling along the dance floor for everyone to see—was improvised?

F: *Loves of a Blonde* was filmed almost directly from the script. Just the dialogue for the last scene, with the mother and father protecting their son from the girl by taking him into bed with them, was improvised. I had that scene written in the script, also. But this was the last day of shooting. And these nonprofessional actors, like the father and the mother (she was a factory worker we found on a Prague tram) kept getting better and better during the shooting. On this last day of shooting I had enough material and enough time, because we were ahead of schedule. And I decided that I'd like to try something different than I had planned. I told them the situation I wanted, but the words are their own.

G: Why did you make *The Firemen's Ball?*

F: The idea of this film started one day when Passer and Papochek and I were in the mountains to write another script. One evening, to amuse ourselves, we went to a real firemen's ball. What we saw was such a nightmare that we didn't stop talking until the next day about it. So we abandoned what we were working on to start writing this script, because it was something really fantastic.

I didn't want to give any special message or allegory. I wanted just to make a comedy knowing that if I'll be real, if I'll be true, the film will automatically reveal an allegorical sense. That's a problem of all governments, of all committees, including firemen's committees.

That they try and they pretend and they announce that they are preparing a happy, gay, amusing evening or life for the people. And everybody has the best intentions. And everybody's prepared to be happy, to help. But suddenly things turn out in such a catastrophic way that, for me, this is a vision of what's going on today in the world.

G: One of the few objections I've heard anyone make about *The Firemen's Ball* is that it rambled and didn't have the central focus of a single character, like Peter or the blonde.

F: I realized in advance that because the film would not be based on the story of one person it would not be helped commercially. Because people like to identify with one person. But in this film it was not possible, because the main personality is a committee, a firemen's ball committee. And it brought problems for me. For example, the shortness of the film is a result of this. I underestimated this fact. When you have one leading character and the audience likes him or her, you can waste a certain amount of time watching just this personality. But when you don't have such a central single personality, you must move quickly.

I shot enough material for a hundred-minute film. But this was for me a new experience. I tried to make one main person, a girl who is in the firemen's beauty contest, the leading character in the film. But I found this was impossible. I got more and more interested in describing the atmosphere and events surrounding the ball. So finally I eliminated most of the scenes with the girl, who now has a very small part in the film. And I concentrated more on this collective hero, the committee. I didn't realize the problems when I was writing the script, just when I was cutting the film. Then I understood that this collective hero doesn't keep the film together as solidly as one leading person. The first cut was about ninety minutes. But then I saw that the film was going too slow. So I cut seventeen minutes.

G: Whenever a new young director makes a great success and he's very hot, obviously all of the money men in Hollywood, Rome, and London are interested in possibly exploiting him. To what extent has this happened to you?

F: Two years were wasted on projects that did not become films. I received several scripts which some producers proposed to Ivan Passer and me. After *Loves of a Blonde* got so much attention, Carlo Ponti had me start working on a script for him—*The Americans Are Coming, The Americans Are Coming*—about a tourist who comes to hunt bears in Czechoslovakia. This went on for four or five months and the results were not happy. What we liked, Ponti didn't like, and what he liked, we didn't like.

G: How did Claude Berri (director of *The Two of Us*) and François Truffaut become the producers of *The Firemen's Ball?*

F: Ponti had agreed to put up $110,000, or about half the cost. When the film was finished, he wanted me to add some scenes. For instance, he wanted me to lengthen the scene in which the plump girl goes under the table to make love. I refused. The film is made just as the script was written and no one changed it. Ponti finally quit. He had the right to, because in the contract I didn't fulfill the length of the film. It was supposed to be at least eighty minutes and the film is only seventy-three minutes. I didn't add seven minutes because it would disturb the film.

When Ponti rejected the film, I was in quite a bad situation. In Czechoslovakia, foreign currency is very well guarded by the state. Ponti had already paid about $50,000 or $60,000 and then withdrawn it, because he had the right to under the terms of the contract. I was in danger of being brought to trial by the state for losing that money. They would have put me in prison for many years. Really. So I was in a bad situation. At the time, I was traveling through Paris. I had met Claude Lelouch before I made *Firemen's Ball*. And he told me he would like to produce and buy my film. I called him and he said, "Yes, yes, I want to see the film and I'll buy it." This was a Tuesday. I arranged a screening for Thursday. But a print did not arrive on Thursday. And Lelouch was leaving Friday for several weeks.

The print came on Saturday. Luckily, by chance, through a French assistant director I met in Prague, I was told that I should show the film to Berri and Truffaut. I called Berri. When I explained my situation it was Saturday evening. They arranged a screening for Sunday. There were Berri and Truffaut and two brothers who run many important theaters in Paris. I showed the film and had to translate into French for them. When the film was finished, everybody told me they liked it and would take it. I was saved.

G: Why do you suppose the Soviets never tried to crack down on Czech filmmaking—which really spearheaded the new freedom of expression—but got so angry by the freedom of the newspapers, radio, and TV that they invaded?

F: I think that the reasons are very practical. It's because just reading a script makes it very difficult to judge how the film will be. And seeing the rushes, it's also not possible to judge how the film will look. And once the film is finished, it may have cost two or three million crowns, maybe more. It's very easy to prohibit a painting exhibition, because it costs nothing. It's very easy to prohibit a book, because it costs nothing. But to prohibit a film costs a lot of money.

You must understand that the reaction against the Novotny regime didn't happen overnight. It took years until he lost so many people that he had perhaps just thirty or forty people loyal to him. And at the beginning of 1968, the rest of Czechoslovakia was happy he was ousted. In the film industry, it was the same way. Before 1962, you always found people who, even if they didn't understand the script, if they felt something was wrong they cut it out rather than take any chances. But more and more you found that people who would read your script preferred to give you the opportunity to make it. And once the film was finished, we were happy to see that we had started five or six new directors in the same year. It's just too difficult to suppress six films, because you would lose five or six million crowns.

G: Do you think filmmaking at Studio Barrandov will return to the degree of freedom that existed in the renaissance of 1968, or will it become cautious now?

F: I don't think things will go back to being as bad as they were several years ago. But we must wait and see. It is very difficult to talk. It's quite possible that freedom for the artists will be absolutely one hundred per cent. It's possible. But it's just as possible that that fantastic atmosphere we lived and worked in for too short a time is finished now. Finished. In one very important way, it's already finished. People felt strong, certain, free. Then incertitude and fear returned. You are never quite the same when you have been dealt such a blow.

G: Your next film, which you're now calling *Dropping Out,* is supposed to be shot in New York for Paramount Pictures. Do you feel any apprehension about making your first English-language movie?

F : I am concentrating more on the images than on the dialogue. I am trying to write the dialogue very simple and very short. It's very important to have somebody whom I trust to really translate the language. I will write first in Czech and then have a translation into English. I will work with somebody not just to translate but to write an English version of the script. If I have a script in English I can trust, then I will have some confidence I can work in the English language. At this point, I am writing with a French friend, Jean-Claude Carriere. He's a scriptwriter who worked on Luis Buñuel's last three films.

G: I understand that the film will be about a runaway girl who drops out and joins the hippie community and that it will concentrate on the middle-class parents who search for her.

F: I found the idea two years ago when I was here and I met a family of such a runaway girl. And we were talking hours and hours, without any intention of making a film. Suddenly I realized what a good idea it was for a film. These poor parents looking for something and being incapable of understanding how it happened or why it happened to them and their daughter.

G: Are you prepared to live away from Czechoslovakia for the rest of your life, to be an expatriate now?

F: Me? No, no. Certainly, I want to go back. Maybe occasionally if it is possible to work here I'll return. But basically I want to work and live in Czechoslovakia. Because I don't like the feeling of being a foreigner. I like to be at home.

ROMAN POLANSKI

"The director is always a superstar."

Child of Kafka and the movies, Roman Polanski was born August 18, 1933, in Paris and spent a rootless youth wandering through Poland as a victim of that "utmost fear" which he was later to evoke again and again in his own films.

Trained at the famous Polish Film School in Lodz from 1954 to 1959, Polanski learned his craft through making shorts. He was twenty-eight when, two years after graduation, he made his first feature film, Knife in the Water. It was nominated for an Academy Award.

He began his career as an actor on stage. Later, he appeared in such films as Generation, Lotna, The Innocent Sorcerers and his own The Fat and the Lean. He played the apprentice vampire hunter in The Fearless Vampire Killers, which co-starred his late wife, Sharon Tate.

His youthful brashness and technical skill have made him a celebrity in Hollywood, his adopted home. The grosses from Rosemary's Baby have assured him of further artistic controls over any films he will be making there.

Polanski's movies are personal, even when he bases them on someone else's book. Consistently fascinated by aberration in human nature, he was spared the doctrinaire boy-meets-girl-meets-tractor social realism at school in the brief euphoria of post-Stalinist permissiveness. His specialty, anxiety that escalates to total panic, corresponds to Hitchcock's own preference for "pure film" that exists independently of moral judgments and has no purpose except to manipulate an audience.

At thirty-six, he is slender, short, and cherubic, and a mischievous crooked smile creases a corner of his boyishly sinister Dorian Gray looks. This interview was held in the spring of 1969 in New York and in Hollywood.

FILMOGRAPHY:

A TOOTHY SMILE (Short: '57)
BREAKING UP THE DANCE (Short: '58)
THE LAMP (Short: '58)
TWO MEN AND A WARDROBE (Short: '58)
WHEN ANGELS FALL (Short: '59)
THE FAT AND THE LEAN (Short: '60)

MAMMALS (Short: '60)
KNIFE IN THE WATER ('61)
BEAUTIFUL SWINDLES (Episode of a four-part film: '63)
REPULSION ('65)
CUL DE SAC ('65)
THE FEARLESS VAMPIRE KILLERS ('67)
ROSEMARY'S BABY ('68)

GELMIS: Most of your films are preoccupied with death and the bizarre: specifically, by sexual obsession and insanity in *Repulsion*; by sexual humiliation and cruelty in *Cul de Sac*; by anticlericalism and the triumph of inhuman forces in *The Fearless Vampire Killers* and *Rosemary's Baby*. What influence on your films, if any, do you attribute to those formative years of yours as a Jewish child in Nazi-occupied Poland?

POLANSKI: I don't know. It's a question I've asked myself many times. There's undoubtedly some influence from it. I was three years old when my parents, both Polish, went back to Poland. It was just before the Second World War. When I was eight, my mother was taken to the concentration camp, where she died. I was in the Cracow ghetto, from which I escaped just before the liquidation. My father cut the wires and I was off. That's how I saw him for the last time, until after the war. He was taken to a concentration camp, but he survived. I was in the country during the war with different families. I survived by wandering from one family to the other.

G: Are you familiar with Jerzy Kosinski's novel, *The Painted Bird*? Because what happened to you sounds like the outline of that story— the boy brutalized and terrified by his wanderings in the Polish countryside during the war.

P: I know the book very well. And Kosinski is a friend of mine, as a matter of fact. But I was much luckier than the boy was. My father was Jewish, but I didn't look Jewish. So I didn't have the same problems that the boy had. I wasn't the painted bird. I was just *a* bird, like other birds in those times. And I was also lucky because I wasn't on the Polish-Russian frontier. I was in the western country, where people are much less savage. The family I was with, the peasant family, was extremely poor. But they were good people.

I went back to Cracow for a while during the war. I was selling newspapers, so I could go to the cinema. I was nuts about movies. I saw a lot of films during the war. They were only German propaganda films. And the Poles had an Underground movement, a Resistance. And they wrote slogans on the walls, like "Only pigs go to movies." But that wouldn't affect me, because I just loved movies so much. I just went and I didn't see any propaganda. I was getting it on the superficial level. As long as there was any kind of action, I just loved it.

I remember that from the ghetto there was one corner, one angle, from which you could see a piece of the town square where the Germans were showing films outdoors. Mostly they were newsreels. And I would go and look at them. I was overwhelmed by the magic of it. Even though they were saying terrible things, like "Jews are lice" or "Jews are dirt." And there were German tanks and machine guns in action and so on. But I was so transfixed by the magic of cinema that I just had to watch it all.

G: How did you get involved with Polish theater?

P: I went to watch a kids' radio show. And they asked me what I thought of the program. I said, "I think the kids are very phony." And this boldness impressed them. They asked me to be on the show. So I did and I worked in radio. And from the radio, they took me to the state theater when I was fourteen.

I only started going to school when I was twelve, because of the war. I was always late. And I was very bad in every subject except drawing. When I became an actor, I also started to go to art school. In the theater, I had a leading part in a play called *The Son of the Regiment*. That's how I started, really, in this business.

For six years, I worked in the theater. I had mostly small parts. I never had theatrical training. I wanted to go to acting school. But they wouldn't accept me. I tried three times. Not just because of the poor grades. It was because I was already acting and the teachers knew me and they thought I was mannered and they didn't like me.

I'm extremely grateful to them now that they didn't accept me, because I'd be acting in some crummy theater in Poland today instead of doing what I'm doing. Some years later, when I had gone through film school and become a director, I was often in a situation where I was running tests with people who wouldn't let me into the acting school. And I never used any of them. Not out of vengeance, because by then I had only compassion for the poor hams. They were just too bad.

G: Were you a good actor?

P: I was always a very good actor. When I was playing in *The Son of the Regiment,* I had fantastic success. The play had success only thanks to me. And I had fantastic writeups.

G: Did your success make you difficult to get along with?

P: No. I was always very proud and vain, so it didn't change me at all. People liked me. The actors did like me. They always treated me as an equal. They told dirty jokes in front of me. And I told them dirty jokes. It was then that I learned what real *ham* means. I met a lot of them. I would skip school very often to go sit in the balcony watching rehearsals of plays in which I was not involved.

g: Did the fact that your father had been an artisan who employed men hurt your chances to get ahead under socialism?

p: Yes, absolutely. It was during the Stalinist period, when things were at their worst. I couldn't get into any university. I was trying anything. I sank lower and lower, unable to get into the acting school, then the comedian's school, and then I agreed to go to the circus school—which was the lowest. But the circus school didn't even give you a waiver from the draft. So I had to go into the army. But I refused to. I just simply decided, "I won't go. I'd rather go to prison."

Somehow, I got away with it. I already had my draft card. But thanks to the bureaucracy, somehow they must have screwed something up. And they simply forgot me. I didn't report for induction into the army. Even my father didn't know I had been called by the draft. I left home. I just wandered all over the country, sleeping where I could, without an address. I was waiting to be arrested any moment. I thought seriously of escaping, of going abroad. I was ready to do it. I was studying different possibilities, though it was a risky thing.

By then, there was something new in Poland—an identity card, a new type they were giving to people. And I had received, at my old address, a notice to present myself to get this identity card. And I went, shaking, because I was sure it was a trap. But they gave me the identity card. And I realized that I was a nonexistent person to the government. They had misplaced my papers.

g: How did you get into the film school?

p: During the worst period of that year of hiding and wandering, I came back to stay one night at my father's house in Cracow. I got a telephone call from a cameraman whom I knew and he said that Andrezej Wajda was making his first film, *Generation*, in Warsaw and that I should come and be in it. I had had small parts in films made by the students of the film school—and in one three-part film, *Three Stories*, I had met Wajda because he was supposed to direct another episode that was never made.

I went to Warsaw and worked on *Generation*. But this was during the period that I still was scared of being arrested and put in prison. I kept going away and hiding. Once I left the set and they couldn't find me. It was a big deal, because they spoiled one day of shooting in sunshine which they had been waiting a long time for. Then, within two months, I got my identity card and things went better. About six months later, I tried for the film school and was, to my amazement, accepted.

What probably helped me was the friendship of a theater director named Antoni Bohdziewicz, who was also one of the professors in the film school, a wonderful, intelligent, great man. I went to see him and said, "Listen, I'm desperate. My life is on the edge. I need help." He said, "Try the film school." And I did. I discovered, to my surprise, that the atmosphere of the film school was a little bit out of line. It was very progressive and people were really groovy. And they dug my attitude, even though I was terrible. After a lot of tests, I got in, though I know I didn't do too well. I think Bohdziewicz pushed for me because he believed in me.

The film school training was five years. At that time, there were three specializations: directing, cinematography, and production. Later, they added screen acting. I studied directing. Only six people were accepted. Two dropped out later. The first year, we studied still photography, developing, enlarging, all of that. It was really well organized. They taught you everything about technique, from scratch.

In the third year, you made two shorts, three-minute films, without sound, but using only 35 mm, very professional equipment. After the third year, you made a ten-minute documentary short. Your story film could be fifteen minutes. When you finished school, you made a fifteen-minute diploma film.

I had no vocation for documentaries, so I tried to make mine a sort of story. Like every school does, we used to organize dances. And I invited a group of bad guys. We used to call them hooligans, and there were a lot of hooligans at that time in Poland. I told them to break up the dance. And I filmed it. I was almost thrown out of the school.

I called the film, *Breaking Up the Dance*. It was ten minutes long. That was my "documentary." I asked them to break up the dance about twelve o'clock. I needed some shots of everything going well, of some preparation. But the sons of bitches broke it up in half an hour. I had to restore a lot of things. I had to restage many things.

Then I made *Two Men and a Wardrobe*, which didn't belong to the study program. You could make more films, if you wanted to, if you had a good script. That was the great thing. So I used two guys from the school as my main actors. And the cameraman was also from the school. It just cost us for raw footage and processing, and staying on location and paying for extras to appear in the film. It had no dialogue, just music and sound effects.

I really did the film with the goal of sending it to the festival of experimental films at the Brussels World's Fair in 1958. And I won a prize there. So that gave me a big break for what I wanted to do afterwards.

Two Men and a Wardrobe is only superficially surrealistic, because it has a content, which surrealism isn't supposed to have. It was the only film I've made that "meant" something. It was about the intolerance of society toward somebody who is different. I didn't give them a piano to carry, because that would have implied a specific difference that set them apart, like art. They just have a wardrobe. And because of this wardrobe, they can't do what everybody else does. They are persecuted. Meanwhile, bad things are happening all around them, things society accepts or just ignores.

G: There were just a few words—mostly just sound effects, like water dripping or toilets being flushed—in *When Angels Fall,* your diploma film. Was there a reason why you used little or no dialogue in your shorts?

P: Yes. Because I think that in a short it's unpleasant to use dialogue. It's like just a *piece* of a feature film. Shorts are either cartoons or documentaries, for me. When you use people in a short, if they talk you expect it's going to last for two hours. It's not natural, not proper, to the form.

G: What good did film school do you, exactly?

P: I think it did tremendous good for me, looking back on it. When I was at school, I thought I was wasting my time—like all my colleagues. You know, when you're young there's something in you. You rebel against everything. And now when I think back I think it was tremendous, especially the time I spent sitting on the long wooden stairs of the school—which was an old palace that used to belong to some kind of wool king in Lodz, an industrial town. We sat on those stairs and argued about films and about life. And we would see hundreds of films. There were constant projections, practically from eight in the morning to eight at night.

G: What happened right after you finished film school?

P: I went to Paris for two years. During that period, I made *The Fat and the Lean,* and then I came back to Poland to make *Knife in the Water.* Then I went back to Paris, where I stayed for three years or more. During that period, I made only one film. It was part of four stories, a film called *Beautiful Swindles.* There was one part by Godard, which was eliminated from the picture. One part was made by Chabrol. One was made by an Italian director who was supposed to have a big future in films, and who's never been heard from again. And one part was made by a Japanese who had been Kurosawa's assistant.

G: *Repulsion* had a simplicity that was almost documentary in style, except for Catherine Deneuve's sexual fantasies—and even they are very detailed with a sort of nightmare reality. You once told me that you preferred realism and detested pretentious or "arty" films.

P: Yes. The older I grow, the more I value simplicity. The more difficult it seems to me to make a simple film. I want my film to be done so the people who see it have the impression it was done without any effort. But, of course, there is a lot of effort behind it, a lot of struggle. And as for realism, the only way to seduce people into believing you—whether they want to or not—is to take painstaking care with the details of your film, to make it accurate. Sloppiness destroys emotional impact.

G: Do you think you sacrificed suspense or surprise—the kind that Hitchcock gets at the end of *Psycho*—by showing midway through *Repulsion* that your heroine's sexual hysteria has turned her into a homicidal maniac?

P: No. Because I wasn't interested in surprising anyone. *Repulsion* was just a case study of the disintegration of a girl with mental illness. I was interested in showing her illness and establishing a mood, not in having any surprises. The ending, the closeup of the family picture, was to show that this girl was like that from the beginning.

G: Was there an implication in the way the little girl in the picture glared at her father that he had rejected her or molested her and that that was the cause of her hatred of men which would lead to murder?

P: I just wanted to show that something was odd with the girl even then. Very often people live among us and we don't even realize something is wrong with them, until the illness progresses so far that they do something noticeable—like killing somebody, for instance.

G: It took four years between *Knife in the Water* and *Repulsion*. Why was that?

P: I couldn't get financing for any of the films I wanted to do. I brought *Repulsion* to Columbia Pictures first. They laughed at me. But after I finally got it made in England, through a small company there, Columbia bought the rights of distribution.

G: After shooting *Cul de Sac* for three months on a desolate island, you told me: "I think I'll become an actor again and get out of directing, because I just can't bear having to work with difficult actors."

P: Yes, that's true. I really considered it seriously. It was no joke. I nearly had a breakdown, I was so disgusted by that experience. I had problems with the actors. There were frictions between them. It was raining. The island was miserable. Food and living conditions were terrible. But what matters is that the film stands exactly as I wanted it to and it's an addition to the poetic language of cinema.

It is my best film. I always loved it. I always believed in it. It is real cinema, done for cinema—like art for art. It's well in advance of anything that has been done in the semantics of cinema. When I sat down to write *Cul de Sac*, I wrote it for cinema. It was written without any story. It was what I like to see in the cinema. It was the utmost fears in the characters that I care about. Characters and utmost fear are the most important thing in cinema.

G: It's been suggested that *Cul de Sac* is a study of sexual humiliation —of Donald Pleasance by Françoise Dorléac, as his young wife, and by the gangster, Lionel Stander.

P: I would accept that interpretation. It's definitely the prevailing element in the film. It's a study of human behavior and how people in very special circumstances react to each other. When I sat down to write the script with Gérard Brach, we had no design or any definite idea what we would be writing about. It wasn't "Hey, I have an idea, so let's write a screenplay." It was "Let's write what we'd like to see on the screen—the kind of emotions, the kind of feelings, characters, atmosphere we'd like to see in a film." And then we just wrote it loosely from that. Then we organized it as happenings.

We didn't start with a basic situation. We simply agreed after we started talking about a film that what we'd like to see on the screen was an intruder. Somebody coming into somebody else's life, where relations and the situation are already set. There is such and such a relationship between a man and a woman. They are living in such and such a place. And here come the intruders.

G: What period in your life was that in which you wrote the *Cul de Sac* screenplay?

P: I wrote it before *Repulsion*, in 1962 and '63. I also wrote *Repulsion* and *The Fearless Vampire Killers* with Brach. We couldn't get it financed until after *Repulsion* was a success, and even then it had to be made cheaply.

G: You had already made *Knife in the Water*, which was about an intruder into an unhappy marriage. The theme seems to have carried over into *Cul de Sac*.

P: Yes, it did. Why is that? Who can say?

G: What influence, if any, was there of Pinter's *The Birthday Party* and *The Dumbwaiter* in the creation of your two Theater-of-the-Absurd gangsters in *Cul de Sac*?

P: I knew Pinter's work very well, and had read *The Dumbwaiter*. I don't know that I was influenced directly by Pinter, but I was certainly influenced by modern theater, by Beckett, by Ionesco and by Pinter, also. By all this type of atmosphere. Above everything else, cinema is atmosphere.

G: What do you mean, precisely, when you speak of atmosphere?

P: It's the personality of a film. It's everything. It's the sound, mostly. If you show a landscape, for instance, there will be very little atmosphere in it. But if you show the landscape and you hear a fly buzzing, immediately the atmosphere will heighten. Everything in a landscape can affect our emotional state.

If you wake up and see the sun on your curtains, you'll feel different than if you're awakened by the sound of rain. In *Rosemary's Baby*, the apartment changed from a gloomy, depressing place to a nice, bright, sunny apartment. It goes in an opposite direction than the story of the film is going.

G: You give as much weight to the sound in your films as to the image. In your school short, *When Angels Fall*, the sound I remember is the dripping and flushing water while the old woman sits there tending the men's toilet in her misery. And in *Repulsion* there was that long orgasm sequence on the sound track from the next room, as Deneuve lay there listening. At what point do you decide how you're going to handle the sound?

P: I know most of the sound effects I will want as I'm shooting. Later, in editing, others suggest themselves through the images. Ever since I was a child, I realized that good sound transported me into a film and bad sound spoiled my pleasure.

G: Do you have someone who works with you from film to film as a sound expert?

P: I'm the expert.

G: Do you feel there are specific emotional equivalents to certain camera angles?

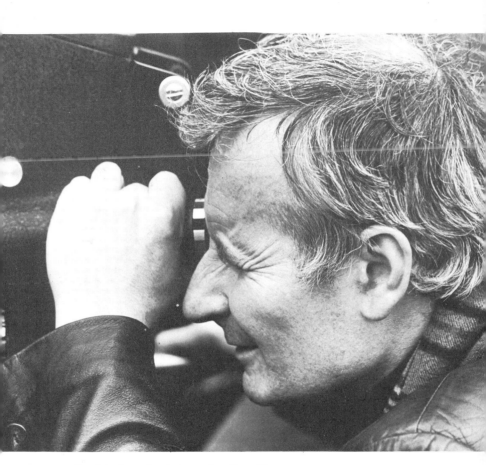

1. Lindsay Anderson shooting *If* . . .
Copyright © 1968 by Paramount Pictures Corporation.
All Rights Reserved.

2. John Cassavetes and Ben Gazzara, on the set of *Husbands*
Courtesy *Husbands* Production Company

3. Francis Ford Coppola on the set of *Finian's Rainbow*
Copyright © 1968 by Warner Bros.-Seven Arts, Inc.
All Rights Reserved

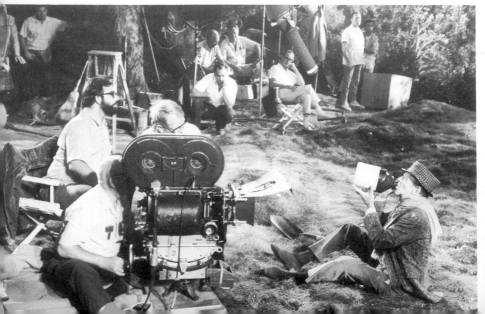

4. Roger Corman on the set of *The Trip*
Courtesy American-International Pictures

5. Brian De Palma
Newsday photo by Jim Cavanagh

6. Robert Downey on the set of *Putney Swope*
Photo by Burt Andrews

7. Milos Forman on the set of *The Firemen's Ball*
Courtesy Foto Oddeleni Film Studio Barrandov, Prague

8. Stanley Kubrick with Gary Lockwood on the set of
2001: A Space Odyssey
Copyright © 1968 by Metro-Goldwyn-Mayer, Inc.

9.   Richard Lester on the set of *Help!*
Courtesy United Artists

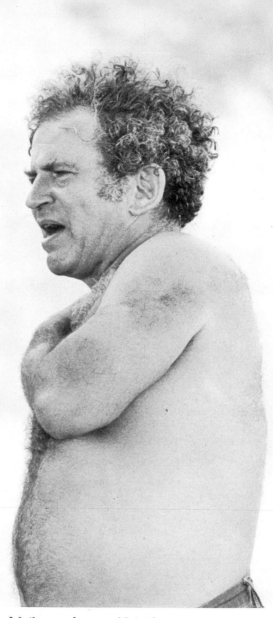

10. Norman Mailer on the set of *Maidstone*
Newsday photo by Ken Spencer

11. Jim McBride
Courtesy Jim McBride

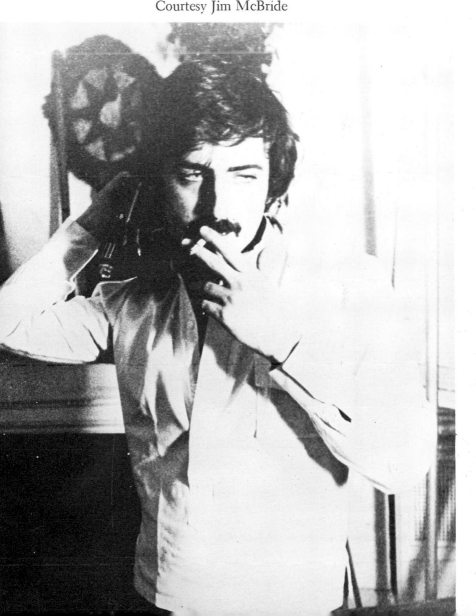

12. Mike Nichols on the set of *Catch-22*

13. Arthur Penn on the set of *Alice's Restaurant*
Courtesy United Artists

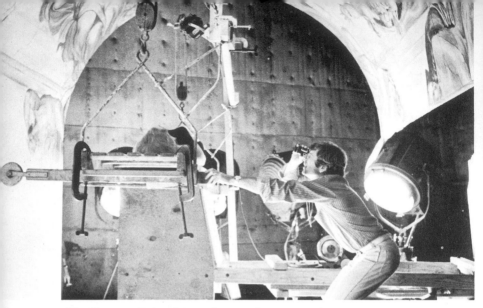

14. Roman Polanski on the set of *Rosemary's Baby*
Copyright © 1968 by Paramount Pictures Corporation
and William Enterprises, Inc. All Rights Reserved.

15. Andy Warhol
Photo by John Chamberlain

p: Yes. As a child of twelve, I remember reading a book about Hollywood. And it was saying, "When you want to make a shot more dramatic or when you want a person to appear stronger and more menacing, you put your camera low and shoot up. And when you want to create an open feeling, you put your camera high and shoot the person from above. Et cetera."

But that really just gave me some rough ideas about it. It took me a long time to develop a film language and to actually understand what I should do with a camera to express *my* feelings. And I realized that the most fundamental way was to observe myself when I'm watching, and just follow what I see when I close one eye, and then to just substitute the camera's eye for my own eye.

g: You've been quoted as saying: "I must confess that I was completely formed by surrealism. Ten years ago, even at the time when I was making my first shorts, I saw everything in the mirror of surrealism." Supposedly, you came to film surrealism by way of appreciation of the work of Dali and other painters, and the chief cinematic influence on you has been Buñuel.

p: This is true. As an actor, I was fascinated by the absurd theater. I was influenced by Beckett and Ionesco and even by Kafka and by a Polish writer, Bruno Schultz, and Vito Gombrovitch, who wrote *Cosmos.* And I've seen all of Buñuel's films. The one that impressed me most was *Los Olvidados.* Like him, I guess I'm an anarchist, in a sense. But it's not what seduces me in his work. Basically, what I like about his films is that they are so *queer.* Other than that, I can't say.

g: Is it true that you wanted to make a film of *Waiting for Godot* but that Beckett refused, so you made your short, *Mammals,* which is sort of your own version of *Godot?*

p: Well, I asked Beckett *after* I made *Mammals,* after I'd made all of my shorts, in fact. He knew my shorts. And when I asked him for the film rights, he said he didn't believe films should be made from his plays. He said they're written for the stage and they're not meant to be adapted for the screen.

g: He did make a film with Buster Keaton.

p: Yes, because he said: "I would rather write an original script for you than have you film one of my plays." He just wrote his own film.

g: Did you choose Donald Pleasance and Jack MacGowran as the gangsters in *Cul de Sac* because they had been in Pinter and Beckett plays?

P: Not specifically because they had done things for Beckett or Pinter. It was because they were the kind of characters I was looking for to do the kind of scenes I had in mind. It was rather Donald Pleasance and Jack MacGowran than Peter O'Toole and Gregory Peck.

G: Some critics damned *Cul de Sac* as being too bizarre and cruel and they mentioned the hot foot that Dorléac gave Stander—sticking a piece of paper between his bare toes and setting fire to it—and Dorléac forcing Pleasance to dress up as a woman and then all the handling of MacGowran after he dies.

P: Yes, I recall the lady critic who used words like *necrophilia, homosexuality, sadism*. That is her problem, not mine. I am not obsessed by these things. It was just a film.

G: How did you happen to be chosen to make *Rosemary's Baby*?

P: The producer who had the rights to the book, William Castle, wanted me, and then so did Paramount's studio boss, Bob Evans. There was no package. Mia Farrow was Evans' idea. They showed me two sections of her TV show, *Peyton Place*, and I agreed. Later, I asked Ira Levin whom he had in mind when he was writing the book. He swore that it was Mia Farrow.

John Cassavetes was my idea. I had seen him in a couple of films. I knew him slightly. And I saw *Shadows*, which he directed. The studio was opposed to using him, and I put up a big fight, with Bill Castle on my side. I won't mention the other names they wanted instead of him, to avoid offending anybody. But they just didn't want Cassavetes.

G: Cassavetes describes himself as a difficult actor to work with.

P: He's one of these method actors who constantly scratch their ear or grin, and it's difficult for him to put himself in the skin of another character, like Guy in *Rosemary's Baby*. It goes against the grain. It caused problems in working. I had to do a big deal of editing.

G: How did you make that transformation of Cassavetes from Guy to the devil—with makeup and then switching actors?

P: Yes. He gradually changes to somebody else, like it happens in a dream. In a dream, you talk to your father and suddenly it's no longer your father, it's the President of the United States.

g: Was that supposed to be a dream sequence or was she supposed to be having a vision of something that was happening in another dimension?

p: To her it's a dream, but it's partially reality. In any case, it's how she sees it.

g: Were those dream figures deliberately supposed to resemble the Pope and John and Jacqueline Kennedy?

p: Well, that's how it happens in a dream, you know. I mean, you constantly see somebody with the elements of myth and yet of being recognizable. It's due to her Catholic background. The girl is Catholic. All her associations are necessarily, in such circumstances, the people who represent married Catholicism for her.

g: How much of the dream sequence did you work out in advance and how much did you decide in the editing room afterwards?

p: I was thinking about the feel of it long before I shot it. I was just trying to follow the visuals of my own dreams, because I believe the way I dream is the way most people do. Somehow the background is not so clear and you have to see what's important in it and not the other things. And everything is floating and everything constantly changes. Nothing is durable. There are no static things in dreams.

It was set on a boat because that's the way it was written in the book. She feels dizzy. The first association must be with something floating. First she sees herself on the raft. And then it becomes nice, and it becomes just a pleasant party on the boat. Then it turns to more stormy atmosphere and eventually it changes to a room where she lies on the bed.

g: Why did the British censor cut part of that sequence?

p: He cut fifteen seconds of it—when they are tying her legs to the bed, and a little dialogue that precedes it. The part where the lady comes down and says, "I think you'd better have your legs tied down in case of convulsions." And Mia says, "Yes, I suppose so." And it's followed by a visual, with two interns tying her legs.

They gave a very vague explanation. Kinky sex, maybe. I think it's idiotic. That's the only country in the world where the film has been censored, and it's been shown in Italy, Latin America, and other such tricky areas without any cuts.

g: How did you approach the problem of adapting the book into a screenplay?

P: Well, when I read a book, I *see* it. I just took the book and wrote the screenplay straight from it. I tried to follow the book as closely as I could. I didn't see any reason for changing it. I assumed that the writer was right even in the choice of the color of a tie. I just tried to be as close to it as possible. I wrote a very detailed script where everything was written except for any camera indications or movements. Technical things I just don't put in a script. I don't even know where the camera will be put when I'm driving to the studio.

It's difficult to shorten a book to acceptable length, because the film would have to be five hours long if you just went straight through the story. But I tried to do it by just eliminating a few things, rather than major cuts. I think it's difficult for someone who has read the book to find out what changes I made in it. The first cut of the film ran nearly five hours, before I got it down to the two-and-a-half-hour running time.

In this particular case, I had to leave a lot of decisions for the last moment. I shot a lot of scenes even though I knew they might not get into the picture, because I wasn't sure they were the ones I should eliminate right away. And that gave me, also, the chance to eliminate the ones that were weaker, that just didn't come out right for one reason or another.

And this is because this film has such careful construction, for the sake of suspense, where you don't really play on the mood so much, or on some sort of poetic approach. You just have to tell the story well. I never made a film like this before. I shot it and cut it very deliberately this particular way.

G: At what point do you decide how you are going to set up your cameras, if you don't know on the way to the studio?

P: After I rehearse with the actors. I rehearse before each shot, each scene. I rehearse the whole scene and then I break it down into shots.

G: Do you ever shoot with more than one camera on the set?

P: Never. I think it's idiotic. You can't be in two places at the same time, unless you jump very far. Being an observer, a witness to what happens, you don't double up suddenly.

G: How much artistic control does the director—do you—have over a picture?

P: I can talk only about my own experience. I had complete control over everything I've made so far, except for the unfortunate accident that I had with *The Fearless Vampire Killers* and, partially, with *Cul de Sac*—where Martin Ransohoff came and intervened after the films were made. He cut *Vampire Killers* just before its release in the United States. My version prevails in other countries. He bought *Cul de Sac*, and he also cut it.

Considering the fact that these cuts were done here, post facto, I've really had, in a sense, complete control of every film I've made. And it was only my naïveté that made me lose control over the versions of those two films shown here. *Cul de Sac*'s been cut nearly eight minutes, both trims and whole scenes. Atmosphere and mood were taken out, because Ransohoff felt that there was no value to scenes without dialogue.

G: Do you think *Vampire Killers* was a good film before he cut it?

P: A beautiful film. But it was redubbed, cut by twenty minutes, the music was moved around. A three-minute animated prologue was added in front to explain some jokes because the alterations had made them incomprehensible.

G: Is that the only film you've ever disowned?

P: I didn't disown it completely, because my version prevails in Europe. It's been a tremendous success all over the world, except for the United States.

G: Would producing your own films give you more power or control over them?

P: I've done most of my films in Europe. And you don't have to be the producer in Europe to be in complete control of your film. This is a Hollywood conception, since they have divided the functions, that really it's the producer that sets up the film and hires the director —who therefore has this subordinate role. But in Europe, it's basically the director who runs the picture. The producer just takes care of the financial arrangements.

G: Some American filmmakers—even those who work abroad—have become producers of their films, like Kubrick, or co-producers, like Lester and Frankenheimer, just to insure that they have artistic control. Can you envision yourself doing that, if you're going to continue working in Hollywood?

P: If the situation occurs where I find that this is necessary to maintain the control, I would have to do it. But I'm not interested in producing. I have *complete* control now. Because I enjoy at this moment the confidence of the studio for which I'm working. I have a contract for two projects. If I had another project, I'd walk into the office of the head of the studio and say, "Let's make a deal."

How far you can expect a studio to go along with a director on the matter of control just depends how much—as they call it in this town —*muscle* he has. I have muscle at this point because *Rosemary's Baby*, which cost $3,200,000 to make, has brought in about $25,000,000 to the company. I have my offices at Paramount and I've worked with them for two years.

I was able to gain their confidence. They know me very well by now. They know what they can count on. If my next film is a complete disaster, however, things can change. I don't think it will be, however. I don't think I'm able to make a complete disaster, if people let me do what I want to do.

G: Is the director the new superstar?

P: To me, the director is always a superstar. The best films are best because of nobody but the director. You speak of *Citizen Kane* or *8½* or *Seven Samurai*, it's thanks to the director who was the star of it. He makes the film, he creates it.

G: What's the best way to learn filmmaking and how does someone break into films as a director today?

P: I think film school may be the best way in our society to learn filmmaking. But there is no one way. I would certainly find a way, if I was just starting out. The most important thing is determination. If somebody wants it really badly, he will do it finally. I would shoot a film in 16 mm, I would try putting things together. Anything at all, just so I didn't sit around and talk about it.

G: Working in Hollywood as you do now, can you judge from the inside how much likelihood there is of the guilds and unions becoming less restrictive and rigid?

P: I didn't have any problem getting past them. It's not a problem once you accept it. Unions will break, because they're against nature. The young are growing up and they are storming and will take care of themselves, whether the unions accept it or not. Life is stronger than the union.

G: What are your next films going to be?

P: There are two original screenplays being written. One of them is *Paganini* and I'm working on it with an Italian writer, the one who wrote *L'Avventura* and *Divorce, Italian Style.* It's more than a biography of Paganini, of course. The other film is *The Donner Pass.*

G: Do you foresee any special problems in making a western?

P: I like westerns. They're part of cinema, just like horror films. The fact that other European directors have tried to make westerns and failed is absolutely unimportant to me. The only possible problem we may run into is from some squeamish people, because we're dealing with material that's never been treated by the movies before. It's a piece of American history that's been written about but never been on the screen. The Donner Pass is in the Sierras near Squaw Valley. The film is the story of people going from Illinois to California. At that time, there were only seven hundred Americans in California. So these travelers were going to this paradise and they were stranded in the snow in the Sierras in very early winter. Most of them died. The few that survived were accused afterwards of cannibalism.

G: *Cannibalism?*

P: Yes, yes, I know, I know. But it has nothing to do with any of my earlier pictures. What makes you think I am obsessed by the bizarre?

PART THREE:

FREE AGENTS WITHIN THE SYSTEM

TRANSITIONAL DIRECTORS

ROGER CORMAN

"I think that had I had the chance
to go to a film school I could have
saved myself a lot of time and a
lot of bother."

*Roger Corman is a one-man film school. Amateurs have gotten their
practical experience in filmmaking by talking their way into odd jobs
as assistants on Corman's hundred or so independent productions.
Francis Ford Coppola (Dementia 13) and Peter Bogdanovich (Tar-
gets), among others, made their first films with the help of Corman.*

*A transitional figure in Hollywood, Corman is the only director
in this book who got his start within the studio system as an apprentice. He now operates as an independent who co-authors, directs, and produces his own films and releases them through either
United Artists or American International Pictures, distributors and
financiers with no studios of their own.*

*Born April 1926, in Chicago, Corman studied at Stanford Uni-
versity and Oxford. He started in the movie business as a $32.50-a-
week messenger boy at 20th Century-Fox in 1948 and worked for
a while as a Hollywood agent. He wrote a script called* The House in
the Sea. *It was filmed, with him as associate producer, as* Highway
Dragnet.

*In 1953 he formed Roger Corman Productions. And with $18,000
of his own and some friends' money, he produced* Monster From the
Ocean Floor. *In 1955 he directed his first film,* Five Guns West. *He
was known as the king of the B movies because he churned out eight
or ten films a year for a while.* Bucket of Blood, *for instance, which
he directed in 1959, was conceived and made in five days.*

*No one really took Corman's films seriously until he directed the
Edgar Allan Poe horror series in the 1960s. He became a cult hero
and his films were shown in retrospectives at revival theaters and
cinémathèques. Yet even as late as* The Wild Angels *and* The Trip,
*his movies were being made on minimal budgets on location or, if
necessary, footage might be shot on a Poverty Row sound stage.*

*His ability to be prolific and keep control of his own films as an
independent appeals to the imagination of student filmmakers. Even
if they don't want to make his kind of films, many of them wouldn't
mind making them his way. In the following interview, which took
place in Hollywood in the spring of 1969, Corman describes the*

difference between working on a major studio film like The St. Valentine's Day Massacre *and a low-budget location film like* The Wild Angels.

FILMOGRAPHY:

1955 FIVE GUNS WEST
     APACHE WOMAN
     THE DAY THE WORLD ENDED
1956 SWAMP WOMEN
     OKLAHOMA WOMAN
     GUNSLINGER
     IT CONQUERED THE WORLD
     NOT OF THIS EARTH
     THE UNDEAD
     SHE-GODS OF SHARK REEF
     NAKED PARADISE
1957 ATTACK OF THE CRAB MONSTERS
     ROCK ALL NIGHT
     TEENAGE DOLL
     CARNIVAL ROCK
     SORORITY GIRL
     VIKING WOMEN AND THE SEA SERPENT
1958 WAR OF THE SATELLITES
     MACHINE GUN KELLY
     TEENAGE CAVEMAN
     I, MOBSTER
1959 BUCKET OF BLOOD
     WASP WOMAN
1960 SKI TROOP ATTACK
     THE FALL OF THE HOUSE OF USHER
     THE LITTLE SHOP OF HORRORS
     THE LAST WOMAN ON EARTH
     CREATURE FROM THE HAUNTED SEA
     ATLAS
1961 THE PIT AND THE PENDULUM
     THE INTRUDER (THE STRANGER)
     THE PREMATURE BURIAL
1962 TALES OF TERROR
     TOWER OF LONDON
1963 THE YOUNG RACERS
     THE RAVEN
     THE TERROR

X—THE MAN WITH X-RAY EYES
THE HAUNTED PALACE
1964 THE DUBIOUS PATRIOTS (THE SECRET INVASION)
THE MASQUE OF THE RED DEATH
LIGEIA (THE TOMB OF LIGEIA)
1966 THE WILD ANGELS
1967 THE ST. VALENTINE'S DAY MASSACRE
THE TRIP

GELMIS: How many films have you directed?

CORMAN: I don't know exactly. I've directed somewhere between fifty-five and sixty. And I've produced somewhere between one hundred and one hundred ten, including some of the ones I've directed.

G: What time period does this span?

C: I think from about 1954 or '55. I produced my first film in '54 and directed in '55. I produced a film called *Monsters from the Ocean Floor*. And the first film I directed was a western called *Five Guns West*.

G: What's the highest budget you've worked with?

C: *The St. Valentine's Day Massacre*. It was budgeted at $2,500,-000, but it only went to $2,100,000. We came in $400,000 under budget. Now that's misleading, however, because that was shot at a major studio carrying 20 per cent overhead charge. You can really figure that if I made that picture at Fox, at $2,100,000, I could have made the picture myself for about $1,100,000 or $1,200,000 independently.

G: A million dollars' difference? That's more than twenty per cent. Where are the other hidden costs?

C: It isn't so much hidden. It's the fact that they work through department heads. When they do a set, for instance, the head of the art department gets added to our payroll. They have a set designer, they have two or three draftsmen, they have a couple of sketch artists. In other words, our film helps pay the studio overhead by having its permanent staff charged to our budget. And then, on top of that, there will be twenty per cent added to all of their salaries. When I do a set, Dan Haller is my normal art director—has been until recently; he's become a director. Dan would just take a pad and paper and sketch out the set. One man can do it.

G: What about the exploitation end of it, and the distribution?

C: There's studio publicity included with it, not distribution publicity.

G: Where would you have made a film like that if you were going to do it outside the studio, in order to cut the twenty per cent overhead?

C: I would have rented a small rental studio. There are a number of rental studios around town. For the exteriors, I probably would have shot them on location in Chicago. We had considered doing it for Fox but to make such a move for a major studio is prohibitive. They would take probably a hundred to a hundred and fifty men on location. I would have taken maybe two or three men from Hollywood and picked up a skeleton crew in Chicago. Now, I'm making it sound overly easy, because it isn't quite that simple. There's an additional problem in that this was Chicago of 1929 and it's a little bit difficult to get the right atmosphere in cars and so on. Yet I think in the long run I'd rather take my chances in the streets of Chicago than the back lot of Metro, which is where I shot.

G: Where would you have picked up the skeleton crew you are talking about?

C: Just out of the Chicago local of the union. There are three basic divisions of the international union, and that's New York, Chicago, and Los Angeles.

G: Is that the way you would usually work on your earlier films—pick up a skeleton crew somewhere, and just go with two or three guys?

C: Right.

G: How does the union feel about that?

C: It all depends on who you pick up. In other words, when I say "pick up," I'll be picking up union people. So there's no problem there. But I'll be going with the absolute minimum. I'll go with a three-man camera crew and that's it. I'll go with a three-man sound crew. Currently I'm trying to get a two-man sound crew because of the newer, lighter sound equipment. You don't need three men anymore.

G: What kind of sound equipment is that you're talking about?

C: The Nagra is probably the standard of today. The Perfection was also a good unit a few years ago.

G: And what kind of camera do you use in situations like that?

C: I still prefer a Mitchell. It really, in my opinion, is the best camera in the world. It's a heavier camera, however. I have shot on location with Arriflex or with Camoflex, which is a version of the French Eclair. They're much lighter. They're more portable. They're not as good a camera, however. If I'm shooting inside a studio, I'll always go with a Mitchell. If I'm shooting on location, I'll probably trade a little bit of the quality of the Mitchell for the ease of handling of the Arriflex or the Camoflex.

G: How do you feel about hand-held work versus a Mitchell? I take it you prefer a more stable platform?

C: For certain scenes. I use a lot of hand-held work. But I use hand-held work primarily when there is movement within the shot itself. I feel that when there's violent movement the hand-held camera leads you into the movement. So if I'm photographing a fight or a chase or something like that, as I did in *The Wild Angels*, possibly a fast group of people dancing, something like that, I'll go among them with the hand-held camera.

Whereas if I have a closeup of somebody sitting in a chair and he's more or less stationary, I want my camera to be stationary also. There's no point in having a hand-held camera bobbing up and down if the man is sitting in his chair.

G: Do exhibitors object to too much hand-held camera work?

C: The exhibitors like it as rock steady as possible, but what seems right for the film is what I do.

G: In *The Wild Angels*, for example, I imagine you must have used a lot of hand-held camera work.

C: Yes. The scenes on the road were all hand held.

G: Did you use special lenses for those scenes on the road?

C: It's very fashionable today to use long lenses, 500 mm, or 1000 mm, and I use them at times. Yet at other times, I like to use the wide lens. I'll use an 18 mm or a 25. In the first shot on the road in *The Wild Angels*, I used either an 18 or a 25, deliberately, to give the sense of the Angels coming out of tremendous depth. There is a 9 but that causes such distortion, I don't like to use it.

G: In *The Wild Angels*, did you use more than one camera?

C: I didn't, much, on *The Wild Angels*, as a matter of fact.

G: How was that possible? You had a lot of people involved in any given scene.

C: Generally I just moved through the scene with a hand-held camera. I would be more likely to use multiple cameras in something like *The St. Valentine's Day Massacre*, when Hymie Weiss sent his parade of cars down the streets of Cicero and blasted Al Capone's headquarters. I had laid something like a thousand squib (simulated bullet explosions) on the front of the building when the cars came through so it was a one-take shot. I think I had three cameras mounted around in different areas, photographing that, because once they shot up the front of the building, that was it. On something like that, I'll use multiple cameras.

Other than that, though, I prefer to use one, on the basis, hopefully, that there's one best way to photograph a scene.

G: Why is there one best way to photograph a scene? Because of the lighting, because you're lit for a particular camera, or is there some other reason?

C: It's a combination. First, simply, my vision of the scene. I say, "I want the camera to be here to photograph this. This is what the scene is about." At the same time, particularly on the interiors, lighting becomes crucial because you light basically for one camera. You can light for multiple cameras, but you tend to flatten your lighting out. Exteriors, you're better with multiple cameras because basically you're using the light of the sun.

G: How much lighting do you think is necessary with either fast lenses or fast film? A filmmaker told me that there's some sort of formula that lighting cameramen have always used.

C: I think that's probably true. Most cameramen have modified not so much their lighting style but the way in which they get the light. In other words, at one time it was necessary to go out there with large heavy equipment, to get the necessary light into a scene. Now you can go out with much lighter, much more portable equipment, and you can light the scene much better. It's very possible the cameraman is still getting roughly the same effect on film. But he's doing it faster and easier.

G: Is it more difficult to shoot in color, in terms of lighting or preparing sets?

C: I think it's easier with color. With black and white it was necessary to cast a certain amount of shadow to give an impression of depth into a scene. You saw probably a more dramatic, sometimes an overly dramatic style of lighting in black and white, whereas color gives its own depth to a scene and it becomes easier.

For instance, you see, the cameramen on European films like A Man and a Woman are using a kind of diffused area lighting now in color which is quite fast to work with and is quite pleasing to look at. That same type of area lighting in black and white would just wash everything out. It would be very flat.

G: When and where did you learn film technique? Such things as how to use a camera, the correct exposures, and how to deal with actors?

c: I learned it simply by doing it. I've a degree in engineering. At any rate, I started in the motion picture business as a writer and then became a producer and then became a director. And what I learned I learned as I went along. I think had I had the chance to go to a film school I could have saved myself a lot of time and a lot of bother, learning to do things on feature films that were then exposed to the public. I think it's much better to do these things on 8 or 16 mm in a film school. I think the film schools, particularly the ones I know here on the west coast, at USC and UCLA, are invaluable.

g: Could you elaborate on that?

c: They are taught to handle technical things. They're taught to handle cameras and sound and light. They know how to cut a film. Before a man is, say, out of his sophomore year in UCLA or USC he is at least reasonably familiar with all the technical workings of making a film. He's not an expert, as I found out, unfortunately, on a few student films I financed. I slightly overrated their expertise.

And they're able to experiment. They know there is no rule that says you have to do any such thing at a particular time. They are simply getting the grounding in making a film. I'm not positive, though, that they are taught by people who *know*. That may be one of the weaknesses of the film schools. I think there are a few veteran directors, or cameramen, older men, semi-retired, who lecture occasionally in the film schools. And I think probably the students will get more out of them than from their instructors. Although I'm not knocking the instructors as such.

g: You worked within the system as an apprentice, to learn your craft.

c: That's true.

g: What did you learn from writing that you were able to use later on? How to mold and shape a script?

c: Yes, to a great extent. Also, to be able to control the type of film I wanted from the inception. Very often the producer or director is somewhat at the mercy of the writer. The writer has one idea, the producer has another idea, the director has another idea, and they do not always mesh.

g: As a writer, have you written most of your own films?

c: I haven't written screenplays recently. Generally, I'll write the original idea. And then I'll work very closely with the writer on the screenplay.

c: How did you learn to work with actors?

c: I learned through the painful process of simply working with them on the set. And then I did do some studying. I went to Jeff Corey's acting school here in Hollywood for a year or two, as a student actor. I was directing at the time and I felt I just did not know enough about acting and I'd better learn.

c: At what point in your career were you finally satisfied you were getting the kind of performances you thought you wanted?

c: I've never been satisfied, or gotten the performances I wanted. I've gotten good performances. I can remember individually good sequences in a film, a good job by a specific actor. But I've never been able to look back and say, "I really did it that time."

c: What's involved in getting a good performance out of an actor? Is it just picking the right person or is it motivating them or is it luck or is it the editing process that makes them look good?

c: It's everything. How do you become a great football coach? You get a bunch of really good football players. You start, hopefully, with a good script. You then find good actors, and then you work with them the best you can to get the best performances out of them. And then you work in the cutting room to cut to what you hope are the best of moments.

c: Is it slower shooting in a studio?

c: Yes. On the other hand, let me say this. The Hollywood technicians are extremely good. They're the best in the world, in my opinion. So although you're working at a slower pace in a major studio, and spending a great deal more money, you're getting technically the best work you can get.

c: When you work within the system, does one do it fairly traditionally—the master shot, for example, and then the various setups?

c: No, it isn't that rigid. They will let you have a fair amount of freedom.

c: What's the difference between the way you shot *The Wild Angels* and the way you shot *The St. Valentine's Day Massacre?*

c: I probably shot a little more traditionally in *St. Valentine's Day*, due to the fact that I was in a studio and had a certain amount of lighting and control and so forth. I was probably a little freer in *The Wild Angels*. That was not necessarily dictated by a studio hierarchy.

The differences are more in what happens in getting the camera and the actors into position. Once the camera is there and the actors are there I can say, "Action," just as easily on the streets of Mecca in *The Wild Angels* or on Stage 17 at 20th Century-Fox. At that point it's all the same. It's how you get to that point that makes the difference—whether you're there with a 12-man crew in the desert or whether you're in a studio with a 120-man crew. But it still ends up with actors in front of a lens.

g: How long did it take to make *The St. Valentine's Day Massacre?*

c: It was about forty-five days. It was the longest schedule I've ever had.

g: How long did it take to make *The Wild Angels?*

c: Three weeks. The budget was about $320,000.

g: The film has supposedly grossed several million.

c: That's right.

g: How much of *The Wild Angels* did you make with a rigid script and how much of it did you shoot on the basis of the locations and the day-to-day conditions?

c: I was very loose with *The Wild Angels*. The script was in a constant state of flux. I was rewriting as I was shooting. I never had a really finished script on *The Wild Angels*.

g: Why was that? Was it because your own feeling about what the film was about changed from day to day?

c: It was partially that my feeling changed from day to day, and partially that I was never really satisfied with the script. I had a definite start date. I was actually under contract to Columbia at the time and I had a leave of absence to do this picture for AIP. I had to shoot it at a specific time, though the script I had I felt was not right. So I said, "I have no choice. I will shoot at this particular time, but I will continue to work on the script, hopefully trying to improve it as I go along."

g: Looking back on it, was there something specific that you know now that you would have liked to have done differently?

c: I probably would have gone a little deeper into the characters of some of the Angels. I had previously done a film that I had believed in very much, *The Intruder*, which I shot in the South on natural locations. It was about white and black relationships. The film was a magnificent critical success but did not make money. Thinking back on it, I decided that one of the reasons the film was not a commercial success was the fact that I believed so much in my subject matter that I pushed my own personal thoughts a little bit too heavily into it and the film became slightly propagandistic. So on *The Wild Angels* I determined to withdraw and to shoot in an objective and documentary style as much as possible. Now of course I was dealing with fiction, so it was impossible to do so. But I did pull back a little bit.

G: What film are you working on now?

c: I'm working on a couple of films. I'm working on one film called *The Labyrinth*, which is a modern suspense or horror story. It's my own original idea. I'm working on another one called, tentatively, *Millennium*, which is a science fiction fantasy story based on another one of my own ideas. I used to do quite a bit of science fiction and fantasy and I haven't done it for a number of years. I've always liked it, and I think I'm going to move back into the field again.

I've got one other film at work at the moment and that's the story of the German ace in World War I, von Richthofen, and Roy Brown, the Canadian who shot him down. A dual story that cuts back and forth between the lives of both men.

G: How far in the future are any of these projects?

c: I'm working on the first-draft screenplays of all of them. As yet I don't even have a first draft.

G: Are you working for a studio at this point, or are you working on your own?

c: I'm independent, but I'm working through United Artists. This is a setup I like, since they give me a great deal more freedom of operation. I am preparing one picture for AIP I might mention, called *The Great Peace Scare*.

G: Is that an original script too?

c: Yes, more or less. A friend of mine and I developed the idea jointly. It startled a few people, and they must understand that we're doing a satire. We will attempt to prove that war is the natural and normal condition for humanity and that peace is a perversion. I got some nasty letters when I said that at one time.

G: You've been quoted as saying about modest budget pictures: "This is an art business, but the majority of people who run the business do not know how pictures are made. Thus a man who brings in better pictures cheaper becomes not only a threat to other directors but also to the committees that give pictures to him." Do you still feel that way about the business?

C: It seems like a rather harsh statement that I made. I don't remember phrasing it exactly that way. But I think it is a threat. For instance, if *The St. Valentine's Day Massacre* could have been made at a major studio for $2,100,000 and it can be made independently for $1,100,000, there must be *some* cause for thought somewhere as to why an extra million dollars is spent on a film.

G: Where, for example, did you shoot the studio stuff, the interiors, for *The Wild Angels*?

C: Everything was natural. There were no studios.

G: You mean that church where the orgy was held was a real church?

C: That was a church. We almost got thrown out for a variety of reasons. I explained that we were going to have a funeral in the church and that there probably would be a moment or two of violence. The preacher would then call the police. Which is a fairly accurate statement.

G: Yes, but he didn't know the minister was going to end up in the coffin or that there was going to be an orgy. Was anybody there witnessing this thing?

C: Yes, there was some unhappiness.

G: How much of *that* was improvised?

C: A great deal was improvised. As a matter of fact, the business of the preacher and the coffin. It's very funny you mention that, because the writer saw the rushes with me and he said, "Why did you put the preacher in the coffin?" And I said, "I just shot the script." And he said, "I never wrote that." And I said, "Sure you did. It's in the script." We looked up the script and it was not in the script. I started thinking it was in the script but it wasn't. But I did not believe that I was making up any ideas.

G: Directors keep talking about instinct all the time.

C: I'm a believer in both instinct and preparation. I think you have to go in prepared and then you have to be able to throw away your preparation, if something better occurs. But if you go in just with the vague hope that something brilliant will happen on the spot you could be in a lot of trouble.

G: Is there a Corman technique for making films so quickly, when other people seem to have to take twice as long?

C: If there is, it would be just what I've said. The idea of preparation. Trying to go in with an efficient, small crew, very well organized and very well prepared. And then be able to throw all of the preparation out if you want to change.

G: What about the independent filmmakers who are coming up right now? It seems to me that the film students who are learning how to make documentaries or how to make low budget features don't have any place to go right now. Unless they start a whole new industry of their own.

C: Well, they do have a place to go. For instance, some of the fellows I've backed on their first films—going back a few years to Irv Kirshner, and Bernie Kowalsky, and Monte Hellman, and Peter Bogdanovich, and Francis Coppola, and a few others—they've all found their way into the industry. You can come into the industry a variety of ways. Maybe by shooting an interesting short subject that gets somebody's attention. Maybe by writing a screenplay that somebody wants and saying, "Look, I've shot some documentaries and if you want the screenplay you must take me as the director." Maybe starting away from Hollywood and working in the style of the New York underground.

G: You mentioned before that you had backed some student films. In what sense?

C: I just put up the money.

G: Students come to you and say: "We want to make a film. Here is our project, our script?"

C: Yes.

G: You seem to think the best young directors are going to find their way into the system. You don't think it's necessary to form a third force someplace between the underground and Hollywood?

C: It would help. But the best men do work their way up. I think it would help to make it a little easier for them, and let them work up a little bit faster so that they can get recognition at an earlier age.

On the other hand there may be something to be said for suffering a few years before you get that recognition.

G: What about distribution and exhibition? Isn't that a tremendous problem for the independent? You probably solved it for yourself with an outfit like AIP, by which you both serve each other. But what's the alternative for the independent filmmaker who presumably has some talent but hasn't had a chance to get much financing and has a very low budget film? He doesn't really have a place to distribute it.

C: There are a number of independent distributors who can handle a low budget film. And he can place his film with them. The real problem, I think, is that most low budget filmmakers and most new filmmakers fall into a trap where they're unwilling to make a straight commercial film and they're afraid to invest theirs or their backer's money in a full art film. And they've come up with a film that's not really quite commercially successful, not really artistically satisfying, and they can be in some trouble on that basis.

G: What do you think about television within the next couple of years, either Pay-TV or some other form of TV, as an outlet for independent films so you don't even have to go through the exhibition stage?

C: I have no faith whatsoever in Pay-TV. I just can't believe for one minute that anybody is going to pay money to see something he can see free. So I don't think there's any chance at all that that will happen. I think, however, there will be an increasing outlet on television on the UHF stations, on educational stations, and so forth for serious works of young filmmakers which will probably never be shown in theaters or maybe only one or two theaters in either big cities or university towns and then straight on to television. Television is today what the second-feature market used to be for films. I wouldn't push that analogy too far, but it's true in a general kind of a way.

G: The last film you made was *The Trip*, and it was released two years ago back in 1967. Why haven't you worked for two years? Is it true that your encounter with big budgets has somehow slowed you down?

C: Possibly just disenchantment. With the industry, and with my own work within the industry.

G: The multimillion-dollar *Robert E. Lee* script, for example, never came to fruition, did it?

c: I have the script. I may yet do it. But I was never really satisfied with it.

G: So are you back to thinking in terms of more manageable budgets?

c: Probably, yes.

G: For realistic reasons?

c: Right.

FRANCIS FORD COPPOLA

"The day I got my first job as a
screenwriter, there was a big sign
on the bulletin board saying:
'Sell-out!'"

*Francis Ford Coppola was probably the first graduate of a university
film school in America to direct a Hollywood movie. Certainly he was
the first to offer a commercial film as his thesis for a degree.*

You're a Big Boy Now, *made for $800,000 in twenty-nine days,
established the twenty-seven-year-old Coppola (born: 1939) as a whiz
kid at his studio. Though he had had to bully Hollywood into letting
him make the film, his willingness to work within the system alienated
him from the student filmmakers whose heroes are rebels like Godard.*

*In some ways, Coppola's love-hate relationship with Hollywood is
the archetypal one felt by many young filmmakers. He sentimentally
accepted the job of adapting a creaky 1940s musical,* Finian's Rainbow.
*Yet before the film had opened, he had coerced the studio into bank-
rolling a personal film he would make during a unique odyssey on the
road across eighteen states in a semiscripted* cinéma vérité *style.*

The Rain People *was shot for $750,000 over a period of about three
months of traveling with a company of twenty in a caravan of seven
vehicles equipped with two-way radios. It was edited en route, with the
film being processed and returned from the lab in New York within
three days. The idea was to capture the actual regional character of
the country while filming a pregnant young Long Island housewife
going AWOL, in her station wagon, from the responsibilities of marriage.*

*And then Coppola's ambivalence expressed itself in still another
odd decision. He announced that his next movie would be another
Hollywood project,* Heaven Can Wait, *starring Bill Cosby in a remake
of the 1940s fantasy* Here Comes Mr. Jordan. *And he simultaneously
disclosed that he was leaving Hollywood to set up his own small
independent production studio in a warehouse in San Francisco where
he could experiment and make noncommercial personal films.*

"I don't dislike L.A.," *he told* Variety, *"but I figure at this age I
should find out where I'm going. I'm from New York, but I wouldn't
want to live there. Los Angeles, I like it—but I want to do what Jack
Warner and Harry Warner did forty years ago. Find the place."*

The first film he wants to make in his own studio is The Conversation, *which he is writing himself. "It's about a man on his fiftieth birthday," he said.*

My interview with Coppola was held in his suite at the Plaza Hotel in New York on October 9, 1968, a few hours before the world première of Finian's Rainbow. *He was nervous and under great emotional stress.*

FILMOGRAPHY:

DEMENTIA 13 ('62)
YOU'RE A BIG BOY NOW ('66)
FINIAN'S RAINBOW ('68)
THE RAIN PEOPLE ('69)

GELMIS: What experience with filmmaking had you had before UCLA?

COPPOLA: I used to play with film like a lot of kids. My father, Carmen, was a flutist with Toscanini and a conductor and composer himself. So we had a tape recorder. And I had sound back as early as 1949 or so. I used to have synchronized movies. Most of them I cut together from home movies my family had shot. I'd make myself the hero. I made money out of them, too. I'd show them to other kids in the neighborhood. I had a little movie company there on 212th Street in Queens.

When I was about eighteen, I became very interested in Eisenstein. I became a disciple. I read all of his work and went to see his films at the Museum of Modern Art. And I was really dying to make a film. Taking my example from him, I went to theater school, and worked very hard. I directed lots of plays and I studied theater and I could light a set, build a set. I wanted to be very well rounded, very complete, to have that kind of background, because Eisenstein had started like that.

And I stayed away from film because I knew it would seduce me. I think most young filmmakers in the schools get so hung up—handling film is so much fun, so exciting—that they tend to bypass content and acting, the other things which eventually the film will make use of. They go into it with just technique. So I tried to stay away from film for four years just so I would really have something to bring to it.

But, in my third year at Hofstra, I sold my car and bought a 16-mm camera. I just couldn't wait. I went out to make a short, which I never finished. It was a subjective piece about a woman who takes her children out for a day in the country and she shows them all these beautiful things. And then she falls asleep in an orchard with them.

When she wakes up they're gone and she goes looking for them. The idea was that everything that had seemed so beautiful before now becomes ugly to her because it represents a possible danger to the missing children. I wanted to experiment with this kind of looking at the same thing two ways. I shot part of it but never finished it. I just didn't have the technical expertise. Then I went to UCLA directly from Hofstra, on graduation. I had done lots of musical comedies and had a pretty rounded stage experience—so much so that the first short I made for the film school was too theatrical.

While I was going to UCLA I became one of Roger Corman's

assistants. He'd call me when he wanted cheap labor. I was a dialogue director on *The Tower of London*. And I was Roger's sound man on *The Young Racers*. Roger has one major weakness. When he pays the money to bring a film crew somewhere, he can't resist making a second film with them because he's already paid for their travel.

We were in Ireland with a movie crew that was just begging to be utilized. I was dreaming up an idea for a story, while everybody else just talked about making a film. The secret of all my getting things off the ground is that I've always taken big chances with personal investments. While the other guys my age were all pleading, "Roger, let me make a film," I simply sat down and wrote a script.

Then I took the little money I had and went out and bought some odds and ends I needed for the film. I talked Roger into putting up $20,000 by raising the matching $20,000 myself. I met an English producer in Dublin and he heard we were making a movie—which we weren't, really, yet—and he was willing to buy the English rights. So, essentially, I sold the English rights for a movie which did not exist to this man. And with the $20,000 he paid me and the $20,000 Roger put up, I was able to direct my first feature film—based on a script it had taken me three nights to write.

I shot it with a nine-man crew and some of the actors who were in *The Young Racers*. At the time, I was twenty-two and still just a student at the film school. Some people—including friends of mine—paid their own way to come over to Dublin and work on the film. That's how I met my wife.

The film *Dementia 13* was meant to be an exploitation film, a *Psycho*-type film. *Psycho* was a big hit and William Castle had just made *Homicidal* and Roger always makes pictures that are like other pictures. So it was meant to be a horror film with a lot of people getting killed with axes and so forth.

G: How would you rate it now?

C: I think it showed promise. It was imaginative. It wasn't totally cliche after cliche. Very beautiful visuals. In many ways, it had some of the nicest visuals I've ever done. Mainly, because I composed every shot. In the present circumstances, you never have the time. So you just leave it to others. *Dementia 13* got very good reviews and I made money on it. In England, it was released as *The Haunted and the Hunted*.

I came back from *Dementia 13* and I got married and a week later I got this chance, really on the basis of the Samuel Goldwyn screenwriting award I won at school, to write *Reflections in a Golden Eye* for Seven Arts (later Warner Bros.-Seven Arts). They liked it very much and gave me a contract for three years at $500 a week, so I left school. The reaction was such a load of baloney. Everyone read the *Reflections* script and said, "Fantastic, who's this genius? It must be Dalton Trumbo writing under another name." They gave me all that junk. Everything is either one hundred per cent or nothing. I'm really fed up.

g: What happened to your script for *Reflections?*

c: What very simply happened to all of them. They finally got placed with a director and actors who brought in their own writers and nothing was used of them. I never saw the film they made. But I know that none of my eleven scripts—*Reflections, This Property Is Condemned,* or any of the films I wrote—ever got on the screen very much like I wrote them.

I was twenty-three and I was making about $1000 a week after the first year. I lost it all, by the way. I wanted to make a film so desperately that I saved all my money. And I had about $20,000 cash. I was really frustrated, because I could buy a Ferrari or I could buy a sailboat but I couldn't make a film. So I decided I was going to risk it all on the stock market and either have $100,000 and make a film, or have nothing. I lost it, every penny of it. In one stock. Scopitone. That jukebox with the little films. Lost every penny on it.

A lot of guys are very lazy. Let me tell you. I meet a lot of young filmmakers, because I'm interested in them. And they're all very lazy. They come and they want you to pay them to write the scripts. The first job I did for Roger I was paid $250 to do a dub on a Russian space picture (*Battle Beyond the Sun*) and I worked six months for that $250. No one's willing to do that anymore. I would have done anything. That's the difference.

g: Your screenwriting stint for Seven Arts ended badly, didn't it?

c: It was traumatic. I was one of ten writers on *Is Paris Burning?*, but Gore Vidal and I got the full screen credit for that fiasco. I quit and was fired at the same time. I was broke. I'd lost all my money. I owed the bank $10,000. And I had two kids and a wife to support. I went to Denmark for some reason. I can't remember why, but I wanted to move there. I was very depressed. Then it turned out that Seven Arts had appropriated my script of *You're a Big Boy Now,* which I had written nights in Paris to stay sane. They maintained that since I wrote it on their time they had the right to keep it. I had nothing. I had *nothing.* Not even a friend. I had lost all my friends because I was such a success.

g: How did you survive?

c: Somehow, 20th Century-Fox hired me to write the life of General Patton for $50,000. (Director Franklin Schaffner finally began work on *Patton*, with George C. Scott in the title role, in Spain in January 1969.) I had a little bit of a reputation as a screenwriter that I didn't know about, apparently. So, with that money, I girded myself, as they say, and I made *Big Boy*. I made very little money on the film. I made only $8000 for both writing and directing it, even though I had been offered $75,000 to just write a script for a different film. So, again, I took the risk. Why did I make *Big Boy* for just $8000? Because that's what they could get me for. I would have done it for nothing. I saw *Big Boy* recently, by the way. I really hated it.

And yet I really had to hustle to get that film made. I buffaloed the whole thing through. I got everyone committed before they even realized there was a package I'd put together. Nobody wanted me to direct a film. I was writing films and I was filling a very definite, awful need in the film business, which was to write scripts quickly and anonymously and have them so they could shop them around and get other directors and have other writers rewrite them. I was filling a real function. And I was being paid for it. And I was being paid more than other twenty-three-year-old guys.

But I wanted to make a film. I wanted to make *You're a Big Boy Now* years before I made it. I finally got to make it after this big uphill fight. I bought the book with my own money. I wrote the screenplay. I rewrote the screenplay. I begged people to read it. I got actors to say they would do it. The whole game. I flew to New York. All that stuff.

I paid $1000 for an option on the film rights, against $10,000. It was a big thing for a young guy. I never had anything much. If it makes the people who think I'm in such a great situation feel any better, I never had anything. I lived on ten dollars a week which my father sent me for expenses when I went to graduate school. I earned the tuition. I haven't been pampered. No one helped me do this.

The important thing is that nobody was interested in making the film, literally nobody. The secret of our society is that it's based on the fact that people should pretty much stay where they are, because then everything works. I was a victim of that, I thought. So I went through all of this energy and I got to make *You're a Big Boy Now*. And by the time I got to make it, I didn't know whether I wanted to make it anymore. Because one of the great pities was that I had written *You're a Big Boy Now* before Dick Lester's *The Knack* came out and yet everyone said it was a copy. It was definitely influenced by *A Hard Day's Night*. But it was all there already before I even saw

Hard Day's Night. One of the troubles of the film business is that you're always sort of forced to do things three years later, like with *Big Boy.*

When I finished *Big Boy,* I resolved I wouldn't make the same mistake as a lot of guys—to suddenly get into projects over their head, films they didn't have complete control over, to take other people's raps, so to speak. And then *Finian's Rainbow* came along and I took it, though I didn't know the play, the book. I only knew the score. When I read the book, I was amazed. I thought it was sort of ridiculous, a cockamamy story.

I was hired because they wanted to zip it up and do it à la *Big Boy,* the direction that maybe that was going in. I tried to be very faithful, and to do all of the work underneath so it wouldn't come out like what they did to *A Funny Thing Happened on the Way to the Forum* and films like that. I really tried to show some discipline, to try to make it work on its own terms and not to make a big thing out of myself—you know, to get fancy. I tried to lay low, and give it a lot of warmth and affection and make it work in a timeless way.

I knew there were pitfalls. If I did it faithfully it was going to look like a twenty-two-year-old show. So I tried to make it faithful and yet make it acceptable for contemporary audiences. I think I always knew that the show, critically, was going to be received ungenerously. A lot of liberal people were going to feel it was old pap, because of its dated civil rights stance. And they were going to say, "Oh, the real *Finian's Rainbow* we remember was wonderful." If they were to look at the material today, they might not love it so much. And the conservatives were going to say it was a lot of liberal nonsense. I knew I was going to get it from both ends. And it sort of hurt my feelings.

G: Why did you take on the burden of a twenty-two-year-old musical?

C: Because I thought it was a lovely old show. I thought there was something warm about it. And I thought that maybe if I could do it right, that if I could find the balance, I could make it timeless. It'd be like *Snow White.* I had always loved musical theater.

G: Why hadn't it been made in the past twenty years?

C: There were political reasons, partly. It came out right before the McCarthy era. I guess lots of people felt there were leftist radical things in it. And the people who wrote it wanted lots of money for it. And by the time that subsided, it was already an old show. People had tried to make it, on and off. John and Faith Hubley were planning to make a full-length cartoon out of it back in the '50s.

And another thing, it's being released now as a big fancy roadshow. It wasn't that when it started. It was just a movie musical. It was not expensive. It cost about $3,500,000. You know, it's competing with $10,000,000 musicals like *Funny Girl* and *Star!* But we rehearsed it in three and a half weeks and shot it in just twelve weeks. It was not a luxury production. I'll tell you honestly, after the second week of this picture I was out of what I had prepared. I was faking it.

The choreography was abysmal, let's be honest. We fired the choreographer halfway through the picture. I staged all the musical numbers, eventually. I didn't know I was going to end up doing quite that. And most of those numbers are faked. For example, after the song "If This Isn't Love" we were supposed to go into a big production number. Well, it was so awful that I finally got little Barbara Hancock (Silent Susan, in the film) and we went back and I shot her with a 500-mm lens going in and out of the trees. She was just faking it. And that's the way the numbers were done. I felt very unhelped in the area of choreography, and I needed help.

I wanted to do the musical numbers. I dreamed up the way the numbers were going to be done. I said, "Grandish." I'll shoot it on a hill and have Petula Clark hanging white bed sheets. And "If This Isn't Love" will be done with children's games. And "On That Great Come and Get It Day" they're going to throw away all their old furniture in big piles. And for every number I had an idea. I figured it out. And I wanted to. But for the dance steps, the "combinations" as they're called, I needed a choreographer.

The whole picture was made on the Warners' back lot, the "jungle." I shot just eight days out of the studio. The location footage was carefully interspersed in the film and used with the titles. Yet look what we're competing with. *The Sound of Music,* where they go and sit on the Alps for a month. Any other picture really took the time to do it right. And, even in fairness to our choreographer—who I think was a disaster and was hired at Fred Astaire's insistence—do you know the months that Herb Ross rehearsed those *Funny Girl* numbers? I mean, that's what we're being compared to.

Do you realize that when *Finian's Rainbow* was first assembled it ran two hours and thirty minutes? And this final print runs two hours and twenty-one minutes. That means that only nine minutes were wasted. I'd like to see what the rough cut of one of those other shows ran. William Wyler (*Funny Girl*) and Robert Wise (*Star!*) are perfectionists. I'm really annoyed about the whole thing.

There's a reason why this picture was shot in twelve weeks while

Star! was made in six months. I'm not so much faster and cleverer than those people. Obviously the reverse. So there was a degree of tolerance in terms of what I could go for in the time allocated. I would shoot a scene eight times. And it would be different every time. And then I'd jump-cut mismatched bits together. In other words, I'd never try to match a picture.

If you look at the chorus during this movie you'll see lots of miscues or flutterings. As you know, kids are very hard to program. And the more you get kids that are programable, the more phony they are. Also, there wasn't lots of time to keep going after every detail. Very often I was going for what I felt was the essence of a scene. I always feel a director directs his movie before it's even done. If the vision is right, then you'll forgive a lot of this other stuff. More time will help alleviate the rough details. But I feel if the audience didn't enjoy it, it's because of the vision.

G: In the case of a musical, the performance is almost everything. There were problems with the performances of several of your people. Do you think it's possible for a director to control such things?

C: Yes. Don Francks never did improve, as an actor. The one I'm really unhappy about was Tommy Steele, because I think I could have done better with him. When we were doing the rehearsal, Tommy was doing his *thing.* And I said to him that I really felt we were going in the wrong direction. Everyone loved him and told Tommy he was so great. But I felt the leprechaun should be more shy and timid and bewildered. When I first came into the picture, I wanted Donal Donnelly to play the part. I wanted it to be an introvert leprechaun, a guy who speaks in this quiet voice and then suddenly becomes a human being.

And at my insistence Tommy started to do just that in the rehearsal, and he really was good at it. But actors are funny people. They have certain crutches that they rely on. And they're very unwilling to let those crutches go when they feel insecure. And somehow during the actual shooting, little by little, he slipped back into his familiar character. And you don't notice it because you're shooting little pieces. And that's the whole game of directing. Directing takes a lot of concentration and being able to be blind to certain problems and just focus where you should be focusing. I did that in some cases. In some cases I failed. With Tommy, I wanted a different kind of performance and he eluded me.

G: Was there more pressure on you as a young director making a big musical than there had been exerted by the studio when you made *You're a Big Boy Now* for less than $1,000,000?

c: I have to say in all honesty that I did both films the way I wanted to do them. I had my way, within the limitations of time and money. I was very responsible. *Finian* cost as little as it did because I was very disciplined. I consider myself a very romantic human being and I really feel I was well suited to do this project. But it's not my personal kind of filmmaking, which I may never depart from again, by the way.

g: Among your contemporaries, especially from the graduate film school at UCLA, there must have been a lot of guys who said: "He's selling out. He made a small film his way and now he's an apostate."

c: Oh, I am the original sell-out. The day I got my first job as a screenwriter there was a big sign on the bulletin board saying: "*Sell out!*" Oh yes, I'm the famous sell-out from UCLA. Dating back to 1961, when I got my job for $300 a week to write *Reflections in a Golden Eye*. There was open resentment. I was making money. And I was sort of *doing* it. I was already doing what everybody was just talking about. You know, more and more I have gained the power, so to speak, to do what it is I want to do. It's like getting here by going there. It's the ancient dilemma. But I've got to be honest about *Finian's Rainbow*. I wanted to do it. I thought it was a very sweet thing. So I can't say the old thing, "Well, I didn't want to do it. The studio made me do it."

g: Do you think that the key to the respect of young filmmakers is to bend the System to suit your personal style, as Jean-Luc Godard did when he got Carlo Ponti and Joe Levine to put up $1,000,000 and then made *Contempt* his way?

c: Yes. But the kids at school are the most narrow-minded of any age group. There are kids at UCLA and USC who are incredible Godard addicts.

g: Isn't it the nature of the revolutionary to be confident?

c: Yes, but it's so narrow. I'm trying not to be narrow myself. I'm trying to bounce this whole marvelous thing of making movies off what I am as a human being. That's why my feelings are very hurt about all of this. First of all, it's very, very difficult to make a good film. When I go to see somebody else's movie, if it was sincere in what it did, I am the best audience in the world. I really am. The only thing I can't stand is when they start getting very pretentious and dishonest. But other than that, I go in with the attitude not of "Show me what you can do," but, "Boy, isn't that nice, I'm going to see a movie." Very few people go to the movies with that attitude.

It's come to the point where I just want to get out altogether. I just want to go do my own thing. And I may do that. I'm fed up. It takes too much out of you. You don't get enough for it, in whatever commodity you're dealing in. I think a lot of people are jealous of me. Basically, my contemporaries. They say, "Well, there he is, twenty-eight, twenty-nine years old, he's got a lot of money and he's making movies."

They wouldn't want it. Not much. They want it. They just think I'm living this golden life and they don't realize that I am really straining and endeavoring to find some honest balance with myself in terms of the work of the future. I am more interested in the films that I'll make when I'm forty than I am now. I'm trying to develop myself. I'm trying not to believe all the baloney publicity written about me. There is no intermediate in this business. They either say, "Here he is, the boy wonder, the best young filmmaker . . ." or they say, "Ah, he's just a load of crap." Why doesn't someone ever say, "Well, he's a promising guy and he's somewhat intelligent and he's really trying and maybe in ten years he might be a really . . ." No one ever says that.

G: Why did you make *The Rain People?*

C: Because nobody else could have made *The Rain People.* Good or bad, it's me, it's my own. If I've got to take raps, I'd rather take raps for my own tastes. That film was a labor of love. We had a very small crew in a remodeled Dodge bus that we rebuilt ourselves and filled with the most advanced motion picture equipment available. I presented the movie to the studio as a *fait accompli.* I told them on a Friday, "Look, I'm starting to shoot on Monday and I need some money and if you don't give it to me, I'll get it from someone else." And they gave me the money. And I never showed them the script.

It's my film, from beginning to end. What it really comes down to is a pregnant woman, sitting in a car, literally walking out on all the responsibilities one associates with a young wife. And putting distance between herself and that. She has a very sympathetic husband. There's no reason she's leaving. He's not ugly, he doesn't have bad breath, he's not intolerable. For her, he is a potentially fine husband. She's a girl you might have known in college, very bright and decent, a good woman.

And she gets married and suddenly starts feeling her personality being eroded, not knowing why. What is she supposed to perform in this thing, marriage? What's her place? A lot of women have a terrible time with this. And she's pregnant. That's the final straw. So all it is, it's a trip she's taking, getting more and more pregnant and getting farther and farther away from her home.

And she picks up a guy in the car. And the guy says to her something like, "Hey, I just have to be dropped off on Union Turnpike because some people are going to take care of me and take me someplace." She drops him off and she realizes the people there who are supposed to take care of him don't want him. So she has to keep him with her in the car. So it's a story of a human being becoming more and more responsible toward another human being. It's like a woman sitting next to the kid she's going to have.

G: What plans do you have to help George Lucas (another film school graduate) expand his fifteen-minute prize-winning student film, *THX-1133-4EB*, into a feature film?

C: It's my most immediate commitment, to produce it this spring, probably for Warners. George was my assistant on *Finian*. *THX-1133-4EB* is a full-length story now about a futuristic society. We're going to go to Japan or somewhere and George is just going to direct it in his own way. It's all based on my strength now. Let's say *Finian's Rainbow* is a big flop. It's going to hurt George more than anybody. I'm giving him my strength. I'm saying, "If you want me, you've got to give George Lucas his break." Well, if suddenly they don't want me, then George has got a problem.

I'm in a position to make lots of money this year. If I would accept two or three of the forty films I've been offered, I could make a million. The word of mouth on *Finian* was very high the last eight months. If the picture does not get very good reviews—and I know it will get some of both—that may tarnish my reputation a lot. (The notices were mostly poor.) I have been very foolish in some people's estimations, but I think, too, very honest, in not having accepted any pictures.

I've been offered a half million dollars for a movie, to direct and write another musical. But I'm not going to do it, because I don't want to do any more. And all I got for writing, directing, and cutting *The Rain People* was $50,000, though it's going to represent a year and a half out of my life. Now what I should have done, which is what everyone else does, is to just keep accepting the big movies before the reviews of the other ones come out. So right now I'd be very securely sitting with a contract for a $500,000 picture and I'd be already committed. Well, I have no commitments.

And in a way I sort of hope it all blows up. I'm disgruntled. I could make a lot of money by just grabbing up three pictures and having writers write them and having cutters cut them, and just—zoom—

go right through them. I could pile up about a million dollars, which I would surely like. Because I have no money now whatsoever. I spent it all.

I lived on what I made on *Finian*. How do you think I made *Rain People?* I bought motion picture equipment. I own the $80,000 worth of equipment in that van now. It's mine. I supported that cast and crew of almost twenty for nearly five months. I'm broke today. I am totally at liberty. I've been offered lots of big pictures. And I sort of hoped, I'll have to admit, that one would come along that I felt I could do very well. Again, it's linked to *Finian*, which is sort of dumb. But it is. So after today, I may not get the offers that I was hoping I would. In which case, it may solve some of my problems, because then I don't have to make a choice.

G: Are you, then, disgruntled because you've somehow got yourself in a position where your reputation rests not on *The Rain People* but on *Finian's Rainbow?*

C: Yeah, that's a big part of it. But let's be honest. *Finian* made *The Rain People* possible. The fact that *Finian* was made and everyone at the studio liked it meant that I could then go and do *The Rain People*. Now, I can't do another one. I need a successful picture sooner or later. Look at (Bernardo) Bertolucci, sitting over there in Italy. It takes him four years to get a film. The same thing could happen to me. My only ace in the hole was that I had a big commercial picture and I was considered flexible, which was a tremendous asset.

What I'm thinking of doing, quite honestly, is splitting. I'm thinking of pulling out and making other kinds of films. Cheaper films. Films I can make in 16 mm. No one knows whether there's a viable market for that kind of film yet. All I know is that I'm tired. It's not just opening-night jitters. I've been thinking about this now for six months. I'm tired. I never knew that so many people wished you failure. I didn't realize. Let somebody else have the headaches.

G: You once used the phrase "the Hitler syndrome" to describe how you had joined the establishment and were tunneling away at it from within.

C: That's what I did. Here I am. But now I don't know if I'm totally satisfied with where it's all led me. I really feel I could make an important film. It may take ten years. But I feel it's possible.

G: When *The Rain People* comes out in 1969, might it start the cycle again?

C: *The Rain People* could be an awful picture. It's very experimental. It doesn't protect itself at all. It's not even sensational. No sex. Very sincere. And I don't even know how terrific it is. But it really tries. And I'm tired. I don't want to have to make success. You know, if it means I've got to work on $6000 films in San Francisco, then I guess that's what I have to do. (Pause.) I don't know, I'll probably do another big picture now. I really need the money.

"Film offers the opportunity for
constant contradiction between
what is said and what is done."

*Born in 1922, Arthur Penn is still trim and boyish, and could prob-
ably pass for a graduate film student on location in his sneakers and
chinos. From years in the theater, he has developed a gentleness with
his actors and an abiding rapport with most of them.*

On the set of Alice's Restaurant *in Stockbridge, Massachusetts, in
the fall of 1968, I watched him become absorbed and absolutely quiet
while preparing a particularly troublesome scene. It was Penn's method
of reacting to something that's gone wrong. There are no outbursts.
He implodes.*

*Later, after seeing the day's rushes, the following interview was
recorded during a leisurely three-and-a-half-hour dinner. Penn is, quite
obviously, articulate, but what may not be apparent is that he laughs
easily at himself. He is genuinely warm and compassionate, and he is
receptive to and stimulated by the irreverence and skepticism of
youth. Between takes on the set, Arlo Guthrie said: "I trust Arthur.
He knows where it's at. That's why I'm making this film with him."*

*Though there are brilliant action sequences in each of his films, it
used to be argued that Penn was an "arty" director influenced by the
Italians.* Mickey One *was dismissed by many critics as pretentious,
and Penn himself is overly modest about the film despite the fact
that it holds up as a strikingly original experiment.*

Penn is best known in America, of course, for Bonnie and Clyde.
But European critics have been fans of his since his first film, The
Left Handed Gun. *Penn's gifts for handling actors, for alternating
the dynamics of humor and horror, and for pure action narrative as the
stuff of legends coalesced in* Bonnie and Clyde.

The world-wide reaction to Bonnie and Clyde, *especially among
those under twenty-five, indicated that the film touched some sort of
psychic nerve. It made schizophrenics of critics, who couldn't decide
how they really felt about it. It appealed to the intelligentsia and to
the yahoos. Penn discusses here some of the things he was trying to
do and his feelings about the furore the film created.*

Bonnie and Clyde *was written by David Newman and Robert
Benton and then, in turn, influenced or shaped by Truffaut and*

Godard—each of whom almost directed it at one time before other commitments prevailed. Warren Beatty brought the screenplay to Penn, who did the final shaping of the shooting script into what he considered the necessary emotional curve.

FILMOGRAPHY:

THE LEFT HANDED GUN ('58)
THE MIRACLE WORKER ('62)
MICKEY ONE ('65)
THE CHASE ('66)
BONNIE AND CLYDE ('67)
ALICE'S RESTAURANT ('69)
LITTLE BIG MAN ('70)

GELMIS: How do you plan to make a full-length feature film from Arlo Guthrie's recording of *Alice's Restaurant?*

PENN: The film really spans a broader period of time than the record. It begins at a point in Arlo's education when he was going to college in Montana. It moves with him cross-country. Because he can't really make it out there. He finds he's not really responsive to it. As somebody said to him the other day, "You were a drop-out." And he said, "No, I wasn't really a drop-out, because there was nothing ever to drop into. Why do you assume that I was the one who was at fault? Maybe there was just no scene out there at all. Why do you call it a drop-out? It suggests that there was something of value there to start with."

It's a very interesting point. Given that as a premise, we start out with a sort of out-group kid. And I'm hoping that in the course of the film we will go through with him those experiences which are not dissimilar from all of ours. The kind of personal identity crisis of dying parents and surrogate choices in parents and love affairs. But on the other hand, we are witnessing something in which rebellion is not the essential characteristic. These kids are on to something much more genuine, much more tender, and clearly loving. I have a lot of admiration for them, I must say. And so I'm hoping that the film will be able to elucidate that part of their subculture in a way that I haven't seen done elsewhere yet.

G: This particular community which Arlo belonged to and wrote about dissolved, disintegrated. Yet he doesn't seem to feel that's an indication of its weakness, or that stability is itself a value.

P: I think that's a valid point. We are in that deceptive position that history always puts you in. When you look back, you recognize that there was a community. I think at the time there was no community. There was a state of being. They were moving through an experience of their own. Only now, by our backward glance, do we define it as a community. It's still there, in one form or another, for a slightly different generation of kids than Arlo's.

G: In the same place? With the same leaders?

P: Not the same leaders. Alice and Ray have busted up.

G: Isn't that a metaphor for what happened, actually? The parents busted up and the kids went to the winds?

P: It certainly seems so. Alice and Ray experienced a sort of crisis in their marriage. And then they decided that by some kind of active reconsecration they might be able to re-establish a bond between them, and, by implication, a bond that was broader than just their marriage and that went out to all the others from whom again they'd begun to experience this separation . . . that is, with the kids. And so there is this big ceremony. It's self-conducted. One of the group acts as a minister. Because there's no need to be married legally. They are already married. But metaphorically they're not. So they decide to do it again. One of them was a photographer, Benno Freedman, and he acted as the minister.

G: Can you just briefly tell me something about the genesis of how you got involved with *Alice's Restaurant?*

P: I had only a peripheral acquaintance with it. I knew Ray and Alice, but only cursorily. I knew Alice's Restaurant as the best restaurant around here. She's a terrific cook. And Ray was a builder who was working around at our theater, at the Berkshire Theater Festival. So we came to know in an odd, tangential way some of the kids who were in the group. Ray is a wonderful builder. And one of the things he was teaching these kids was how to build. He's a kind of architect-designer-sculptor-manqué. He's manqué in everything. But he's talented in all his directions. And he was teaching the kids to build. A lot of them make a living as builders around here now.

G: Were these all disaffected kids, by the way? Were they kids who had left home, run away?

P: There is such a multiplicity of backgrounds, it's almost impossible to isolate a single characteristic. They were kids who were, in a certain sense, repudiating an ethic and a moral value they felt was somehow hypocritical at one level or another. Either personally and emotionally or politically and socially. At some level, there was a disaffection with the extant standards of their parents. Some of them were fairly advanced in scholarship. One of them was deeply engaged in a doctoral thesis in the Greek language. Another is just graduating from Radcliffe.

G: They weren't just drop-out kids who hadn't been able to make it?

P: Oh no, anything but. The intellectual level of the group was quite high, I would say. But they were feeling somehow that their own thing was being overlooked, whatever that need was, that their personal need was not being dealt with by society. A lot of them were bright enough to be in the community and then buzz back to Radcliffe to knock off the exams and then get back to the community. They come over here and live all week long and go back for perhaps two classes and somehow make it.

One of the kids brought the record to our house one night. I recognized it. I had heard some fragment of it at a party, but had paid no attention. It had just gone by me. But when I heard it at home, I had an instantaneous response: "I just know I have to make that film." What that film would be or what it would be about, I had no idea.

When we started out writing, we wrote about four or five variations on the record. That's all we wrote. And we kept coming up with a thirty-page, forty-page script, which was just not enough. I couldn't find a purchase on the material, until I began to delve back into some of these remembered conversations with the kids and realized that there was a kind of constancy in it all. Which was the constancy of identity being unachievable in their given birthright circumstances, but somehow achievable in these surrogate and chosen circumstances. And that seemed to me to be a very interesting phenomenon. But then I raised the question with myself and with Venable Herndon (Penn's co-writer), which is, if it's that easy, why haven't we all done it, why haven't other generations done it? There must be something about this generation which is particular.

And I think there are several things involved. One, growing up in the atomic generation is a sort of bottom line. Nobody makes any mention of it. But it's the bottom line for a certain instability, the sense that the world really may not be there on a given day, if Curtis LeMay has his way. I mean, that's perfectly within the lexicon that all of us employ. It's not simply that a nut out in the middle of Illinois says that the world is going to end in eighteen days. It's really possible. I don't mean that these kids verbalize this at all. That's one. The other is the draft. The third is that it's a draft in a really absurd war. I can only tell you about my own experience in relation to war. I went to war—and I think of myself as a relatively pacific man—but I went to war with passion, because I believed in it. These kids have no belief in it. Not only that, but they have contempt for the people who instigated it. And whether we're willing to accept the onus or not, it represents all of us in another generation.

In Arlo's particular case, there's still another dimension to it. His father (Woody Guthrie) was, after all, in a way the voice of his generation, of the insurrectionists of his generation—the Old Left. Now, Arlo is not actually part of the New Left, in the sense one could characterize as political. He simply says, "I just will not go to war. I just don't intend to go to war. I don't care what they do to me. I'm just not going." He can say that now at twenty-one. At age eighteen, it was not such a clear-cut decision. So one of the things that I think is happening is that the social conditions have helped these kids anneal an identity. Under these kinds of pressures, it was either put up or shut up. And he couldn't hang out here and not put up, in relation to the draft.

So Arlo didn't. He went through the whole thing, received his induction notice and was prepared to go to jail. It's a very hard-nosed decision for a nineteen-year-old kid to make. I don't know if, believing as I do now, I would necessarily have that kind of guts as the kid I was. I can't translate my own experiences into theirs. But I can have a certain admiration for them, I must say.

It seemed to me that this capacity to repudiate what they didn't like, to have the freedom—which is also characteristic of this generation—to choose what they do like, that those kinds of liberties on both ends of the spectrum put them into a benign new life that I don't think any of us has experienced before. All I can say is that my recent experience with it and proximity to it has filled me with admiration for it. They are loving kids who have found a way of dealing with their hostility, of dealing with living together, of dealing with some of the absurdities of life, in a way that doesn't reduce them to immobility or keep them from functioning. They just don't necessarily function in the orthodox way, but they function. I think *that*, for homeless kids, is a remarkable accomplishment. That's sort of what I'm shooting for in the film.

G: Do you think that one of the things that characterizes these kids is the need for drugs?

P: Very little. These are not hard users. They resented, as a matter of fact, that we portrayed somebody in the script who used hard stuff. In point of fact, I happened to know of somebody up here who was not of the community except peripherally, though he did cross it in a way, who was a hard user and eventually did kill himself. He went down to New York and OD'eed (over-dosed). It was a very sad case. He was a brilliant kid. But very few of the kids in this film even need to turn on. They have a work responsibility that I find admirable. The kids from this community have signed on for this picture and there's not one who's failed us, not one of them.

The ones who've failed us have been, oddly, the kids from the OK establishment, who said, "Oh, yeah, I'll be there." And then never showed up. For instance, the guy who was supposed to look like the cowboy today had come from an elegant Connecticut family. He had brought his horse up here and had ridden for us in a riding shot and said, "Yes, of course I'll be there" (mimics prep school upperclassman accent). Not a chance. Never showed this morning. We used a production assistant with long hair, put a hat on him. But our kids—our cadre of about fourteen—are responsible; we have not had one failure in presence or their being on time.

G: How do you deal with non-actors like these, in terms of getting what you want out of them?

P: I let them do their thing. I try to take as much of the literary value away from the script as possible. Actors are equipped to do the literary thing. But movies are not necessarily about literary utterances in the way that the stage is. So I'm perfectly willing, as Venable is, to suspend our written dialogue in a given instance and say, "Go with your own words, whatever would seem amiable here." And that's true of Arlo too. Certain of our ways of speaking are clearly not his. Although Venable did a very good job of researching them, and he lived in that church with those kids for months and really got their sound. But it's not necessarily Arlo's sound. When Arlo read the script, he said, "Hell, this guy sounds like he comes from Oklahoma. I come from Brooklyn." Well, in a way it's true. But on the record he sounds like he came from Oklahoma. He was using something from Woody's presentational style.

G: Why did you choose Venable Herndon?

P: I read a couple of his plays, *Bag of Flies* and *When the Monkey Comes*. They struck me as very interesting and with-it. He's very responsive to these kids. He had almost the same experience, only more intensive than mine. You fall in love with them as a group.

G: How do you intend to transform the record into a movie?

P: Clearly the incident, as told in the record, is not how it happened. What's involved is essentially the clash of value systems. Arlo is telling it from his point of view. He admits he took liberties. He's the first to say it didn't happen that way. So I thought what might be interesting was to do a kind of *Rashomon*. What we'd do is recount the incident that's on the record and then we would talk to the people individually, get their version of how it happened, and then maybe that would be interesting. I persuaded myself of that for about ten minutes. But it was manifestly dreadful.

So I went to see David Picker and Sam Gelfman at United Artists and told them I really didn't know how I would do it, but that I did know there was a film there somewhere. I asked them to give us the money for Venable to work on a script. And Venable came up here to live. (Penn has a home in Stockbridge too.) We met every day; would meet for five or six hours a day and just talk. And we started from as sophomoric ideas as the *Rashomon* one and then we got into the most erudite and abstruse, impossible versions of this film . . . "typical of the new sexuality" and all kinds of nonsense. None of that settled in.

As we began to really *groove* on the record, as Arlo would say, we began to find what it was about—which was clearly the identity question, "Who am I and where do I belong? And what are the limits of where I belong and what are the limits that impose themselves on me, that cause me to fall short of where I belong? Am I experiencing all I might experience?" Which then brings me back to your question about the drug scene. I would put these kids on the level of experience which is that they're not users, or in any way hung up on drugs. But I think that almost anything that they can find, within the sensual as well as intellectual and spiritual experience, they would like to reach out to. It's an act of repudiation of what exists around them, of whatever this ethic is we're living in.

G: The up-tight ethic?

P: Exactly. It's a sort of enlightening experience to be around them. I mean, I don't happen to be particularly interested in astrology. I don't give a damn about it. But, okay. However you choose to categorize or identify people, that sort of belongs to each generation. I can remember my generation saying, "Well, you have a father fixation or a mother fixation or an inferiority complex." There are as many short cuts and shorthand expressions to try and describe the human experience in one generation as there are in another. The wonderful thing about these kids is that they don't want to be limited in the way that my generation was. There are various reasons. Economic, political, social, and evolutionary, if you will. The evolution of society and a certain culture. It simply was not possible for us. It is possible for them.

And I think they're taking the best advantage of this affluent society—not by using the affluence, but by using the freedom which is obtainable through the affluent society. So if you want to go out and do a few days' work a week, which is enough to keep your life together, and then spend the rest of your time finding out how to live, I think that's admirable. They're not taking any money from home. They're out there doing the Thoreau thing, building a greenhouse for somebody, or building a house for somebody else. They're first-rate builders. My generation grew up admiring Thoreau. But these kids are coming closer to him than we ever did. On every level, including civil disobedience in the case of the draft.

G: How were you able finally to avoid making the film just an extension or illustration of the record?

P: What we have in a way is an almost too-good story. Historically, it's too good. Imagine, if you are part of a certain generation which says: "I am repudiating the values of the older generation—that immobility that I feel in my parents." And imagine having this characterized by a man (Woody Guthrie) who's experiencing increasing paralysis (Huntington's Disease, the deterioration of the central nervous system) as a sort of dramatic event which ends finally in death. It's almost too perfect, too well chosen. Point two, it's a hereditary disease. And it's possibly going to affect Arlo, or his kid brother. Three, that your father was the voice of the Old Left. It begins to resonate like a really well-toned bell, because it begins to tell all kinds of stories in all directions.

G: Still, everybody doesn't already know who Woody Guthrie was.

P: Right. So part of our problem is how do you do that without saying: "There was this man named Woody Guthrie . . ."

G: At the beginning of *Bonnie and Clyde* you set up little biographical police cards to place your characters in historical perspective.

P: Right. But those were dead criminals. Arlo is alive and functioning. On the other hand, we did want to tell a little bit about his father. So we have some scenes up front. They're fictional. But I would bet you anything they're not inaccurate. There's a sort of record industry man, not really an A & R man, but a kind of manager guy with whom Arlo has a scene. And he says, "Yeah, we can set you up. After all, you're what's 'is name's son. You get yourself tied in with the New Left, the SDS or something, get yourself busted a couple of times, sing at a rally here, sing at a rally there, and we'll fix you up. Then we can get you a record date, and you know, we'll go from there."

Well, in a certain sense, you're beginning to pick up a little bit of it. Then there's a woman he meets later on who runs a club that he sings in. She's sort of sentimental about the Old Left. And she recalls, "You know, Woody still owes me for a train ticket that he borrowed the money for." And then she ends up making a pass at Arlo. In this way, we build up the charisma of the man.

We also meet Woody in the film, in the hospital room, with Arlo's mother, who really nursed him and worked with him during the decade he was confined prior to his death in 1967. Arlo's mother will be played by an actress. I'm hoping Pete Seegar will play himself. He frequently would visit Woody in the hospital and he and Arlo would sit there and play Woody's songs for Woody to hear. And we have a couple of scenes like that where they go through Woody's songs of the period.

I must say that I wish I'd listened to that Allan Lomax tape of Woody Guthrie before I did *Bonnie and Clyde*. He solved the whole picture for us, in a way I finally worked out, but without knowing it. He gave the sociological background in terms of people's attitudes towards the banks in a way that it had taken me months of working with Benton and Newman to finally come around to. Which was that the banks did a sort of stupid thing. They foreclosed on the farms to the degree that they finally indebted themselves to nothing and had to be dissolved.

c: This is what you once described to me as cannibalism.

p: Yes. Exactly. The banks were pursuing the nineteenth-century retaliatory posture—"You didn't pay your mortgage. We're going to foreclose." They followed the textbook rules gloriously down the road to perfect oblivion. Well, Woody, in this tape with Allan Lomax, talks about Pretty Boy Floyd. And it's another capsulized version of exactly this principle. Unfortunately, I hadn't heard it until after we had worked it out the hard way for ourselves.

c: I'm not familiar with Lomax's record.

p: He's the man from the Library of Congress who went around recording folk songs. He did a three-hour interview with Woody, with songs and history. And one of the things he asked Woody about was the gangsters of the '30s. I wish I had heard this. Woody had even written a song called "Pretty Boy Floyd." A wonderful song.

c: But you solved the problem—with the gun, the farmer who shoots his house when he's forced by the bank to leave it.

p: We found those same symbols. But I wish I had had the luck to listen to the record first. There was the answer beautifully contained. Somebody could turn around right now and make a marvelous film based on Woody's view of Pretty Boy Floyd.

c: What was Woody's view of Pretty Boy Floyd?

p: That he got into this situation because of a hassle with a deputy, and then went off and was protected by the populace. Then the police began to blame things on him, like bank robberies. And he said if they're blaming them on me, I might as well do them. And then it got worse and worse. When the banks started failing, they said they were failing because Pretty Boy Floyd had robbed them. But he had never been near them, he'd been 350 miles away. (Penn slips into almost unconscious mimicry of Woody Guthrie's Oklahoma accent.) And on he goes, talking this half-lyric, half-Oklahoma droll.

Well, isn't that fascinating? Supposing a bank is going to have to go bust because they followed this nineteenth-century Keynesian economic morality and you follow it down the line and say, "An eye for an eye." You close up somebody's farm, you close up enough farms to close up your own bank. And you have to appropriate an excuse for it. So you say you were held up by gangsters: Pretty Boy Floyd and Dillinger.

The FBI came into being as a result of these banks. In a sort of comic book published by the FBI, they supposedly recounted the exploits of these terrible bloodthirsty killers and bank robbers—Bonnie and Clyde, Pretty Boy Floyd, and Dillinger. What they were really doing was promoting the FBI into a national phenomenon. The G-man came into being on the reputation of these gangsters. They managed to inflate the reputations to such ominousness that the citizenry quaked in their boots, when, in point of fact, they were really petty criminals by almost any standards in the world.

But because the FBI was attempting to create a sort of national police—which they succeeded in doing, and very well—their propaganda was staggeringly well done. You could make a fascinating story of how someone creates a national police force. Anyway, this is part of what Woody talks about in the Lomax record.

G: I'd like to bring us back for a moment to how you got into the actual process of putting together *Alice's Restaurant*. You are using Arlo in the film as the personification of the new young sensibility. How much is truth and how much is conjecture?

P: I would say much of it is truth. I don't know if it's specifically truth. But to go back to the old analytical, Freudian terms, one begins with a child, aged four, whose father becomes visibly afflicted with a malady considered terminal. I think he would probably end up mistrusting the existence of the father. The father figure would be something of the life-into-shadow, a mythic character whose life certainly hangs over you. You go to a particularly rigid, authoritarian school. You repudiate that. You go in quest of a kind of father, and you find a very amiable one. He finally found a perfectly wonderful society, in his terms.

I don't know how wonderful it is—I wouldn't make exactly that kind of value judgment. But it probably represented a kind of salvation to him. It brought him into a community of peers who were doing things which he felt were not available to him elsewhere, and through the personages of parent figures who did not resemble his parents. Here was a robust, hard-living kind of father who was, yes, permissive, but he was also full of a kind of sexuality which was probably not—and I'm just guessing here—available to Arlo's father.

And it may be too psychoanalytic, but a child growing up in a certain kind of household knows of sexuality, or does not. He can sense it. It's a kind of "ongoingness." I think if you grow up in a house, as I did, for instance, of divorced parents—where I lived with my mother when I was three and a half—I knew that something was conspicuously absent. And on the rare occasions when it was present, I was doubly alert to it. And doubly hostile to it, probably. I don't know anything about Arlo's situation, but I would suspect there's something correlative between our two lives. Anyway, here you fall into a church where people are really doing it.

It's a building, incidentally, that was constructed by the Salem shipbuilders, who were brought inland. Apparently there were two structures on that same foundation. One burned down in part. There are two cornerstones in the wall. One is about 1827. And the other is about 1860. It probably represents the rebuilt church. It's an Episcopal church of the St. James Parish, Great Barrington, on the Housatonic, of a little village once called Van Deusenville. And a couple of the names that are up there in the stained glass are Van Deusen. Probably in its day it was a very distinguished church. But then, of course, New England went through an economic crisis. The textile mills folded. And the paper mills had not really come into existence in sufficient quantities to employ the local populace.

So they drifted from Van Deusenville through Housatonic and the old village of Great Barrington. And this church finds itself now on the very periphery of the Great Barrington community. There are no longer enough parishioners to support it. About six years ago, it was deconsecrated, or rendered unholy. We have that scene in the film. I guess it's necessary, if you're going to have a church which is supposed to be sacred, to say this other place is no longer a hallowed, sacred place. But then if you think about it in terms of these kids, what is sacred to them? What is unsacred? And isn't what they're doing there perhaps more sacred than what was done there in the old ethic?

G: You spoke before about the almost too-perfect film. Here you have a situation where these people are living their ritual, in the shell of the old society's empty church. They're living the sacraments.

P: Exactly. They not only live it, they create it. They took an antique American hymn, "Amazing Grace," put it to their own use. They sing it when they turn on or sit around of an evening. The first time I heard that was when—in the early stages of talking about the film—Arlo called me one night and asked if he could drop over. I said sure. Eleven people showed up.

G: His retinue?

P: Not really. Just the gang. They don't travel alone. They live together. So we were sitting around, had some food. He sat down at the piano in our house and started to play "Amazing Grace." They just drifted into singing it, without preparation. I heard this beautiful hymn, sung with real soul. And when I asked Arlo where he got it, he said: "We sing it all the time. We sing all the old, old songs of the church and the early settlers."

G: What is Arlo's relation to Alice? In the daily rushes we saw today there's a certain ambivalence, almost a sexual link between them— mother and son. But more like Hamlet and his mother.

P: That's the name of the game. Alice is a young woman; she's twenty-seven now. She was an earth mother at age twenty-four. And she was not that far away in age that she wouldn't want to fall in love with him. Here she is, really a beautiful woman . . . She has a wonderfully sexy orientation toward life.

G: How large a community did she and Ray attract?

P: The word "community" doesn't really describe it. It was always in transit. A lot of the kids have houses up here. Arlo had a house. Some of them still do. A lot of them come from around here. So it's never been in that sense a clearly circumscribed community. I would guess—and it's just a guess—that there may have been up to thirty or forty people orbiting around Alice and Ray. Very few lived in the church itself. Kids would drop by for food at night. To smoke a little bit. Live a little bit. Or during the day to work on some projects around the church. Or to fix their bikes. They're hard-riding motor-cycle racers. We have a shot of them driving their bikes right into the church on Thanksgiving.

G: Why was Thanksgiving such an important event in their lives?

P: It wasn't really. Every ritual is important to them. They love ritual. They make ritual, if there is none. They have a lot in common with Indians. Tribal life. Ritual. Totem is a very important thing to them. Every day has a certain character to it.

G: How are you going to use the record in the film, if at all?

P: We use it almost intact, actually, as an episode near the end of the film. As Arlo goes into a sort of identity pressure, we take off from the Thanksgiving Dinner—which in itself takes off from a crisis between Ray and Alice. Everything they do resonates down with increasing strength within the community. Even today, if Alice says something, it gets a different kind of response than if anybody else in that room had said it. And there isn't one of the kids who, on his way out, didn't pay some kind of obeisance to Ray. They are very important figures in their lives. Each of us has had in probably one way or another such a figure. We may not have had it in such a formalized way. Or we may have had, in the form of a teacher or a friend. Somebody other than your parent. Somebody with whom you relate in that relationship which is quasi-sexual, intellectual, moral, spiritual, philosophic, etc. Just so you have that kind of transference in life with somebody. In retrospect, you realize you had it, or that you were in a community.

G: We were talking earlier this evening about what theme, if any, runs through your films, and it seems that your chief figure is always an outsider. Billy the Kid in *The Left Handed Gun*. The Warren Beatty character in *Mickey One*. The Robert Redford victim in *The Chase*. Bonnie and Clyde. And now Arlo.

P: And the blind girl in *Miracle Worker*. It's not a conscious theme, but it certainly is a theme. If you come out of a divorced family and you grow up, as I did, in a highly migratory life, moving from one section of New York to another every six months—the Bronx, Brooklyn, back and forth—and if you're poor, really hurting during the Depression, it has to have an effect on personality. I went to live with my father at age fourteen. But he was a man I hardly knew. So once again I underwent an alienation experience, whatever that was. And as I came of age, I realized that the Germans were killing the Jews, which shook me up considerably. And I was prepared to really go over and die for the good and just cause.

When the war was over, I was somewhat surprised, I must say, by the return to business as usual. I went off to a community school called Black Mountain College in North Carolina, which doesn't exist anymore. It was a self-supporting, absolutely remarkable school. It was a community. I think its largest enrollment was sixty-five students. It happened to attract people who are now the very pillars of society. Teaching at a given moment that I can recall we had John Cage, Merce Cunningham, Buckminster Fuller, Willem and Elaine de

Kooning, Isaac Rosenfeld, Josef Albers . . . And I've probably left
out three conspicuous names. This is out of a faculty of about seventeen, and a student body of at the most sixty-five. Among the students
there was James Leo Herlihy, the writer, Ken Nolan, the painter . . .

It was just an incredible pressure group of talent and turned-on
minds. It was a two-year school which had grown out of the Bauhaus
in Germany after Hitler discredited it. This tiny community in North
Carolina welcomed the political refugees. And so we had this wonderfully heady brew of teachers there. Albers now runs the Arts and
Architecture department at Yale. Gropius runs the Arts and Architecture department at Harvard. One great painter after another,
dancers, musicians, came out of there. But at that point, they had no
accreditation. And it was really self-supporting. We raised our own
crops. We built our own buildings. We were living on the GI Bill, a
little bit. But it was hard on seventy-five dollars a month, and we
really had to stretch it. Still, we managed. And then eventually the
school closed because it wouldn't accept endowments. They didn't
want to be beholden in any way. It was self-destructive, I suppose,
and perhaps necessary.

I studied psychology, philosophy, literature, and whatever I could
overhear. The second year I was there they wanted a performing arts
department. Since the class was about three, you really couldn't call
it a department. But they had nobody in the performing arts, except
in music. I had some experience in theater, so I asked if I could
teach as well as be a student—which was not all that unusual at
Black Mountain. The faculty allowed as how I could, so I taught a
class in acting.

c: What kind of theatrical experience had you had?

p: I'd begun in amateur theater. And I'd had one session of stock,
before the service. Then, at the end of the war in Europe, I was suddenly summoned into that soldiers' show group, stationed in Paris,
with Josh Logan. I toured as a stage manager of *Golden Boy*. (Penn
later directed the musical version on Broadway.) We toured around
Europe with it. Then I got a job with the Army directing shows for
a year. I directed the soldiers' show program in Germany for the occupation troops. And I ran theaters in Wiesbaden and Hamburg and
Frankfurt and Stuttgart. When I came back, I went to Black Mountain.

c: What is the transition point from being a spectator to becoming
a director, from being an interested party to calling yourself a director?

p. I'm not sure. I would say that one is responsive, as a director, to the connective tissue of living, as different from being a central participant. I suspect that it probably comes emotionally out of trying to synthesize adult human experience in some fashion so that it makes sense, is bearable. Naturally, I have to specify it personally. In my case, the idea of divorce was so intolerable that I tried to make up a new kind of family, a new structure. And so I made one up. It's very elaborate. It has to do a good deal with my older brother, who's very talented, a photographer. He taught me a great deal. Being a director is a reorganization of the material of living into a better form than one can experience. I guess I took the world and remade it into the best of all worlds.

The first time I ever had a sense of experiencing directing was when I was a part of the Neighborhood Playhouse in Philadelphia. I had begun to hang out there. It was around the corner from where I lived. It grew more and more attractive to me. I didn't know why. I was working on the technical crew, for the most part. The switchboard, electrical work, building scenery. I've always been hung up on that part of theater life anyway. I enjoy it a great deal. I do it regularly up here now (at his theater in Stockbridge). And at a certain point they said they would be interested in seeing the work of student directors. This was in the heyday of radio, when Arch Obler and Norman Corwin and those guys were doing radio shows. And they were pretty terrific, given the form, given the medium.

I took a radio show—it wasn't by either of those two guys—and I thought it would be interesting to flesh it out. The playhouse had a kind of contest, which I won. I don't remember all the details, but it was such a success experience for me that it was really intoxicating. I think my show was the second one on the program. And everybody said, "We won't even continue." It was a wipe-out. I was in my own medium. I didn't know it then. It never occurred to me as a medium. And I really never paid any attention to it. I really was not serious about directing until many, many years later. I went to Black Mountain. Then I went to Italy. Nothing connected with theater. Studied literature, Dante. Came back, got involved in television, at NBC, as a floor manager.

G: How did you get involved in TV? What did it teach you?

P: When I got back to the states, I managed to get a job on the floor at NBC. I eventually was sent to California to work on the Colgate Comedy Hour—the Martin and Lewis, Eddie Cantor thing. A different comic every Sunday. And I was doing fine. I worked up from the third floor manager to the second to the first to the assistant director. And then Jerry Lewis said, "Next year you direct my show."

And Cantor came to me and said, "You're directing my show next year." So I said, "Great, I don't know why, but I'm delighted."

G: How did they spot you? Were you setting up a good shot?

P: It was more than a good shot, I guess. They had known me out on the floor when I'd worked with them. And, you know, comics are like thoroughbreds. You have to calm them and cool them before they go on. And I thought, "What the hell, if I'm standing here and all my job is is to point my finger and say: 'You're on!' that would be too dreary." So I started talking to them before they would go on. "Listen," I'd say, "you're about the funniest guy I've ever met. You're going to be wonderful tonight." All of which was true. I had never heard of Dean Martin and Jerry Lewis until I was assigned to the show. And I thought, two snot-nose comics from the Copacabana. I couldn't care less. But after the rehearsal, the next thing I knew I was sitting on the floor trying to recover my breath. So I would tell them, "Listen, I'm a nice, square intellectual and I don't really care very much about comics, but I think you're as funny as anybody I've ever met." And that meant a lot to them, I think. It meant a lot to Cantor, who was not so funny. But it was not dishonest to say that he'd really been a big influence in my childhood. We listened to him every Sunday.

G: And you had us all listen to him in *Bonnie and Clyde*.

P: Exactly. It meant a lot to the guy, I must say. Anyway, this particular year, quite independently of each other, they both came to me and said, "Next year I want you to direct my show." I was flattered, of course. And then suddenly the phone rang one day and it was Fred Coe, whom I had worked for during my Army days in Columbia, South Carolina. Fred had become the producer of Philco Playhouse, which was *the* prestige dramatic show.

And, although I was caught in the comedy world, all my fantasies had always been directed toward drama. Bud Yorkin and I used to work together. Bud was the first floor manager and I was the second. Bud became a director and then I was going to become the next director. That was the logical line of progression. It was not all that unusual for us to move up in those days, because television was moving, expanding fairly quickly. Bud and I used to sit around and say, "Some day, if we're really lucky, like in five years, we'll get a shot at a Philco show." And then one day I went home and the phone rang and it was Fred Coe and he said: "Do you want to come East and direct an experimental dramatic show?"

G: Were you even thinking about making films then?

p: Never. Not only was I not thinking films, but I'd had a bad experience with a film at about age five. Some scary movie. It sent me right under my seat. And I was so frightened I didn't go back to the movies until I was about fourteen. And then I saw a couple of movies, one of which was *Citizen Kane*, which absolutely lifted the top of my head off. I was stoned. I just didn't know how to respond. Suddenly I was onto something that made the theater look ridiculous. But I couldn't admit it.

I was into the theater, and the theater was very nourishing to me at that time. But my God, *Citizen Kane* just staggered me. And I went back, time and time and time again. And I never have done that since. I don't see a movie more than twice, at the most. I've seen *Citizen Kane* a good six, eight times, easily. And I'm not counting the recent years, you know?

Anyway, Fred Coe called me, said he was doing a new experimental series the summer of 1953 on NBC called *First Person* as a replacement for the William Bendix show, *The Life of Riley*. It was live. The camera played the central figure. We had Paddy Chayefsky and Robert Alan Aurther and Tad Mosel and Horton Foote and those people writing for us. I came in and was supposed to alternate with another guy.

We started in and he just couldn't do it. I began to dig it, though I was in way over my depth, way over, in terms of the actors. The first rehearsal I came to, I had Joe Anthony, Kim Hunter, and Mildred Dunnock. I didn't know what to say. I finally turned to Joe Anthony and admitted, "I don't know what to tell you, Joe. You're all so good. You know so much more than I do, why don't you tell me what to do? And I'll try to work out the cameras. Would you help me?" And he said, "Gladly." He was very sweet. He really told those people what to do. And I took credit for it, without any hesitation at all.

But what was interesting about it was you got that invaluable experience where you hear somebody tell somebody something and you think: "I could have said that, had I known the technical thing to say." That insight was important. I didn't know the language. But I knew the feeling. So after about two of those shows, I did one with Kim Stanley, written by Horton Foote. I was about thirty-one or so. And I realized this was my time to plunge in and start directing. So I told Kim what I wanted. And I found out, years later, something that made me feel very close to her. When Fred Coe asked her after the show whether I knew what I was doing or not, she said, "He's good."

So at the end of that season, instead of doing four of the eight, I'd done six of them. Fred came to me and asked if I wanted to direct

Philco. It was like rolling over backward. I couldn't believe it. Philco
was the heights. He had two directors on Philco, and he said, "I'm
going to make it three directors: Delbert Mann, Vinnie Donahue,
and you." In those years, Philco got to be quite good. We had all those
fine writers, all those extraordinary actors. The actors were, in a way,
the best part of it. They taught us all more than we knew. They
taught the writers a lot, although the writers will never admit it.
They're remiss in not doing so. One after another, Kim Stanley and
Geraldine Page and E. G. Marshall and Rod Steiger worked with us.

G: What was the basic difference, in your experience, between
directing on television and directing in movies?

P: We were directing live television, which is like flying four air-
planes at once. It's hard to describe. We had three and four cameras,
each with a complement of four lenses. And we had to remember
where they were placed in the studio, so they wouldn't photograph
each other—a fundamental problem in live television. How do you
shoot a scene with two actors standing face to face and not photograph the camera? It seems simple now. But that was the basic
problem.

Then you had to remember what complement of lenses the camera
was carrying. You were carrying sixteen lenses in your head. One
would have a long lens, one would have a 100-mm, one would have
an 85, one would have a 75, one would have a 60. We had odd-milli-
meter lenses that we've never heard of since then. We also had to
watch out so the cables didn't cross. It was really like flying a space
ship. We'd take off at the point of the hour and then go.

And poor Bob Mulligan, on his first show, said: "Okay, fade up
Four." And cameraman four said, "I just blew." His camera blew.
The director had to start with three cameras instead of four. Now
the nightmare of what that means: twenty-five per cent of all your
lenses are gone. For a guy who's got to get from this set to that set
in order to start the next scene, it means he's got to start thinking,
"Who do I have to release? And who can carry the shot? And what
boom?" There is simply no describing that experience. It's really
another world.

G: What did you learn from that whole experience on TV that, for
instance, John Ford never learned from making westerns?

P: I learned a lot that John Ford never learned. I learned how to
direct actors. Which he never learned. John Ford is goddamned good.
He's a *movie* director. But he doesn't know anything about how to
direct actors. He has them doing prototypical behavior. There's *this*

kind of guy, and there's *that* kind of guy. There's *this* kind of a barroom brawl, and there's *that* kind of barroom brawl. And they're wonderful. But you can predict every single piece of human behavior about them.

G: Do you feel that's because he was dealing with basically a stock company and his favorites were all that kind of actor? John Wayne and Ward Bond and Harry Carey?

P: In a way. Yes. They're not actors. They're simple *personages*.

G: Ford was making his last picture, *Seven Women*, in Hollywood when you were there filming and editing *The Chase*.

P: I never edited *The Chase*. I must have been shooting it or listening to Sam Spiegel write it. Sam chose to edit the film because I was locked into a prior commitment, rehearsing *Wait Until Dark* for Broadway. After weeks of editing it, he called me. I said, "Sam, I don't know what the hell you're doing, but please let me come and see it." I flew to London on a Friday night. Saturday they screened eight reels which were already scored. I couldn't believe it. I went upstairs to the cutting room to see what they were doing with the automobile junkyard scene. And I kept saying, "Where's this shot?" They looked through the logbook. "We don't have it." And, "Where's that shot?" Again, "We don't have it." I demanded to know, "What do you mean you don't have it?" They couldn't find anything. I said, "Somewhere"—and we went through the logbooks— "there are six reels of exposed, printed film missing that belong in this one scene alone."

G: Was this subterfuge? Or was it clumsiness?

P: Clumsiness. They didn't add scenes. All they added were some nice sequences under the titles directed by a guy in England who's famous for making titles.

G: Was *The Chase* meant to be a restructuring of the Lee Harvey Oswald killing?

P: Yes, but only in the most oblique way. It was really an analog about violence. About the concept of taking violence as the instrument of your vision of law and order into your own hands. Do you remember the guy who shot the sign in *Bonnie and Clyde*? Six guns in the trunk of his car all the time. All the time. And he was illiterate. He used to stand there and interpret for the Negro, who was in the same scene and was twenty years older than he was and twice as bright. And I would say, "At this point would you look over here?" And he'd say, "You understan' that, boy? He means to look over thair!" Anyway, this fellow, Red, had six guns in his car, and when I wanted to know why, he said, "You never know what you run into down here." I said, "You mean hunting?" And he smiled and said, "Well, you could call it that."

G: Why does the symbol of America as a junkyard recur in *The Chase, Mickey One,* and *Bonnie and Clyde?*

P: I didn't really mean that. *Bonnie and Clyde* really has to be made independent of that. The fact that old cars were prominent in *Bonnie and Clyde* is only really indigenous to the area. I don't have a hang-up about cars. It never occurred to me that I was using them that way.

What we needed in *The Chase* was a sort of self-destroying area. And we hunted and hunted for what that might be. The art director suggested an automobile junkyard. We all passed it by, saying the hell with that, that's no good. This went on for weeks, and we came up with nothing. Then I remember going home one night and trying to lay out the last part of the film. And I accepted the idea of the junkyard from Richard Day, the art director.

I remembered there were old gasoline pumps in which the gasoline was stored very near the surface. There was only a thin layer of concrete. And I thought, "Why not use that? That would give us a terrific blow-up." So I wrote that up one day and gave it to Sam Spiegel, who got very excited and said, "That's the answer, that's it, it's perfect."

G: What about the symbolic use of water in *The Chase?* In the beginning, you see Robert Redford racing across his reflection in the swamps and then when he realizes he's going in the wrong direction, he dives into the water and that aids his escape. And ultimately he's caught knee-deep in water by the sheriff.

P: Let me see if I can honestly separate the conscious from the unconscious use of the symbol. There is something about any reflective surface in film that's intriguing. You're constantly confronted with the problem of how to shoot a straight image. You do four- or five-hundred basic shots in a movie like that, straight on. If you can get a kind of billiard shot of an image—whether it's through glass, through a mirror, through water—it's always intriguing, as long as it's not overdone or intrusive.

The other thing was that the water seemed to be a strong symbolic correlative for both purification and entrapment. It's corny, I'm afraid. I try to lean over backwards not to use symbols. But it's hard, because

symbols are implicit. They jump at you, even when you haven't consciously set them up. It can happen merely through the arrangement
of scenes or the placement of actors or props or in the editing process.

Like with Venable Herndon constantly sidling up to me now while
we're shooting *Alice's Restaurant* and saying, "I mean, man, the
idea of that thing in the pulpit (a carving of a nude man and a
woman) and this guy and this chick sitting there talking, it just blows
my mind." And I have to tell him, "Venable, there are a bunch of
kids sitting around in a building which happens to be a church. I
don't even want to know about *that*." I'm trying to put it behind me
during the shooting.

Given a culture, given an ethic, given a morality, given a basic
system of philosophy, the imagery within this framework is relatively
limited and bound to recur. I mean, you can do a *Through a Glass
Darkly* and get pretty dense with double and triple meanings. Yes,
it's true that water has figured very strongly in a lot of films. The
reflective image is a popular one. The symbolism of *Mickey One*,
for instance, I could discuss for an hour and a half. It's an allegory
about a man's trip through Purgatory, and a lot of other things.

G: Was there any conscious use of symbols in your first film, *The
Left Handed Gun*? Did it start with his being left-handed?

P: Absolutely. There's one famous photograph of Billy the Kid that
shows him left-handed. There are those historians who claim that it's
printed backwards. That starts you off wondering immediately about
the truth, versus appearance. Was he left-handed, or has the passage
of time reversed reality? Aside from that, though, *The Left Handed
Gun* was full not of symbolism really but of displacement of figures.
I finally got my own 16-mm print of the film recently to show at
home to my kids and myself.

G: What was your reaction?

P: Staggering. Because I really understood it finally. I didn't understand it when I was making it. Your instinct says this is what the
next relationship is. Or this is how he relates this man to himself.
He picked up alliances and allegiances. I tried a great many difficult
things in that movie because I didn't know any better. I didn't know
how to make a movie. Fred Coe had this script from Gore Vidal,
which had been a television show. Bob Mulligan had done the show.
It was called *The Death of Billy the Kid*, I think. Anyway, Fred
got a contract with Warner Bros. and I think he tried Del Mann
and Vinnie Donahue first. Then he asked me if I'd like to make the
film and I was enthusiastic.

G: After working in live TV with four cameras, what made you think you knew how to make a movie—especially with just one camera?

P: I had no idea. The script was lousy. It had nothing to do with the final film. And I didn't know I'd be working with only one camera. It turned out that I did use more than one camera, after all. I brought in a writer named Leslie Stevens. Leslie and I rewrote the script from top to bottom. How did I have the guts to make the kinds of choices I did on my first film? I just didn't know any better.

I was being paid a munificent $17,000 for the whole picture. Not bad, though in retrospect it doesn't seem particularly good. By that time, I was doing Playhouse 90 and making a pretty good living in live television. And I was pretty fancy, making maybe $25,000 a year. So at that point, $17,000 for my first movie seemed absolutely delicious. I shot it like a television show. I went out with the assistant director to the Warners' ranch weeks before we started shooting. We took Dixie cups with us and nailed them down. We said, "This is the camera position for this shot" and so on. We worked out every shot. I went through the whole script and figured out every shot and lens, right off the bat.

About that time I was supposed to direct A. E. Hotchner's television screenplay for Hemingway's *The Battler*. James Dean was playing the battler and Paul Newman was playing Nick Adams, the kid. Jimmy Dean got killed the week before we went into rehearsal. And Paul switched from playing the straight part that Dewey Martin finally played, and took the role that Jimmy Dean was going to play, the punch-drunk fighter. Robert Wise saw Paul in that TV show as the punch-drunk fighter and decided he'd be right for the Rocky Graziano role in *Somebody Up There Likes Me*. Paul had been dropped by Warner Bros. He had been unable to get work. Between that TV show and *Somebody Up There Likes Me* which made him a star, we hired him for *The Left Handed Gun*.

We shot the whole picture in twenty-three days. The cameraman was a guy named Pev Marley, now dead. Here I was this upstart young twit from television. And he would ask, "Well, what do you want here?" (Penn mimes a golfer practice-putting.) And I'd say, "What about a two-shot?" And Marley would swing the club and call out: "Give him what he wants, a two-shot." It was really frightening. Those were wild days. I said, "Why don't we have a second camera?" And he'd look at me as if I were crazy: "Because I'm only lit for one camera." I tried to persuade him that it wouldn't make that much difference if we set up a second camera off fifteen or twenty degrees. He said, "I refuse to be responsible for anything but the one camera I'm lighting for."

That shook me up. I thought, "My God, he refuses to be responsible." So the first day I suggested it, I didn't do it. The second day, I said: "Hey, listen, Marley, it seems to me so simple to shoot two cameras on two different lenses. We would cover so much of the action, instead of having to break up here and move over here where I want to move next. Why don't we do it?" Marley said, "I refuse to be responsible." And so finally I said, "Okay, all right. I'll be responsible. I don't even know to whom I'm being responsible. But whoever it is, I'm responsible. Okay? Let's shoot the second camera."

I couldn't figure out to whom we had to make the disclaimer. And that was one of my greatest insights about Hollywood. We set up the second camera and, if anything, it was better than the first camera. It was spectacular. We used an Arriflex slaved to the Mitchell. They rolled together and they shot in tandem. In the dailies, one shot after another on that Arriflex knocked me out of my seat. And the Mitchell was nice, standard stuff. So I decided to go on with the two-camera setup from then on. But Marley complained that the lighting was terrible and he wouldn't be responsible.

I kept asking to whom he wouldn't be responsible, but he wouldn't say. I finally began to figure it out. It took a long time, because I had never been through this experience before. It was simply that the head of the studio saw the dailies before we did. Steve Trilling and Jack Warner used to see them at eleven o'clock in the morning. We'd come in from a day's shooting and then we'd see them. The cameraman didn't want to be responsible, so on that slate there would be a disclaimer in code. I didn't understand the code. But Warner knew it.

It said, in effect, "Slave camera unlighted. Arthur Penn, director." Supposedly it was for the timer in the lab, but it was really for Jack Warner's information. I never heard a beef about it from him. I went on and finished in twenty-three days, which was a little over schedule—though I don't know how it could be, in retrospect. It cost about $700,000. It made a bundle. We didn't own it. Paul had a per cent of the net.

G: Would you describe how you decided on that grotesque shot of the cowboy being blasted out of his boot and having the child laugh and the mother slap her?

P: The actual shot was easy enough. It was done with a cut. He's shot in slow motion, hit by a blast from Paul's shotgun. It's the guy who's been tormenting him. And the shot is into the sun, and you can barely make out the figure. He's against the sun. Paul looks up and says, "Hey, Arlinger." And he hits him. Arlinger does that slow motion turn—that actor, incidentally, was the sheriff in *Bonnie and Clyde*.

This shooting sequence was a medium shot, a little above his belt. He did the slow motion turn, then we did a speed-up, so he hit the ground at about eighteen frames—BAM. And I said to my assistant and cameraman at that time, "I want something that has the effect of a guy *blasted* against the ground. How do we get it?" Somebody suggested his vest could be torn off. And I said, "No, we've already got his vest all smeared with blood." Then I remembered that in the war I'd seen the remains of a guy who'd been blown out of his boot. A guy who'd got it, and whose boot was still standing there.

G: Buck Barrow loses his shoes, too, in *Bonnie and Clyde*.

P: Yes. However, you can't do something as raw as that without it being a sort of plea for attention as a director. In reconstituting the conscious memory of it, you have to disclaim the mere attention-getting aspect of it. So, in *The Left Handed Gun*, we tried to figure out some way of showing we were conscious of the effect we had produced to give it a functional purpose. It was suggested that somebody could make fun of it. Who could make fun of it? A kid. If a kid makes fun of it in the presence of death, the parent is going to have to respond with some kind of violence. Even though there *is* something funny about the grotesquerie of death. And this thing escalated right up out of my hands into what that shot finally became.

G: I understand that you are going to be making another western, in 1969, with Dustin Hoffman?

P: Dustin is going to play Jack Crabb. *Little Big Man* is the story of a guy whom we meet at the age of a hundred and twenty-one, and who says, "I'm the only white man who survived Custer's last stand." And of course the reply is that that was a big wipe-out, so how could he have survived? And Dustin says, "Let me tell ya . . ." Then he goes on to spin the biggest yarn of all time. It's a monumental lie. But in the course of telling the lie, he tells the story of his life.

He was captured as a kid by the Indians, grew up with the Cheyenne, was then caught in a battle against the whites, was taken prisoner by the whites, then grew up in the white society to a certain point, then moved over to the Cheyenne, then over to the whites again, all the way up to Custer's last stand. This is a guy who has two identities. He constantly weighs one identity against the other. It's a wonderful story. Calder Willingham did the screenplay from a marvelous book by Thomas Berger.

In telling Dusty's story, we're going back to very primitive film technique now. We're starting with the narration, and flashback. It's not farce, nor black comedy. It's closer to social comedy. What kind of comedy is it when a guy who is searching for his white wife, who's been captured by the Cheyenne, joins up as a scout for Custer and is sent on a mission which is really a slaughter of all the Indians? In the course of that slaughter, he finds himself protecting an Indian woman who is about to give birth to a baby.

He can't find his own wife. So he goes back to the Indian life with her. He stays with her for a year. She's again pregnant, this time by him. But so many braves of her tribe have been wiped out that her three sisters are now living with her and she expects him to service the three sisters because there aren't enough men to go around. He's finally forced to do his duty. In the course of the night, he says to the second sister, "I'll be back." He says later, "That was one of the biggest lies I ever told." That's the kind of comedy it is. It'll be a roadshow for CBS Cinema Center, with Dustin and Faye Dunaway.

G: There were some critics who ridiculed *The Left Handed Gun* as a psychological western with a neurotic cowboy hero. What effect did the reaction to that film have on your brand-new career as moviemaker?

P: It had a bad effect, I suppose. I hadn't understood what "first cut" meant, which was in the contract. First cut seemed to us to mean getting down to the first serious cut. But that was not at all true at Warners. They were turning out product and they wanted to get it out fast. They took a look at our so-called first cut, which was really only an assemblage of the rough-shot film. And they said, "Okay, you guys have had it." And we were kicked off the lot, to all intents and purposes.

We had at that point production plans for *Two for the Seesaw* for Broadway. I hadn't done any Broadway plays before. The show was one of those big smashes, one of those dream hits. So Fred Coe and I said the hell with movies, who needs it? We were into the big scene here. Broadway was a gold mine. It was wide open for both of us. We were offered every show on the road. We figured: No more movies. Broadway was where we were appreciated. I didn't like what was done to *The Left Handed Gun*. I finally saw it at the Loew's 86th Street, on the bottom half of a bill with a dubbed Gina Lollabrigida film. I barely recognized it. They took scenes I had meant to run five seconds and made them a minute long. Other scenes that were meant to be a minute long were running only five seconds.

G: Precisely how does someone reassembling footage destroy the intent of the director?

P: Let's use the dailies we saw tonight on *Alice's Restaurant* as an example. Suppose we just put the master shot in. Would that represent as good a scene as we could do?

G: I suppose it would lose all the nuances of the subsequent closeups.

P: Right. All the subtext that you read into it about incipient sexuality between Alice and Arlo, something odd between Alice and Ray, and between Ray and Arlo. All that triangulation that is underneath the surface of that scene is not visible in the master. You start seeing the dailies and you realize from a look in someone's eye in a closeup that there is more going on than the master shot can show.

So, in *Left Handed Gun* there was a scene that I had shot a quick version of—this woman calling into the window to Billy while he's locked in jail: "I want that boy. I want that boy." They managed to stay on that shot until the woman disappeared all the way down the end of the western street and around the corner. We had done that thing on the assumption of "Start the shot and let's see. If something miraculous happens, if she trips on her butt and falls, maybe we'll use that piece of film." You let it run, because you always hope for the accident. But they put in every foot of film. I couldn't believe it. I started slipping under my seat in embarrassment. It was on the screen, it seemed to me, about a week, a full week. And it was meant to be a flash cut, just a *flash* cut.

So, anyway, to get to your point, what happened? I paid no attention to film any longer. I was on my way, established on Broadway with six hits in a row: *Two for the Seesaw, The Miracle Worker, Toys in the Attic, An Evening with Mike Nichols and Elaine May, All the Way Home,* and *Fiorello!,* which I wrote originally. And they were running simultaneously.

G: Where did *The Miracle Worker* as a movie fit in during this period?

P: The reviews from Paris of *The Left Handed Gun* started to trickle in, from Bazin, Truffaut, the Cahiers critics. Then it arrived in volume. Suddenly there were twenty clippings on my desk, everything from the most cursory kind of affirmative review to the most in-depth penetration. I couldn't believe it. Certainly the sense of recognition was startling. By then I was already in the midst of adapting *The Miracle Worker* for the movies. And I regret now . . .

If I had to pick a movie that really represents the duality of my feelings about being *with* movies or not being with it, it's *The Miracle Worker.* It's half stage, and half film. It could have been liberated in one instant from the stage, and I didn't dare. I was committed to the stage play, which had been so successful. But if I did the same project now, I would have enough film sense to realize that we don't have to make the father the antagonist. The antagonist is Helen's condition. It's sufficient, cinematically. If you just show a deaf, blind child, as we did under the titles, we had enough antagonist to carry us for three hours.

G: And yet there was a very cinematic sense when she was touching the water from the pump and makes the connection in her head between the word for a thing and the thing. How was it done in the play?

P: It was done cinematically in the play, oddly enough, only I didn't know. There was actually a pump that was rolled out onto the stage by the stagehands, and she actually pumped water.

G: It was touch, sensation, as opposed to literary qualities?

P: Exactly. But the scenes of confrontation between Annie and Helen's father were dreary. They didn't belong in the film. They were entirely lifted from the stage and put on film because I didn't dare make the transition to *film*. I wasn't impelled enough toward film to say, "I really have to find the cinematic equivalent." The nine minutes of fight scenes were part of my unconscious cinematic staging of portions of the play itself. For nine minutes we really were good, we were filming.

G: What's the difference between the cinematic and the theatrical?

P: In theater, the reliance is on the verbal. Film is how one looks, as against what one says. On the stage, you can't document that. You're too far back. So what one says is what one is.

G: Is the key, then, distancing? What does the nearness of the camera do?

P: It permits a kind of contradiction and complexity that you don't have on the stage, unless you have the most poetic of utterances which contains its own imagery and self-contradiction as well as its self-enunciation. That's only true of the best poetry. Otherwise, you get simplistic statements that can only work at a distance, on the stage. Like: "I want my *daughter* to be able to have the best in life." Now, when a mother has to say that, she's unnecessarily underlined and announced the fact that she's the child's mother. You don't have to say it in a film. A look, a simple look, will do it.

G: You say poetic dialogue might be all right. But poetry is antithetical to contemporary literature and drama. We deal in street language and the terse Hemingway prose, rather than in poetry.

P: Which may be why cinema is so relevant to this age. Poetry must be kinetic now to be relevant. We respond to the direct experience, and to the contradictory experience as a more subtle statement of the human condition. Film offers the opportunity for constant contradiction between what is said and what is done. It's closer to how we really experience life. I'm saying *that*, but I'm really feeling *this*. And these two things are going on at once. Ambivalence is closer to the human feeling than the simple Eugene O'Neill statement: "My father was a bastard." That sort of statement that says everything and says nothing. Well, film is the exquisite medium for expressing ambivalence. A man says one thing, but his eyes are saying another thing.

G: And the music may be saying something else.

P: And the symbolism and the resonances are saying a fourth thing. Nothing can match the cinema. I didn't understand that, however, at the time I was making *Miracle Worker*. I went to see it the first time and sat there smothering myself in self-congratulations on doing this marvelous transition to the screen. And everybody was delighted. Anne Bancroft and Bill Gibson (the author) had come to see a rough cut and just hated it. I told them to wait until I finished it and they'd change their minds. They had no choice, of course. But they were suffering. Then they saw the finished print and said it was the best film they'd ever seen. But about the third time I saw it, it jumped off the screen at me as a near-disaster. We got away with it because there was just about nine minutes or so of cinema in the whole picture.

G: The next film, *Mickey One,* was your conscious attempt to explore the possibilities of the medium. What were you aiming for and do you feel you succeeded?

P: Yes, it was much more experimental. I may have overshot my mark. I was aiming for a metaphorical film. But I really overlooked the essence of what I think of now as film, which is, first of all, engagement. I was really operating on the symbolic and metaphorical level without engagement between audience and screen. I figured, "To hell with the story, the story will take care of itself. People will read into the story what they want." Yet it would have been so easy to tell a really simple narrative, but a binding one. And we have only to look at any good literature to recognize that the binding narrative is really what holds it together.

G: How do you explain the apparent disdain for narrative in film-makers like Godard?

P: I think he's telling a narrative that seems to be sort of a secret code and people are responding to it. There is a narrative, for the most part, certainly more than in *Mickey One*.

G: You used speeded-up sequences in *Mickey One*, just as you had used slow motion in *The Left Handed Gun* and would do again in *Bonnie and Clyde*. Did you manipulate time in *The Miracle Worker*?

P: Only under the titles. When Helen comes out as a child and drops the Christmas tree ball off the Christmas tree. It falls in very slow motion. It wasn't done in the editing stage. It was shot that way, just as it was shot that way in *Mickey One*. In the final sequences in *Bonnie and Clyde*, I wanted a balletic quality. I thought that after we had seen a succession of realistic, rugged killings what I wanted to dramatize in those last ten seconds was the movement from life into myth.

Just shooting them down, as we had shot down other people in the film, would have simply terminated it. It would not have suggested that there was something that was going to go on into an extended sense of time, movement, myth, resonance in the culture. I felt I had to do this balletically. And when I started talking that way, naturally the camera people didn't know what I was talking about. Not that they weren't bright, but they simply didn't understand those terms. That's the first time I had a really finished image in mind. It was shot and done in the editing room, both.

G: *Mickey One* was a non-Hollywood experimental movie, made for about $1,000,000 in Chicago and New York. What did you learn from it that you were able to use in *Bonnie and Clyde*?

P: I learned two things. I learned how to work with Warren Beatty, which is no simple problem. I don't mean to suggest anything pejorative. Warren is a covert personality. There's a distinct quantity of him that's hidden. It took a whole film for him to trust that he could be bad on film and that I would take it out. The other thing I learned was the alternation of emotions and moods on the screen. I feel that *Mickey One* was boring. *Bonnie and Clyde* was a distinct and conscious effort not to be boring, by alternation of effect. The unexpected in the sequence of scenes is as important as the unexpected in affect and behavior.

G: How did you get involved in *Bonnie and Clyde?*

P: Warren sent the script to me. I had read it about five years ago. It had been making the rounds for some time. Two people were producing it at that time and it didn't sound very appetizing, although it was an interesting script. Warren bought the script for $10,000 against $75,000 final payment. He called me first off the bat and I said: "I just don't think so. I've read the script and I don't really want to do it." But he kept urging me to do it. I was working on *Little Big Man* at the time and it wasn't ready to go. I don't know what changed in me, but *Bonnie and Clyde* got more and more attractive. It suddenly seemed a jazzy kind of film. I began to respond to it.

G: What did Robert Towne do with the Benton and Newman script? How much, if any of it, is his script, since he didn't get any credit?

P: Bob Towne is Warren's closest friend. He's very learned, very talented. So much so that when we were working on this script (*Alice's Restaurant*) he was on his way to England and I asked him to come by and spend the weekend at the house and read the script and talk with Venable and me about it.

Bonnie and Clyde was built in a different way, originally. Bonnie's meeting with her mother took place very early in the film. The kidnapping of the couple also took place much earlier than it does now. I worked on a number of scenes with Benton and Newman for a while and they were very willing and able workers. They were good. Then I got to California and was about six weeks away from shooting. Benton and Newman had been out in California for a couple of weeks, but were now in New York. Warren was also back East.

I called him and said, "I want to come back and talk to Benton and Newman. I feel there is something distinctly missing about this picture. I cannot grasp the closure of the issues here. It just seems to me to be a bunch of incidents which are relatively parallel, emotionally and actively, and that it doesn't come together." Warren said, "I don't think you should talk to Benton and Newman any further. You've talked to them for six months. Do you have any idea what you'd like to do about it yourself?"

And I said, "Yes, I do. I think the scene with the undertaker should be a foreshadowing of the death. The comic scene should end abruptly with a chill. Bonnie has to be impelled to go home to see what is there, to see whether there is anything left." And Warren said he thought it was a good idea and suggested that I talk to Bob Towne. Bob was in Hollywood then, so we talked. I asked him what he thought about reorganizing the material in this way. And he said, "Absolutely right.

Why don't you write out an outline of the new organization of the material?" So I holed up in the hotel and did the reorganizing necessary.

G: It was mostly a reshuffling of scenes?

P: Yes. Reshuffling and saying, "This is the important point of this scene." And then putting in several scenes which were not in the script. Like right after the scene with her mother, where she and Clyde are on the bed and she says, "I'm so lonely, I have no family." And he says, "I'm your family." And she sits up and embraces him. That was an outgrowth of this restructuring. Also, the foreshadowing of the coming death proceeding out of the comic scene with the undertaker and the big family reunion scene.

I felt that was the heart of the film, right in those three scenes. As Benton and Newman accurately had it, Clyde had no identity crisis. When Bonnie asks him how he'd do it if he had it to do over again, he says he'd do it substantially the same way. Clyde never confronts the problems that lie before him. He simply says, "I would do them slightly differently, and perhaps more or less successfully." Well, that's marvelous. That's one whole character. But that could not be both characters. Yet, in a way, both characters were living that way.

So what we did was to reorganize Bonnie to the point where she really underwent the identity crisis in the film. She knew the character of the oncoming death. She sensed it, and was willing to accept it to be with Clyde. And that seems to me to have given the film a kind of underpinning that it didn't have originally. For instance, Benton and Newman had written an excellent family reunion scene. But Towne added to it that wonderful exchange between Bonnie and her mother in which Clyde says to her, "Bonnie and I were just talking the other day, Mother Parker, about how she wants to live no more than three miles from you." And the mother says, "She lives three miles from me, she'll be dead." That was Towne.

Those were valuable contributions to the film. But it would be inaccurate to suggest that it's not Benton and Newman's film. It's basically theirs, no question about it. If American film were different than it is, in the sense that it were not so high-priced and so high-pressured, maybe we would have come to these same reorganizations with Benton and Newman. But the fact that they had to be flown to California, supported there at a certain amount per week, in an elegant hotel, left us no genuine room for the kind of discussion out of which this sort of thing could grow. Bob Towne lived up the road. He dropped over and all day long we talked and talked and talked.

G: Was that scene with the mother supposed to be fantasy or reality and what was the point of the change in texture, the diffuseness, if it was actually happening?

P: It was supposed to be happening, but in the sense that it was unreclaimable, that it was disappearing like an ancient photograph. That it was there and yet it was all dealing with values that belonged to the past and not to the present. And I thought that it would be very interesting to change the textural character of it. That's why we put a filter on it.

G: Was the kidnap scene filmed exactly as Benton and Newman wrote it?

P: Exactly, right down to that look between Gene Wilder and Evans Evans when she admits her age.

G: Were Bonnie and Clyde, in your view, supposed to be star-crossed lovers, participants in a romance in the tradition of Romeo and Juliet?

P: No. I'll tell you what I really thought about it. Originally, Benton and Newman wrote that Clyde was a homosexual who was making it with C. W. Moss. It seemed to me to be a dreary story. I felt that if three people could live that sophisticated a sexual life, I couldn't envision them doing those really primitive sensational acts they performed. And so I talked to Benton and Newman at length about it and they became persuaded of that with me. I said, "I don't know what the history books say"—because we went through them and they're extremely skimpy on this . . .

G: She was supposed to be a ravenous sensualist.

P: That's the tale that is told. But there's so little documentation that it's highly suspect that anybody was even privy to that kind of information. And I felt that if she was that ravenous and that Clyde was in fact making it with C. W. Moss and that Moss was satisfying all these insatiable appetites, however bizarre, they wouldn't have time to rob banks, let alone an inclination to. On the other hand, I thought it was about time that, at least in American films, somebody talked about the heterosexual experience as being less than the heralding of angels, which it is always presented as.

The man pursues the girl. The girl pursues the man. They finally get to bed and the movie ends, because everything is perfect from there on. But it struck me as everything but perfect. It's the beginning of all kinds of complexities, the best and the worst. Everything in life comes out in the bedroom. And it's highly inappropriate to suggest to the kids that it's all marvelous, that all you have to do is get the right man and the right woman into bed and it's all going to be perfect.

And certainly the character of the American male's impotence—not physiological but psychological—struck me as something that had not really been touched upon. I don't mean impotence, really, in its physiological sense, but that kind of guilty failure because we were brought up to believe there must be that simultaneous climax or else you're an unworthy man. That thing hanging over the bed is a kind of sword of Damocles. And it makes a guy say, "Jesus, I shot before she did. I finished too soon. I'm not a man." And that begins to build up.

It struck me as being a part of an American myth about sexuality and as being inaccurate. We don't talk about gratification as just one act of loving, with one act of loving, however it's achieved and by whatever tricks and stunts. You know, we always talk about the Europeans as being so bizarre. And yet the American sex acts seem to me to be puritanically representative of medical books on sexual enlightenment.

So I thought it would be relevant to show a love scene in which the level of appetite was different, the level of ability to gratify was different, the levels of tension were different. And that seemed to me to be more related to these kinds of people. I don't mean to suggest that it was causal. Some writers—like Frank Gilroy in the *New York Review of Books*—have said about the film that the sexual portrait of the man was ludicrous. I would question that. It may be ludicrous, but it's valid.

G: Since they finally do make it before their deaths, does the word romance have any bearing on the film?

P: Yes. What I was using as an abiding rationalization was that in a certain sense the emerging romance of their characterizations as people in their own times was beginning to be sufficiently self-sustaining so that Clyde could maintain an erection long enough to have some kind of contact with her. That was it. And I'll admit it's a rationalization. But I don't know that it's wholly inaccurate.

G: What was the significance of the final sequence, that look that passed between them when they both realized they were going to be ambushed and killed?

P: "This is it." The surprise of this being the moment we've known was coming. "This is it."

G: You physically tied Dunaway down to the car so she wouldn't fall out during the scene?

P: Yes. One leg to the emergency brake, so she couldn't fall out, although she could lean out. I wanted her to lean way over when she was dead. And she couldn't do it without falling out of that car. We shot a whole variety of speeds. I have no idea how long the whole sequence lasts.

G: Why do you think that people like Bosley Crowther used *Bonnie and Clyde* to focus on violence in American films?

P: I think they were being confronted by a violent society and they were looking for a causal factor. People have often decided in the past that films are a causal factor of sexuality, violence, juvenile delinquency, and crime. I think that's simple-minded. Films, it seems to me, are one of the least of many, many causal factors, certainly one of the least pernicious. It's absurd to suggest that film is *the* central issue in violence in a violent society which has been repressing the black race for two hundred years and which has been ridden with prejudice and violence of the most flagrant character through all its history—the West, the '20s, the '30s. It's a violent society engaged in a violent and ridiculous war. To turn around and say that *Bonnie and Clyde* is the cause of the violence is simply mushheaded. If anything, *Bonnie and Clyde* was a rather mild reflection of the culture of the '30s. And I think that one of the functions of art is to purge or exorcise the crap that encrusts society, to blow out those undesirable capacities in all of us.

G: Does it bother you that so many yahoos enjoyed the violence in *Bonnie and Clyde* in a different spirit than perhaps you intended?

P: It bothers me, but I don't know how to be responsible for it. It titillates people because it titillates people. People project onto a given situation all kinds of personal responses.

G: Is there a favorite Arthur Penn film, emotionally and intellectually?

P: I'd say *Bonnie and Clyde*. Financially, too. I own ten per cent of the film after it recoups about $8 million. It's expected to gross about $28,000,000.

G: What is an actor, and how do you get the best out of him?

P: I like actors. I spend a lot of time with them and have a lot of fun with them. I think they're pretty courageous people. They deal out in the open with private feelings that most of us don't like to have exposed. And that's pretty gutsy, I think. The ones with the ability to really deliver that emotion again and again are also pretty remarkable artists.

G: Do you consider someone like Michael Pollard a "natural" who just does his thing on or off stage and that very little can affect it?

P: Oh, no. Pollard can be good or bad. Pollard is a pretty finished actor. Off stage, he's quite a different character. Shy, somewhat depressed, very little to say, very little *behavior*, almost no acting out of any impulses. You very rarely see him *do* anything.

G: How did you get what you wanted out of him?

P: I'd just keep teasing him into it. I mean, I said: "Come on, Michael, what happens if somebody drove up to you right now and told you they were bank robbers?" And he'd say, "Ah, sheet, they wouldn't, I mean, they wouldn't, they, ah, sheet . . ." And I said, "Why don't you act that?" And he said, "What do you mean? Like, 'Ah, sheet.'" And he started to hit the post. And I said, "Boy, that's exactly what I mean." Interestingly enough, in the cutting, I cut that scene in half and it was not one bit funny. So I put back another quarter, and it was still not funny. I finally put back the whole scene and it was hilarious. He needs that room to go beyond where anybody would dare go with a response and then, finally, it gets hilarious.

G: What about Faye Dunaway? She seemed the most theatrical performer in a cast of naturals.

P: She is. Her training is theatrical. She's a good actress. I could count on her for take after take after take.

G: Was Beatty more erratic in giving you what you needed?

P: With Warren it's not a question of being erratic so much as it is just saying : "Okay now, do it more, you're on the right path, just have the courage to do it more." He builds up to it. He has a natural fear of directors and a natural fear of exposure. He underplays terribly to begin with. And if you know him, you know it's there and you say: "Come on, come on." And he's very candid. He says, "Listen, if I really bomb out, will you cut it out?" And I assure him, of course, he can trust me.

G: As the producer of *Bonnie and Clyde*, was Beatty in a position to do more than ask politely?

P: No. Warren was a producer in the best sense. He sold that film and made it possible and then he fought the studio to give it a better distribution deal than they had planned; he went out on the road to sell the film to the public and the exhibitors, and he managed to get it secondary bookings in which it grossed more than it had originally. At no point, if it ever got down to the nitty gritty of an aesthetic choice, did Warren ever intrude with any more muscle than the muscle of a friend who had an opinion.

G: Did you know while you were making *Bonnie and Clyde* that you were onto something big, was there a mystique of a hit in the making?

P: No, we didn't know.

G: How did you work with Burnett Guffey, your cameraman on *Bonnie and Clyde*?

P: Essentially, I just said, "Turn out the lights." Historically, there is an existing body of norms in Hollywood for the levels of light. So, in a way, the cameramen themselves are really interchangeable. The technique is constant from film to film. The lab can take up Burney Guffey's work and Ted McCord's work and put them together and there's almost nothing to distinguish them. Because they stay within the same foot-candles, essentially they follow the same simple ideas. What is the light source? What is the secondary light source? They're pretty simple-minded formulas.

For years they've been the Hollywood norms. And the cameramen have been ignoring the fact that film has gotten so much faster, that still photography has advanced into a completely new direction. Indeed, *cinema* has advanced. Decae and Coutard and Lassally have broken new ground in cinematography while Hollywood has stayed in the same place as before. So when I would see Burney Guffey lighting a set, I would say: "Hell, Burney, do we need all these lights?" And he'd say, "Well, if you don't want them, we don't need them." And I didn't want them. So I'd say, "Let's turn them off." And that's the way we did it.

G: Could you see in Paul Newman's first film, *Rachel, Rachel*, touches of Dede Allen, your editor on *Bonnie and Clyde* and *Alice's Restaurant*? How does she work as a collaborator in the cutting room?

P: I could see her touches everywhere. She asks the very pertinent questions that sometimes you don't dare ask yourself. Such as, "What do you really mean here? What do you mean, where is your emphasis, really?" In a series of dailies like you saw tonight, with a possible thirty opportunities to cut it—maybe more—she'll want to know

"What do you really want to say?" She's very insistent. She won't be put off. She won't be conned. She keeps asking. And it makes her a superb editor. I think she's absolutely without a peer. She's an *unknown* editor who edited *America, America, The Hustler,* and the films you've mentioned. She formed the editing union in California and was Robert Wise's assistant for years.

G: What route should an eighteen-year-old who wants to make movies go today? Does he make six-minute shorts on his own? Does he go to film school? Does he try to hustle his way in as an errand boy on the set of a movie to be near the action?

P: I don't know of a good film school. But that's only because I don't know a great deal about film schools. I would think the best way would be to make shorts, 8-mm shorts. The silenter the better. So that the question of sound, which is what a lot of the young filmmakers ask about right off the bat, seems to me to be a relatively academic question which is best answered by "Suppose you don't have any sound? Why don't you start and make the history of film, all by yourself? Start with silent film. See if you can tell a story that way. Certainly if you can tell it that way, you can tell it with sound." And that would seem to me personally to be the best way. It's the way I recommend to most guys to start.

On the other hand, there are a lot of people who spring full-blown from whatever that crazy material is out of which film directors are made. They're just natural. So to those guys, I would have no hesitation in saying: "Go to the top, start right at the top. Walk in the front door and say: 'I intend to direct a movie for you. I think I can do it for this much money. In fact, I will promise to do it for this much money.'" And I wouldn't be surprised if the odds are probably more on the side a certain audacity and verve in dealing with the establishment than most people suspect. That would be my guess.

RICHARD LESTER

"A director's job in this period
of filmmaking—and I know
that this may change, as it
has in the past—is to be an
absolute dictator and produce a
personal vision on a subject
that he has chosen."

*Richard Lester has one of the nimblest wits of any filmmaker of his
generation, and he has transmitted it through a number of films of
dazzling virtuosity. Some critics have found him facile and flashy and
tricky. Yet Lester's favorite film was the deadly serious* How I Won
the War, *whose technique he describes as Brechtian.*

*Born in Philadelphia in 1932, Lester quit a secure job as a television
director to escape incipient suburban complacency and he embarked at
age twenty-two on a bum's tour of Europe and North Africa, guitar
on his back, sleeping on floors, benches, borrowed beds, hustling
meals and rides. He has lived in England for the past fifteen years,
and is temperamentally an anarchist and citizen of the world.*

*As a filmmaker, he is fiercely independent and he feels his only
obligation is a logistical one—to get two minutes of film in the can
every shooting day. When this interview took place in the summer
of 1968, Lester was filming* The Bed Sitting Room *at a refuse dump
in beautiful downtown West Drayton, England.*

*He contended, at that time, that he hadn't shown the script to the
studio and that he had absolute control of his films. "I don't know how
long it will last," he laughed. "Probably until, like Icarus, I fall from
financial grace with promissory notes flapping about me like feathers
coming off."*

*Lester began his career directing live television with four cameras,
went on to make a short film, then learned film technique from
directing TV commercials. He has continued to shoot all of his movies
with three or four cameras filming simultaneously. The influence of
the TV commercial—especially in pacing, with cinematic sprints
and quick climaxes—is frequently evident in his films.*

*His experience in directing commercials and working with every
phase of production had made Lester a consummate technician. He
admires the films of Buster Keaton for their exquisite use of space*

and form. And he feels that the best way to direct a movie is "to actually operate a camera and with your eye see the performance happening, with film moving between your eye and the performer."

FILMOGRAPHY:

THE RUNNING, JUMPING, AND STANDING STILL FILM (Short: '59)
IT'S TRAD, DAD (U.S. title, *Ring-a-Ding Rhythm:* '62)
THE MOUSE ON THE MOON ('63)
A HARD DAY'S NIGHT ('64)
THE KNACK—AND HOW TO GET IT ('65)
HELP! ('65)
A FUNNY THING HAPPENED ON THE WAY TO THE FORUM ('66)
HOW I WON THE WAR ('67)
PETULIA ('68)
THE BED SITTING ROOM ('69)

GELMIS: Did you have any theatrical preparation in school for television or stage or movies?

LESTER: I wrote music for the Masque and Wig, which is a University of Pennsylvania student theatrical organization, and wrote a musical comedy that the University's dramatic society, the Pennsylvania Players, did. That was all. During that time, I was beginning to work as a singer in a vocal group and as a not-very-good composer. The vocal group had been appearing on a television variety program. We were fired and I stayed on. So while I was still at university I was working in television, progressing from stagehand to foreman to junior assistant director and then director.

G: Was it your family or a girl or the city itself that made you, like W. C. Fields, run away from Philadelphia?

L: I didn't want to be bogged down in being a successful television director at the age of twenty-two and having two cars and a big family and a horse in the paddock—all those things that were financially possible because the money was quite good—and never having the opportunity to find out whether there were better things outside the continental United States. So after two years of working in television, I left America. It was in early 1954.

G: I've heard that you played the guitar and sang at army bases in Europe to support yourself.

L: I've never really learned to play the guitar. I was unique in Spain in that I seemed to be the only person in the whole country who couldn't play Spanish guitar, and therefore I was a novelty at parties. I used to hammer out three chords, and was treated as a sort of golliwog that sat in the corner and played.
I played the piano at an army base outside of Paris. And I played the guitar in a cafe in the south of Spain. I didn't do it very often. The first time I did it for an evening it was to get a free meal. And I'd also put a plate down beside me in which I'd put three of my own pesetas to encourage others to do likewise. I played folk songs and sang for the whole evening. After dinner, I went to pick up the plate and there were only two pesetas left. So I thought, "There isn't much future in this as a career." But I did have free food.

G: How do you think that the experience of wandering and being away from America in the '50s helped to shape your attitudes and anarchical disposition?

L: Well, I think that having the urge to go was already the beginning of the shaping of that. I think it was just useful for me to find out if I could live by my wits, meager though they may be. I think it is always necessary for people fairly young in life to find themselves suddenly in a country where they are ignorant of the language, where they have absolutely no money, and they have to just survive. Once you find that you can do this, it gives you an enormous confidence to carry on, to experiment, to gamble in the future.

If you've never tried it, you're never sure whether you're able to do it. So you think, "Well, I better be secure. I'd better have a steady job." And if you have a steady job, "Well, I'd better not try this effect, because it may not come off and I'll lose my steady job." I've never had a contract, never in my life, for any length of time. I've never had any security. I've never searched for it. I've always consciously rejected it, never worried about where my next paycheck, my next film, is coming from.

G: How did you finally settle in England and get work as a producer on commercial TV?

L: During the year of wandering about I had written the words and music to a musical comedy. Since it was in English it became clear that I'd have to bring it to England to try to sell it. I managed to have it produced as England's first original musical that was put on commercial television. By accident, my visit to England coincided with the time that commercial television was about to begin and there was a need for television directors who had experience. So I was able to sell the musical and also to get myself a job as a television director. I directed a jazz show. And I did an ad-lib television program with an out-of-work actor named Alun Owen, who has since become a very successful television writer and who wrote the screenplay for A Hard Day's Night with me. He and I ad-libbed a half hour comedy and music show which was a terrible experience for an audience and for us.

Everything was live in those days. There was no tape. There was a primitive sort of telerecording, but that was too expensive for the likes of us to use. So all the programs that I did were live. There were three series of surrealist comedy shows which starred Peter Sellers and Spike Milligan. We had all the elements of the Rowan and Martin Laugh-In show, in that we used catch phrases, and something called an Idiot's Post Bag where people kept appearing, flashing on, and doing one-liners, and were taken off generally against back projection screens of total non-sequiturs. Like the Belgian riots or a bed traveling through the sea in the wake of a motorboat, and things of that sort. We also did sketches, some of which were running gags from week to week. It was a totally anarchic program.

G: Why did you leave England for a while in the '50s?

L: I left England in the beginning of '57 as a sort of reaction against Suez. By this time I had married and I went and worked in Canada for four months. My wife was a choreographer on some television programs in Canada, and I was writing gags for a program that Norman Jewison was directing. Next we went to Australia. We stayed there for seven weeks and then we slowly worked our way back to England through the Barrier Reef and India.

It was basically a reaction against the politics of Suez, but also a chance for my wife and I to work our way around the world and see as much as we could before we bought a house or a flat or furniture or possessions. We returned to England in late 1957 and I did some more television work.

G: How did you happen to make *The Running, Jumping, and Standing Still Film?*

L: The film was an outgrowth of the filmed inserts we had been doing for the live TV shows. I'd enjoyed those inserts, because they were so flexible to work with. So the film was two Sundays shooting in a field with friends and chauffeurs and wives. It was written in equal parts by Peter, Spike, and myself. We shot only one take for any gag. It was shot silently, black and white, using Peter's 16-mm Bolex with a zoom lens. The total budget for this shooting was seventy pounds.

When we got the rushes, we took them to Peter's house the next Sunday to edit in his study. The editing, which was really just topping and tailing, took two hours. Every gag we shot, every piece of film that we shot, is in the finished film. We showed it to our wives by projecting it onto a wall in the living room. They liked it, so we decided to finish and polish it up. I wrote a musical score for it and conducted it, with a huge orchestra of four. I put sound effects on it.

It was shown to someone from the *Daily Express* who said he had a friend who was looking for material for the Edinburgh Festival. It went to Edinburgh, was seen by a man from the San Francisco Film Festival. It won first prize there. Then it got an Academy Award nomination. And it's still running. We never had any plan to distribute it when we made it. We were just friends who wanted to make a film to enjoy ourselves.

Having made *The Running, Jumping, and Standing Still Film,* in 1959, I decided to concentrate on film rather than television. But there were no job offers to make feature films until the end of 1961. In the interim, I started making television commercials as a means of earning a living and to learn about film. Not having had any traditional schooling in film at a studio, I've learned what I know by making commercials. They are an excellent way to learn about film-making. The problems are the same, in miniature. Ideally, you should know everybody's job, how to lay in a musical score, what the lab does, how to handle film and cut it. And you learn to use film to obtain instant impact, not to waste frames, because you've only got thirty seconds or a minute to make your point. I've probably made about five hundred commercials so far. And I've managed to keep making commercials while making features, because they're stimulating and keep you in touch with what's happening. But I was able to make only two in 1967 and one in 1968.

G: When did you make your first commercial?

L: I made it about two months before my first feature, *It's Trad, Dad*. Just while I was talking about doing that picture, I made my first series of commercials. They won the World Prize of the best commercials that year in Hollywood. But they were banned by commercial television in Britain because they were considered to be too violent. They were about children, but they were naturalistically made and in those days that wasn't permitted.

G: Since film work was apparently hard to come by in those days, how did you get to direct *It's Trad, Dad?*

L: Someone had seen *The Running, Jumping, and Standing Still Film* and another short I'd made, a thirty-minute pilot television film called—forgive me—*Have Jazz, Will Travel*, which was a mixture of documentary techniques and modern jazz. My handling of those two themes seemed to be interesting to the producer. He wanted someone who was not highbrow and who'd be willing to take a twenty-five-page story outline and make a feature film out of it in three weeks. Which we did.

It was a pop musical that ran seventy-three minutes and had twenty-six musical numbers. I used three cameras, which I've continued to do ever since. By changing the camera setups three times during each musical sequence, and making sure that the key light was always coming from the same direction for all the cameras, I had in effect shot nine setups of a performance in an hour. Coming from live television, where we used four TV cameras, it seemed a natural procedure.

To save money, we used one set and a white cyclorama. The set could be rearranged in various shapes, like a Chinese puzzle. We just shipped in band after band and shot five and six sequences a day. Some of the film was shot in New York. In retrospect, it was an insane experience. Not only was I given a minuscule salary, but I had to pay my own air fare.

Overall, I've had the best reviews out of *It's Trad, Dad* that I've ever gotten. They were uniformly encouraging. The film was made for sixty thousand pounds, and on the Third Circuit, which was a bunch of fleapit theaters in England, it made three hundred thousand pounds in the first run. It was therefore totally successful on all counts.

Then I made commercials for about nine more months and nothing was really being sent to me. Having made a pop musical, I was offered three or four more pop musicals to direct. But I didn't want to be caught in the trap of doing one kind of filmmaking. Then the opportunity came to make a picture on a slightly larger budget, in color. And I didn't realize at that time, being a fool, that you should never make a sequel to somebody else's film because you have no control over it whatsoever.

In making *The Mouse on the Moon*, I had to use the sets and characters from *The Mouse That Roared*. All the actors were already cast. All their mannerisms were stereotyped. And since the first film was apparently financially successful, nobody would dream of changing anything in it. That's a desperate way to make a film. But it enabled me to shoot for seven weeks in color, so I did it. It was useful experience. But I don't think it was in any way *my* film, looking back on it.

G: Do you feel you learned anything in particular from your mistakes on the first two films that was useful in making A *Hard Day's Night?*

L: Well, I don't say that *Hard Day's Night* was that much better than *It's Trad, Dad*. I was able to shoot for seven weeks, instead of for three. I had a better class of performer to work with. Of course, one learns from one's mistakes. The sad thing is you attempt less the more mistakes you make. So that one tries almost anything on the first film, and having seen it go wrong you then try a little less. You experiment a little less with the second one. So now with the tenth one I'm almost paralyzed with fear because I've seen in ten films what can go wrong.

G: What were the circumstances that led to your directing *Hard Day's Night?*

L: I had made *Mouse on the Moon* for United Artists. It was made on time and on budget. The producer of that picture was approached by the United Artists music corporation to make a quick film with the Beatles before their popularity declined. The Beatles had seen *The Running, Jumping, and Standing Still Film* and liked it a lot.

G: Was it difficult to keep your identity and equilibrium working as a fairly new director with superstars like the Beatles?

L: Not only were they not superstars, but United Artists advised us to get the picture out as quickly as possible because they felt that by June 1964 nobody would have heard of the Beatles. They were expected to have been a passing phase. It wasn't until we started shooting the picture and the Beatles had come back from their American tour that they were recognized as an important force. I feel that there was a reasonable blend of my personality and theirs in the picture because we seem to share the same interests and we liked and laughed at the same things.

G: As non-actors, how were they to work with?

L: They hated getting up in the morning, and they hated the whole principle of filmmaking as an orderly craft. But they were quite willing to do it, because they were intelligent and realized the importance to me of following a schedule. They are very trusting and quite loyal people and if you'd explain to them why it was necessary for a certain thing to happen and it made sense to them they would do it from then on without questioning it. Like most intelligent people they suffer fools badly and I was fortunate enough not to be considered a fool. They suffered mindless discipline not at all. And since I react in the same way to discipline, we managed to get on.

What I was trying to do was to capture the feeling they managed to give to people around them and therefore I had to make them as natural as possible. We decided on the approach by going to Paris and watching them do a radio show. They were revolutionaries in a fishbowl. Once I asked John Lennon, who had just come back from Sweden, "Did you like Stockholm?" And he answered, "It was a plane, a room, a car, and a cheese sandwich." That was the extent they were able to experience the landscape of the places they performed in. So that became the claustrophobic nexus of *Hard Day's Night*.

The shooting of the concert sequence was astonishing. We used six film cameras and three television cameras to shoot the final seventeen minutes of film in a single day. The fans cut their way through iron bars to get to us. The only way we could defend ourselves was upending the Arriflex camera tripod and holding it with the spikes outstretched against their charge.

G: A writer has said of you, "Tricks are his one indulgence. Sometimes he lets them go on too long and runs them into the ground." He mentions *Help!* What's your reaction?

L: If that's the only indulgence I have, I'm very pleased. *Help!* had to be what it was because of what we were not allowed to do with the Beatles. We didn't want to repeat *Hard Day's Night*, so we couldn't show them at work on tour. They were not allowed to have girl friends, to drink, smoke, or do what they really did in their leisure time. Therefore, we had to end up making them totally passive—making them, as they've since complained, guest stars in their own film story—and to create a story that revolved around them without seeming to. The camera had to be the star of the film. And it had to be an extremely indulgent picture. And I hope that it didn't spoil most people's enjoyment of the film—that my indulgences were reasonably entertaining. I'd hope that other pictures of mine would not be considered indulgent.

I think that what's happened is that critics have said I'm tricky because of the Beatles films, and since then they've been looking for that in all of my films and continuing to say, "He's tricky." But the truth is that most of what is called style is simply solving problems, getting out of trouble. One only uses a cut because a take doesn't really work. The cut is an after-the-fact attempt to correct your mistakes, to put in something or take out something that should have been done differently.

G: What kind of problems did you have to solve in making *The Knack?*

L: It was a one-set stage play which we wanted to make into a film. I hadn't seen the stage production—I usually don't see a thing in its original version, if I can help it, because I don't want to be irrevocably influenced. We knew what we liked in *The Knack* but we weren't quite sure how that could translate. So we started by removing almost everything that we felt we could from the stage convention and wrote a total fantasy based on some of the mood of *The Knack.* Then, slowly, version after version—and Charles Wood reluctantly wrote seven scripts—we worked our way back towards the stage play. We found what we couldn't do without, and in that way we found out what we liked about the original version of *The Knack.*

G: You've said that the Beatles films were about four people who could communicate without having to say anything and that *The*

Knack was about four people who kept talking all the time but weren't able to communicate at all.

L: That's pompous, and quite true.

G: Some Americans complained that they couldn't hear or understand the dialect or were confused by the speed of the brilliant one-liners in films like *The Knack* and *How I Won the War.* Why does it seem that in scenes like the clucking, disapproving, bourgeois voices commenting on the young people trundling the bed through the streets in *The Knack* that you are unconcerned with whether your audience clearly understands the words or not?

L: Well, my wife, who is English, found it difficult to understand most of the dialogue in *Bullitt,* so it works both ways. Nowadays, with a world-wide audience, somebody is going to be hurt somewhere. Because a lot of films are shown on the continent in English versions, and you have audiences that understand a great deal of English, but not all the nuances. But the alternative, which seems to be to create a kind of mid-Atlantic film language, where people speak very clearly, distinctly, and with a limited vocabulary, seems appalling. It would have been absurd to ask the Beatles to speak more clearly or to use words that all America could understand.

In the case of *The Knack,* often there are four or five different effects going on at the same time. There were subtitles, music, the natural dialogue, overlay dialogue of people complaining, and visual effects. They created an overall effect, without my worrying specifically whether the audience understood every word of each of the themes of dialogue running through.

I think that pictures, after all, create a mood. If you have to be specific, you can be specific. If you want to just create the mood, let's say, of a cocktail party, of snatches of dialogue overheard and indistinct comments of people in the street as you pass them by, it is perfectly legitimate that the audience also can't hear everything. In life, we seldom hear more than sentence fragments, and sometimes they are more interesting than hearing the whole sentence.

G: What weight do you assign to words in your films as compared with visual images?

L: I always see things before I hear them. I am visually oriented. I like painting. Yet I think equal weight should be placed on dialogue, though not necessarily synchronized with the pictures. I would like to be able to move dialogue, so that it doesn't become just visualized theater. And so that words don't always have to come out of the mouths of people who are on the screen.

Or, if they do, they don't necessarily have to come out of the same time span as they were recorded. Sound is as important as pictures, because we are in the '6os and not in the '2os. But it is nice to be able to emancipate sound so that it does not absolutely correspond to the visual image. Because there seems to be more of an opportunity in that way to create a wider range of effects.

G: I was intrigued by your use of sound in *Petulia*. Would you discuss how you made that film?

L: I went to San Francisco, about eighteen months before we started shooting, with Charles Wood. He did a rough script based on what we'd seen. It was a sort of free interpretation of the material given to us as the original novel and a first American screenplay. In place of a long series of notes—location notes—we adapted the script very freely in terms of what we'd seen, expressions that we'd heard, lines of dialogue that were interesting, places that had unusual qualities—both for me returning after fifteen years and for him, since he'd never been in America.

Then, over the next year, we worked with an American writer, worked with an American unit, and tried to balance those first stunning impressions with those more accustomed to that genre. In no way was San Francisco chosen because of any sensationalism associated with the hippie movement, because there wasn't any, really, when we chose it. My feeling was, in fact, the reverse. The book was set in Los Angeles. But I felt that Los Angeles itself was—to a foreign and semi-foreign eye—so bizarre, such a positive experience, it was so powerful and demanding, the city itself, that sort of billboard quality, that I felt it would push the characters too far into the background.

Secondly, I felt the kind of people whom I met in San Francisco when we first went to look for locations and met the civic leaders—people who had dropped out of the New York and Los Angeles rat race and were vaguely apologetic and defensive and genteel—seemed to me very much like the kind of people that I wanted to put into the film. Their manners, their code of behavior, seemed to correspond to the families in *Petulia*.

G: Is there a theme, a phrase, an idea, which expresses what you were after in *Petulia*?

L: The phrase would be cheap, because it's just a phrase; it's two words where you'd need many more. But, I think, it's this: "Casual violence." Somehow it seemed that the flashpoint, the burning point, of American life—either in political discussions or general relationships between people in a family—is much lower than it is here in England. I set a scene at four o'clock in the morning in a supermarket where people started to scream at each other over the question of whether a tin of sardines had been brought in or opened there. I was constantly being shouted at, in one way or another. And, making personal films, one takes what happens to you and puts them into the film. That doesn't happen here in England. There may be the same anxieties, the same bigotries, the same inability of people to get on with each other—but their melting point is higher.

G: You were American born, American bred. Yet, along with a number of other American filmmakers in England, France, and Italy, you no longer make your home or films in the U.S. Do you, therefore, consider yourself an expatriate?

L: I don't, in the sense of the '20s and '30s, because I think that they were people who were trying hard to be Americans living abroad. I would prefer to think of myself not as anything; not to be totally of one culture, not to have any particular allegiances, either political or sociological or in any emotional way—and just to be where I am, and not to be considered American or English or European.

I don't honestly know what to consider myself. I'm a resident of this country, my wife is British, my son, Dominic, is British. I still am an American citizen. I still have an American passport. I've thought about becoming a British citizen, but that seemed to be, again, a positive step of becoming nationalistic, and that's something I don't want to do. You can't become a citizen of the world, because people won't let you. You're just not able to do it. I would, if I thought one could survive.

G: At least one critic felt that *Petulia* was a savage, scathing, vilification of Americans, or at least of California culture.

L: Well, I didn't come to attack these people. I personally felt compassion towards the people in the film. They're interesting. They are trapped, and desperate, because they're aware of their problems. Mike Nichols is the only American director I know. And I admire and like him. While I was making *Petulia* he was making *The Graduate*, and we knew a little about each other's films—we'd had an evening together. And we both felt we were making the same film.

We still feel, in a way, that we made the same film, with a difference. The only difference is that most of the people in his film were smug about their inability to recognize their own doubts. My film is, I think, less comic—I don't find it comic at all—in that the people are aware of what's wrong and therefore not only have the problems of being, but the problems of knowing about being—the double agony.

G: *Petulia* seemed to me to be an oblique film, in that the confrontations or resolutions never quite materialize as in the "well-made" film.

L: I think that the story could best be told in an oblique way. I think that everything that has happened to me was a mosaic of trivia, of unimportant periphery, which, in looking back, becomes important and jells together and becomes a whole. I think that it's only by taking those pieces apart and rejiggling them do you come to the sort of realization that the Julie Christie character came to —that probably at the end she realizes that by demanding so much of a man she makes him impotent. So she decides that her responsibility is to learn to settle for 60 per cent of someone, which is the only way she can go on living. And nobody in the film is able to find a way to live up to his or her full potential, which is the tragedy.

G: Was it really her who made her husband impotent, or was he an incipient homosexual before she met him?

L: I think there may have been tendencies that way, because no man is all black or white, but she was the contributing factor to the impotency. Because she kept saying, "You're fantastic, you're the most marvelous man I've ever known." And he says, "Don't say that," on their wedding day, "I won't be able to compete with myself." You know, put a man on a pedestal and the quickest way for him to go limp in bed is to keep saying: "Oh, my God, look at that, it's fantastic." And she finally realizes that. And she says—in that scene where she stays in Joe Cotten's house and George Scott leaves without her—she says, "I'd turn those marvelous hands of yours into fists" to Scott. And, to Richard Chamberlin, her husband who's tried to kill her, she says, "When I married you, you were the gentlest man I knew, David." And he was.

G: I thought she was cruel and destructive and not terribly intelligent or compassionate.

L: She *is* destructive. Because she is such a nail biter. She is a compulsive liar. "My mother was a whore and my grandfather was killed in the First World War in the trenches . . ." Well, the dates are wrong. The mother couldn't have been a whore. It was a rationalization so she wouldn't have to drop her pants. "I stole the tuba." And then he finds out that she's rented it from somebody. She's just constantly lying. Her willfulness in doing the oblique thing—this obliqueness is essential to understanding the problems of these characters.

They don't make speeches or pronouncements. You see them and must understand them in terms of their environment and of what happens to them and by the way they react and by the casual things they say. They would only become aware of a pattern in their lives by taking this mosaic of little images and putting them together in another order. I don't impose a simplistic statement of what makes them behave as they do and say, "This is the reason or the motive."

They don't say, "This is the great revelation of my life." Which is what the original book was about. Which is what everything in life is about. Which is what art has traditionally been about. That "moment of truth." I don't believe in it. I haven't ever had a moment of truth. I've had twenty-eight quarter-moments of truth, which, if you shuffle them together five years later in an interview like this, you can justify and say, "I left America because of Joe McCarthy" or "I left England because of Suez." It's too easy to oversimplify in retrospect. So it's up to one to take those pieces apart and to say, "What really happened?" Don't forget the fact that a bus driver was rude to you. Don't forget the fact that you had a fight with your mother-in-law. Or whatever else might have happened to influence you.

G: The traditional function of the artist used to be, presumably, to make meaningful and make ordered, structured, a vision of the universe out of what, essentially, is a scattershot of experience. How do you feel that's changed?

L: I want to offer the scattershot of experience to an audience and make them work. I want to make each person sitting in a row see a different film.

G: Does that mean you've been very selective with this scattershot?

L: The selectivity comes in the editing. For example, there are five things that happened to me that have nothing to do with the story in *Petulia* but just have to do with making the film. *One:* on the plane going to make the film, a boy in the seat in front of me was in the army and the elderly man next to him said, "Where are you going?" The soldier said, "I'm going to Vietnam." The old man said, "You must be terribly upset about it." The boy said, "No, I'm not actually going to fight; I'm in the Quartermaster Corps." The old man said, "But, still, a lot of people are being killed out there." The boy said, "No, I really don't mind; I'm really looking forward to going. I can't wait to see the Bob Hope Christmas show."

Two: Twenty-five American Indian children, age seven, are being taken for an outing in Muir Woods—the National Park—by a large, redheaded Anglo-Saxon city guide. The Indian children, walking in a file along this native path, turn to the guide and ask, "What happens next?" He is confused, can't think, and answers, "Spring." And they walk on.

Three: Overheard in a bar in Sausalito and written down on a napkin: "So Chiang Kai-shek says, 'God damn, how can I make a nickel? It costs two and a half cents to put the average Chinee up the soap boiler but it costs $2000 to put an average V.C. underground.' That seems to be a basic flaw in the capitalist society. Don't you agree, Ed?"

Four: An image just of a group of nuns walking across by a bandstand, those trees broken off.

And, *five:* Another image of a girl who's pregnant sitting playing solitaire with oversized cards in a park all by herself.

All those things—the first four, anyway—were images I saw. The fifth one, of the girl playing solitaire, I just imagined. I put them all into the film. I cut out the first and second, and put the third one right on the edge of the frame and put more dialogue over it so that you only get a vague impression. It was there to pick up, if anyone wanted to. But I didn't want to make a big point of it. As a piece of non-sequitur dialogue it seemed so perfect that I felt it was worth including.

The fourth and fifth I left in because they were visual images, and were easy to do. I can't tell you why I did them now, but I felt that within what I was saying in *Petulia* it was necessary to take the first two or three out. It is the selectivity of the editing which is what I do, but I will shoot anything that seems to be relevant, seems to be part of the fabric, seems to be extraordinary.

G: Would you say that you film as a reporter takes notes and then edit as if writing the final report on your typewriter?

L: Absolutely. Directing is an editing process. You tell an actor what he shouldn't do, edit out what you think is not good. You try a whole series of visual images, you edit out what doesn't seem to be honest or doesn't seem to be fair. In many films, I spend a

lot of time photographing these non-sequiturs so I can learn about
the place and about myself and about my feelings toward the
subject by learning what I keep out. I go with very little preparation into the actual shooting and work by instinct. In the editing,
it's a matter of painful self-analysis.

G: Isn't there sometimes gratuitous distortion, like the image of
the nuns in a sports two-seater in *Petulia?*

L: I saw nuns in black Cadillacs. I thought there's no reason, if
they're in black, why they couldn't be in white.

G: Yes, but the sports car seemed like an extra zing, the implication of a whole other kind of life. What about the hospital?

L: The selling of those striker flotation pads for the prevention
of bed sores was real. And so was the dummy television set. The
first place we went to try to get permission to shoot, there were
dummy television sets. And the officials explained that before a
patient had their operation, at the time they sign in for the room,
they're asked if they want a television set. A concession offers them
for, I think, ten dollars a day.

If they say no, the hospital officials always leave a dummy television set in the room because they think that when the patient
starts to recover they'll stare at the bare screen and they will think,
"I'm missing something." Absolutely true.

G: There was a moment when a loudspeaker in the hospital
said, "Doctor so and so report to . . ." what sounded like "the
set" or some film unit. Was that intended to imply that this was
the kind of hospital where one would go to shoot a film because
that's one of their sidelines?

L: Precisely. Every time we went through any of the hospitals
to get permission to shoot, the public relations men—who were
always in attendance—would say, "Yeah, we had ABC television
here last week and we did quite a big thing." Hospitals are show
biz, because they're competing in the money stakes.

G: You conveyed the quality of the life around your characters
in *Petulia* with overheard fragments of conversation—between two
lesbians, or neighbors who commented with detachment on Julie
Christie's bloodied head. We never really knew for sure what was
going on inside them. Are these things we're shown a reflection of
what's going on inside their minds?

L: Often in films you have a great dramatic story in which, say, four people exist within a kind of set, in a kind of theatrical background that is paper. And all we're asked to care about is what they are to each other. I like to feel that we can do that as well by showing them always as part of a total environment. Because you're saying, "This girl is what she is not because her mother was a whore—because anybody's mother can be a whore; your mother could be a whore and my mother could be a whore, but it doesn't mean that we're going to be any different together from what we are here and now—but that this girl is living today, in America, and she must be influenced, either to fight against all these bits of background or to accept them."

I didn't want to have a crowd call of fifty extras and just ask them to walk up and down the street when Julie is carried in the stretcher down to the ambulance. They must be part of the film, because, as neighbors who would have a variety of reactions to the event, they must be given an existence beyond mere presence in the scene. They are people, hopefully real people.

Petulia is the only three-dimensional film that I've ever set out to make. The characters are three-dimensional. They react against each other. They correlate, as opposed to *How I Won the War* or *The Knack* or this new film, *The Bed Sitting Room,* where I use cardboard cutouts of cliched people as devices to run through the film and bump into each other and continue on. They're not affected by what happens to them. They're not affected by their meeting.

But the people in *Petulia* are changed, so much so that they reverse roles. They are involved in each other's lives. If the two main characters are involved in change because they meet each other, they should also change when they meet the little bits of mosaic, the oblique things that happen to them. When they meet a bus driver, when they hear a snatch of conversation, when they are at a penguin pool, when they are at a roller derby—that piece of commercialized casual violence.

G: Can you define people by their environment? By showing what they have to deal with every day, can you say, "This is what brutalizes them, this is what dehumanizes them"?

L: I don't think you can define them. I don't think you can do it all by the environment. I mean, if the major characters had never spoken, you would get an idea, but you wouldn't get the total idea. But I think it is better to use the environment as part of what is happening to the principals, rather than just have four main characters and a group of extras brought in for the day. I think you have to balance it. And I think, as you are suggesting, that perhaps the difference between the way I work and the way the audiences expect films to be is that I put more of a burden on the periphery to build up a pattern of what I'm trying to say.

G: Is the "meaning" then in grasping the emotional context?

L: Yes. Nobody's making pronouncements. Nobody in the film speaks and says, "I believe in such and such" or "I love this, I hate that" or "I am what I am because . . ." I don't do that, even in interviews. But you try to understand why these people are what they are, basically by their casual speech and the casual speech of people around them. It's the difference between the heightened drama, which is basically theatrical, of a man on the stage with cardboard around him and you know it's cardboard, and you know he's a real actor who's playing the part of something. And when he says, "I love you," you can see the spit coming out of his mouth and he, in that time, has to get through all this area of stylization. Because he has to make you believe that this bit of cardboard in the background is really Hyde Park and so he has to say, "All Gaul is divided into three parts—and that's it, don't forget it." Whereas, on film, you see that Hyde Park is Hyde Park because it looks like Hyde Park.

G: Do you believe you could make a viable "wordless" picture, with just a few key dialogue scenes?

L: Yes. But I don't want to reduce words from my films because we spend all our time rabbiting away to each other, using words. And therefore, if you want to be realistic, a silent film is as unrealistic as a black and white film. We exist in color. And we exist speaking to each other. And we generally try to get over feelings and attitudes by words, though not through the theatrical technique of making pronouncements. The use that film can make of words is that you can build up a pattern of trivia, if you need to, and still express a clear-cut feeling.

G: Since you want your audience to live and feel what your characters are feeling—rather than saying it explicitly—do you think of your films as more visceral than intellectual?

L: Yes. I certainly don't plan my films by intellect. And if I don't then it's going to be very odd if they turn out to be that way.

c: Does it disturb you that people usually want you to tell them directly what your point is?

l: No. Because I think very few of us have a point that is so startlingly accurate and relevant that we are justified in saying, "This is the truth." There are twenty people sitting in the audience, each seeing a different truth. As long as you put it all there. This is how I felt about *How I Won the War*. It's not a case of preaching. It's a case of telling the audience, "You have been involved in a certain kind of attitude, as exemplified by a certain kind of film and a certain kind of propaganda. This film is an alternative to that. I don't say that it is totally right. And I don't say that it gives answers. It won't solve wars. It won't even give you the reasons why a war is fought."

How I Won the War in no way goes about explaining the economic or sociological or political things that led up to Hitler. It wasn't trying to be a film that shows a Hitler becoming powerful and invading countries or the reluctance to fight him at a certain time and then the overwhelming urge to fight him at another time. It just said, "Right, all wars are justified, until the first shot's fired. Then the obscenity begins. We are going to show just the obscenity." All we set out doing was to offer the possibility that it is nothing but an obscenity, whether it be necessary or not. As the character in the end says, "I knew we had to fight—there was a good reason for fighting—I just couldn't. I leave it to people like you who didn't really have a reason."

There it is, if people want to find it. But I'm not going to say I have the answer, because I don't. That would be presumptuous, and it is not the purpose of an artist to have that kind of presumption. I, for instance, find even the much-admired *Paths of Glory* sinister because it intimates that if only Kirk Douglas had complete charge of the troops they'd have been able to get on with killing the Germans and capturing the fortress more efficiently. It certainly wasn't an antiwar film, and it was one of the films against which *How I Won the War* was aimed. There was a direct reference in our film to *Paths of Glory*: "What we want are more humane killers."

c: What was the point of those tinted, or monochrome, sequences in *How I Won the War*?

l: It was a device to draw direct parallels between the battles of this surreal unit and actual World War II disasters such as the Dieppe raid, Dunkirk, and El Alamein and to underscore military thinking—that individuals are interchangeable and a platoon is immortal, in the sense it is constantly replenished with new bodies. So, for the officers, they began and ended the war with the same men—which is why Michael Crawford kept calling new replacements by the names of the dead men.

G: I understand that the film that distresses you the most, aside from *Mouse on the Moon*, is *A Funny Thing Happened on the Way to the Forum*. Why is that?

L: I've cut every film of mine the way I wanted to, except *Forum*. Since that film I've had it in my contract that I get final cut. And I've been co-producing my films, too, for additional protection. As for *Forum*, I cut it myself but the producer had the right to recut it. So we had a fight between the two cuts. *Forum* was a battle from beginning to end. We were fighting version versus version rather than trying to do the best thing for the film. I hadn't been allowed to rewrite the script the way I wanted to before we started—though I did spend the two weeks before shooting in Spain tinkering with the script. And then after it was shot the producer locked pieces of the negative away and said, "You can't use them."

It wasn't really, in the final analysis, a question of cutting. It was simply, I suppose, a case of different outlooks in filmmaking. The producer wrote it and had also planned at one time to direct it. I don't know why he chose me to direct. He understandably saw the film one way and I saw it quite a different way.

I think he was surprised at my, let's say, dictatorial attitude toward filmmaking. Because he had been a Hollywood producer at a time when the producer was the major figure—between, that is, the producer and the director. I had never come from that school of filmmaking and I rejected it totally.

I must say that I rejected it long enough in advance to make him know what he was in for. But I don't think he realized the terrible reality. And we just violently argued from six weeks before shooting until the picture was out. And when there is this disagreement, no one gives of his best because little problems of filmmaking become mountains.

I found myself being far more inflexible in defending my decisions than I would have been if I didn't have to defend them. Normally, I am considerably more pliable. And since I wasn't able to rewrite the script very much, what I did write was quite different from the rest of the piece.

G: Which parts did you write in *Forum?*

L: I had done some research by reading Carcopino on the squalidness of imperial Rome. The brutality of the film—as a reflection of what, historically, Rome was actually like—was mine. Scenes like the one in the arena with the slaves being teed up like golf balls to test the swing of the gladiator's spiked ball. And in building the set, I had it stocked with fruit and vegetables which were allowed to rot over two weeks to attract hordes of insects. And then I had Spanish peasants brought down from the hills to live in the set and work at specific jobs for the duration of the shooting, to give it a sort of authenticity.

G: Zero Mostel and Phil Silvers, I've heard, were already cast in *Forum* before you were hired. What's your reaction to criticism that Mostel was overpowered by the jump-cutting, instead of just having the camera pointed at him and letting him be funny?

L: I feel that whatever was done with the film was necessary to try to salvage a basic problem. That is, that farce is the hardest thing that I know to make work on film. Because the one thing that seems to be basic to farce is that you let the audience see three doors. They know that at one point somebody's gone in one door and then you surprise them because he comes out another door. The minute you use film and you go into a closeup they've forgotten which door is which. And you have to try to rebuild the excitement by artificial means.

I suspect that Zero is so overwhelming on the stage because of his grace—that you see a very large man moving in full figure all the time with an amazing balletic grace. And that's part of his charm. If you show him any closer than that, on film, you're losing the most successful part of his personality. I admire Zero very much. I'm sorry the film wasn't better, for his sake.

G: Why are you going back to pasteboard characters in *The Bed Sitting Room?* Don't you sacrifice some emotion with abstract humanity?

L: A world filled with just twenty people, a world destroyed and decimated by The Bomb is too big a subject to grasp realistically. You have to use stylized parallels. Instead of trying to pan along forty million dead, I would rather have a twelve-foot high mound of boots being sorted into rights and lefts. If you take a real person with real fears and real tears and put him in this, he won't be able to cope. And if he does cope, he'll sound like Bertrand Russell.

G: How do you plan to turn Ralph Richardson into a bed sitting room?

L: You see the man, then you see the room. Atomic radiation causes the mutation, turns him into what he deserves to be. If he were going to turn into a building, this arrogant aristocrat would hope to turn into Woburn Abbey. But he becomes a bed sitting room—a sort of furnished efficiency apartment—which has no dignity. His terrible premonition has come true.

It's a sad film, a sort of nostalgic view back to the days when we used to be frightened of the bomb. Seriously, it's based on the concern that, because of all our other problems, we have sufficiently pushed the bomb into the background, that it's become a period piece, a piece of nostalgia from those days when we were all marching and organized and worrying about the fact that there were B-52s overhead.

It is such an impossible condition for the mind to grasp that we have to use the techniques of absurdity—an accidental war lasts two minutes and twenty-eight seconds, including the time it takes to blot the signatures on the peace treaty. So we push man's perversions and foibles to the extreme. And then take those twenty people who have survived and let them carry on exactly as they might do.

We're trying to reproduce what Hiroshima was like, but stylized. One of the camera operators was at Hiroshima three months after it was bombed and he took a lot of photographs. We're reproducing that, in some ways. We spent the last two days at a reject pottery dump. It was entirely filled with broken plates, bits of fused glass.

G: Would you describe the alienation effect of your pasteboard characters in this film or How I Won the War as Brechtian?

L: Not in this film. But in How I Won the War, absolutely. Consciously and determinedly. The alienation that I meant in How I Won the War is that at the moment that a character was in danger of attracting your sympathy because of his performance, you turned on the audience and said: "Don't forget this is a film you're watching and I'm an actor and I'm playing this part. And it's not this I want to get over. It is something bigger than Corporal Transom I want to talk about." That, in a sort of

Arturo Ui feeling, is what I meant by alienation in *How I Won the War.*

In *The Bed Sitting Room*, there is no direct relationship between the film itself and the people. In fact, it's being made as a sort of 1930s documentary on the WPA, if you like. It's made very simply. We're using only the lens that would have been used in a very early film.

G: Did you have any problems getting approval for the script of *The Bed Sitting Room?*

L: Nobody's approved the script, as far as I know. They've learned now not to be disappointed and read scripts. It just depresses them.

G: On what basis, then, does a studio make a decision to approve millions of dollars for a film if they can't see something in writing in advance?

L: I think they use prayer . . . I don't really think they knew what it was going to be. I did mention at first that it would be about two young men and two young women in Candide-like circumstances. But we wrote two screenplays on that subject and gave it up. So we then said, "It's not going to be that." And they said, "Oh, I see." That's as far as we're able to explain it.

G: Did you have carte blanche on *Petulia* too?

L: Yes, I had a contract which said I had final cut, total artistic control. Once we signed that I don't think anyone really believed it. I think Warner Bros. were rather surprised with what they'd done. They said something like, "Yes, I know we signed it, but we didn't actually mean it." Too late.

G: As a director, therefore, you've achieved absolute control of your films?

L: I have, yes. I don't know how long it will last. Probably until, like Icarus, I fall from financial grace with promissory notes flapping about me like feathers coming off.

G: Where does your next film, *Send Him Victorious*, come from?

L: It comes from a novel written by two people who were in the foreign office, one of whom is now Edward Heath's private secretary.

G: Why are you making it?

L: I'm not sure that I am making it, at the moment. I hope I am making it because it's an opportunity to examine in thriller form—in commercial form—four or five different types of racism. I think we're very involved, all of us today, in racism. In government, in the manipulation of people by government, and the manipulation of governments by big business.

G: What are the problems you foresee with the film?

L: Getting the money to make it.

G: What energies does the business side of making a movie drain off of you as a creative artist?

L: Well, I think it's impossible to separate them. Every day when I go to the studio I feel: "I must shoot two minutes of film today, otherwise we're going to go over budget and that is unfair." I work on the principle that the distributor shouldn't interfere with the creative side of it and, conversely, it's my responsibility, having given him a budget, to stick to it and to treat it as a bank loan.

G: When you're in production, what kind of routine do you follow?

L: I normally spend about three to four months in pre-production, working with a writer on the idea. Then about three months shooting and about four months in the editing and music stage. Just before I start shooting I do about a month of floor exercises to get myself physically fit and to build up enough stamina to get through the three months shooting.

During shooting, I usually look at the script in the car on the way to the location—not having looked at it before then. And in that way, I plan in my head what I will do that day. This changes when I see what the weather is like or what shape the costumes or sets are in.

I arrive half an hour before anyone else, just wander about the set looking at the things that have changed since I last saw it, and see if I can make use of any of these changes or aberrations. I have no camera angles planned, nothing planned at all. I just shoot as it comes. I shoot probably until six or six-thirty at night, then come back to the studio, look at the rushes of the previous day, go home and ignore the picture as much as I can by involving myself with my family.

G: For you, is filmmaking pleasant, boring, maddening, or painful?

L: Everything but boring. It's certainly painful, certainly maddening. It's very exciting. I have never found it fun. The actual day's shooting is bloody hell. To work with a hundred people looking on, saying, "Go on, show us something, you're getting the most money, you smart ass" is an appalling thing to do day in and day out. It's very physically tiring because you have to charge a hundred people with your own enthusiasm in order to keep the film together. You have to have a thousand personal love affairs with prop men and with actors to keep them happy. And at the end of it you are filled—I am filled—with self-doubt and without any real feeling of confidence that I *know* what I'm doing.

To watch rushes is a very painful experience because it confirms the mistakes you think you've made. In fact, I would prefer never to see any film that I've shot until the whole film is finished. Because I'm inclined to spend the day after seeing a certain piece of bad filmmaking unconsciously correcting that in the new work I'm doing, instead of taking the new work the way it comes. So I'm inclined to avoid what I made wrong the day before.

G: What part of filmmaking do you enjoy the most?

L: I enjoy the editing process the most, without any doubt. The recording of music and the final dubbing, the mixing of all the sound and music together, is enormously pleasant. I enjoy that because there are no demands of time, and I'm very involved in time in filmmaking. I feel total responsibility to do the amount of work that I'm supposed to do in a day—those two minutes of film in the can a day.

Fatigue can spoil one's work. The hardest thing to do is to be physically strong in the last two or three weeks of a long shooting schedule. If you're not physically up to it, if you haven't taken care of yourself, if you haven't produced a peak of condition like an athlete before you start a film, your mental judgments will suffer because you're just too tired.

G: Actors often use their personal experiences in their work, in evoking specific emotions. Do you draw on your own personal life, past or present, for your films?

L: I'm sure we all do, but I think it becomes harder and harder. You're cut off by the barrier of success. I don't travel in a bus or take a subway anymore. Because of various television appearances, I'm instantly recognizable. And I seem to be a bit cut off from people, because of being somewhat of a celebrity. They're inclined to act in a rather bizarre way. I don't have the opportunity to sit quietly and observe people in their natural state as well as I could before I was known.

G: What's your view on the director as technician, and knowing as much as his experts?

L: It's useful to know as much as possible about the technical aspects of filmmaking. Television commercials helped me learn the techniques. But, if you intend to really involve yourself in the physical aspects of filmmaking, you must be able to observe an actor acting through the film plane. That is, to actually operate a camera and with *your* eye see the performance happening, with film moving between your eye and the performer. That seems to me the only really satisfying way of directing. I hate the idea of going to an operator after a shot and saying, "How was it?" He might say, "Yes, that's all right." Or, "It isn't all right." And you ask, "Well, did you see her leg?" And he says, "Oh well, we better do it once again."

Ideally, film should be one person, doing it all. And I think that the closer a director can come to that, the better the film he makes. So, as much as possible, I like to know everything I can about photographic techniques, about how a picture is graded, and about what laboratory effects are possible. Sometimes, it is just not feasible for a director to perform all these functions. I'm not a particularly skillful operator. In *Petulia*, I operated on about twenty-five per cent of the shots that are in the finished film. And in *Bed Sitting Room* about the same. Some things I can't do because I've not practiced enough to do them well. But to me the finest film should be made by one person, alone, doing it all.

G: Some directors claim all they have to know is how to handle actors and they're content to leave the rest to experts. What's your opinion?

L: Well, I think it's very nice if you do know how to handle actors. I'm not sure that I do. "Actors" becomes a sort of great generic term, as if they were all beasts from another planet. Each actor has to be approached separately, and with caution. But I do think that handling actors is one tiny part of filmmaking. The minute the actor is photographed, he becomes part of the space that is photographed. There is space around him, beneath him. And the things he uses, and the way he looks, and the way he behaves within that space, is important. And I think it wrong to just concern yourself with the actor and not concern yourself with the space around him.

I think this was one of the great skills of Buster Keaton as a director—that for the first time in comedy a man was able to make use of the space between the camera and the performer, or between the actor and the edge of the frame. Chaplin, on the other hand, was always just photographing the fourth wall of a stage set. You were not concerned with what was around him, except perhaps a prop that he held in his hand. Whereas with Keaton, the camera very delicately was always at the right place at the right time and the space around the performer seemed to matter. It matters terribly to me. And because of it I feel that I must be involved in the creation of that space. I must choose the setups, I must choose the distance the camera is from a person, the way the person looks, what kind of sound is coming out of his mouth.

G: How did you learn to handle actors, incidentally?

L: One doesn't learn how to handle actors in any way except experience. It is a bit like lion-taming. And I don't think you can read a book on how you should get on with an actor—any more than you read a book on how you get on with your neighbors. You have to set up a series of individual love affairs with each performer, male and female, and just be able to find a shorthand that will get you through the complexity of the day's work. I don't direct actors from an acting point of view. In other words, I am not someone who says, "Look, don't do it that way, do it this way," and then act the part myself, for the simple reason that I'm not a very good actor.

But what I would like to do is to be able to say to an actor: "Don't do it like that; offer me something else. You create something for me. I'm not going to do an impersonation of you impersonating me impersonating the performer. I will get rid of what I don't like in your performance. You provide for me another way to make up for what I've cut out." And eventually, out of that—and I hope that this process goes on while the camera is turning—we produce something that is satisfying and which is really the creation of the actor. The actor is forced to create, because I won't let him impersonate me impersonating him.

G: How active a role do you play in shaping the script?

L: I don't sit down and write anything on my own. I'm lazy and I'm not a good writer. What I feel that I can do fairly well is to shape the writing of other people. I suppose it's the same way that I deal with actors. It's allowing the writer to create, while I'm working as a kind of dilettante editor, saying, "I don't think this is working," or, "I think we might need a bit more of this."

G: How much hand-held camerawork is there in your films?

L: The style follows the content. If suddenly you want to be in a crowd, fighting, observing a riot, it seems more natural to use a hand-held camera, because you're representing one of the people involved in the crowd. If you feel as if you'd like to look at the crowd as if they were ants, from above, you would use a fixed-camera position in a helicopter. Or, if you couldn't get a helicopter, you would put the camera on a building site. You wouldn't hold it in your hand.

I only used hand-held cameras when it was logical for the observer to be moving. There is no other reason for using a hand-held camera at all. The image looks better when it's photographed from a tripod. To use hand-held camerawork as a style, I think, is absurd. And I have never consciously tried to have a style in any form of filmmaking that I've done. I feel that anything I've done with cameras has been done because I had to do it—often what's called a deliberate jump-cut style is merely something that's got to be done at the editing stage to correct a badly shot scene.

If you're trying to re-create newsreel footage, as in *How I Won the War*, it is useful to use the same kind of camera that was used by the newsreel photographer during World War II—to use the same lenses, the 35- and 50-mm lenses, that were normally on the turrets of a newsreel camera. And to disport yourself in the way that a newsreel cameraman would. That is, to spend most of your time crawling along the ground. And that's what we did with *How I Won the War*.

I normally use two Arriflexes, both in blimps. I use Arriflex cameras, rather than the Mitchell, because they're slightly smaller. But they are not hand held. I generally have a third camera, which I operate myself, and which is, for mobility, inclined to be carried in my hand. But I don't think it is noticeably hand held, since I'm not attempting to use an effect.

G: Does it help in editing to have footage from more than one camera?

L: It only helps in that you have twice as many images, or if a piece of extemporaneous business happens. For example, if your actor breaks his leg in the middle of a take, you're able to use some editing control because you have two cameras photographing the scene at the same time. This allows you to cut out the moment, for example, where the actor is writhing in pain. And it allows you the ability to move from a long shot to a close shot of the same action, without having to re-create the moment when the actor broke his leg. I always use multiple camera technique in this way. But I do it so that I don't have to shoot closeups afterwards and re-create moments of either splendor or agony artificially. It's all done once.

G: Could you trace the reasons or the origins of your reverence for slapstick comedy that emerges so clearly in your own films and in touches, like the casting of Buster Keaton in *Forum?*

L: I have always enjoyed slapstick comedy. I have always enjoyed surrealism. I enjoy surrealist novels. I like the paintings of Magritte. I like visual cartoons that have a surrealist nature. In fact, though, the casting of Buster Keaton was only partially my idea. It was only by accident that Stephen Sondheim, who wrote the music and lyrics for the original Broadway show, mentioned that the stage role of Erronius had been offered to Buster Keaton but that he had not accepted it.

I immediately jumped at it, but perhaps wouldn't have thought about it had Sondheim not mentioned it when we were trying to cast the part. I have enormous regard for Keaton, and for all of his films. I would prefer, I think, if I had the choice, to see a film of Keaton's that I had never seen before more than any other director's work that I know. That's for pure pleasure. But I can't trace the influence any more than that. It's like having a penchant for asparagus.

G: Is the key to the Dick Lester film—as it is to almost every silent slapstick comedy—the chase?

L: I don't think so. I don't really like chases. Because so many of them are unmotivated and are put into a screenplay to be able to finish it. There is always a desperation in contemporary chases that seems unnecessary, and somewhat contrived—and I include my own films in that. It's one of the easiest ways of ending a film. But I don't think it's necessarily the most satisfying or satisfactory.

It's easy to do a chase because I'm visually oriented and a chase is generally filled with visual ideas rather than verbal ones —and I'm inclined to create sequences with an overall musical feeling about them, and a basic rhythm. But I've never really been satisfied with any chase that I've done. I didn't mind the one in *Hard Day's Night*, because it was very short. I didn't like the one in *Forum*, because it seemed artificially contrived. Had I a choice, I would not have had a chase.

There is, certainly, something that I feel is very useful in film. And that is what I'd call—for want of a better phrase—the "time clock" element. It's useful, in other words, if the audience knows that there is a certain time in which the picture has to be accomplished. One of the best examples would be *Cleo From 5 to 7*. At the beginning of the picture you know that you have two hours to wait before the answer—does the girl have cancer or not?—will be revealed. And the audience is always aware that the time is running out, the time is passing.

Therefore, scenes of the most extraordinary banality take on poignancy. You know that within an hour of the time that the scene where she tries on a hat takes place she will know whether she has cancer or not. This kind of clock—"we only have three days to accomplish the mission; we've got to get there before the Germans do, and they're going to come in twenty-eight minutes"—I think this element is very useful in filmmaking, because it allows a kind of spine on which you can put irrelevant details and still make them seem important.

c: Why is slapstick your favorite expression of comedy?

l: Because visual comedy seems to be the purest form of comedy and can be translated into any language. Words are always suspect because they don't mean the same thing to one person as to another. But somebody being punched in the nose means the same thing to every person in the world.

c: What's your opinion of film schools?

l: It's a terrible thing to generalize, but I'm against film schools because I feel that you can't teach someone how to direct a film. And most of the film schools are geared to producing not technicians—who probably couldn't get jobs anyway, because of union restrictions—but to producing directors. I think the only way to learn how to direct is to actually direct. And I think that for the time one spends in a film school you get precious little chance to actually direct.

c: How could a young man, then, who wants to make films, get started?

l: I can only look to my own experience. The way I started making films was to go out with a camera of a friend and, for as little money as possible, actually expose film. It seems to me that the best way to become a director is to direct. And film is not all that expensive these days, nor are good 16-mm cameras. You ought to be working in some other profession for a year or so and save enough money to be able to shoot your first film.

G: What role do you foresee commercial or pay television playing as a possible outlet for new, modest-budgeted films by independent filmmakers?

L: Let's wait and see where pay television succeeds, first. It's failed in England, and the experiment has been called off, so there is no pay television that I know about. I think the time will come where you can buy tapes, instead of films. The films will be transferred to tape and you'll buy them in a supermarket and you'll plug them into the wall at home. And the filmmaker will decide whether he's successful or not by the number of tapes he's sold in the supermarket—like LPs.

G: You've been quoted as describing yourself as a "lying bastard" and a "happy pessimist" more interested in your failures than your successes. And you've said, "I don't feel successful." Could you elaborate?

L: I think we all lie. I'm providing you with half-truths, because I think we all avoid real honesty. It is much easier to just prattle on, as we all do, half-truths to half-questions. As far as being more interested in one's failures than successes, I think it's a wiser course. Either to avoid what happened in them, or to examine the reasons why you produced a failure, and cherish them. Success is terribly ephemeral and failure is lasting. And I like values that are lasting. And I don't consider myself successful because I feel that life is extremely short and there's an enormous amount to do. And I find that I have just begun.

G: Would you say that you're happy, satisfied with your work, your life, and your career?

L: Far from it. No. I don't think I have ever been satisfied with my career or my work. I've never really felt that I've done enough in any film. I felt the closest I came to it was *How I Won the War*, which I cannot look upon as a success because not enough people saw it. I'm more satisfied with that film than with any other film that I've made, and I'm quite dissatisfied with a great number of them.

Just quantitatively I'm disappointed, because I've always hoped to be able to do more than one film a year. But because of being totally involved in all the technical processes of filmmaking, I find that I cannot do more than one film a year, and that means no more than one idea a year. And if those ideas only work fifty per cent, then fifty per cent of my working life is wasted.

G: Do you have an ambition or something you'd like to do now that you've made it, in the sense of being able to choose your films and control them?

L: Only to continue exploring ideas that seem to be relevant to our times. Exploring major subjects—either by comedy or by serious films—exploring my own feelings, trying to expand my own life through film, and to expand the technique of filmmaking, to stretch filmmaking, to make it more satisfying to a wider audience. I think we all must aim for that. And that is almost an insurmountable task.

And it implies that filmmaking is a totally personal art, when, as we know, it is tied up in finance, banking, marketing, research, front of house posters, cold cinemas, rude usherettes, bad projection, insensitive distributors—all these things that come into play apart from one's own inefficiency and inability to totally commit to a project correctly. All this makes for partial failure. It would be marvelous if we could avoid it.

G: What do you want to be doing five years from now?

L: Well, I hope not making films. But I can't tell you what I would want to do. What I don't want to do is easier to say. And that is, I don't want to be out of touch with an audience—which is likely—and wandering about trying to set up a Senegalese-Upper Volta co-production, because I can't get financed properly for an idea that is five years out of date because the audience has moved on and I haven't. I don't want to be scrambling about on the fringes of filmmaking. I also don't want, in five years, to try to examine what I think my audience would want, at the exclusion of what *I* would want. I have always made films for myself, and hoped that they would be interesting to an audience.

G: What do you think is your function, or role, as a film director?

L: A director's job in this period of filmmaking—and I know that this may change, as it has in the past—is to be an absolute dictator and produce a personal vision on a subject that he has chosen. He is paid too much because he has that responsibility, and what the people who pay him are buying is that personal vision. He must be absolutely ruthless in producing an accurate vision. He must be a dilettante and interfere in every part of the production, and it must finally succeed or fail on the success or failure of his own personal vision.

G: Someone has described the film director's job as the best job in the world. What's your reaction to that?

L: I agree with it. Provided he is being allowed to do what he wants to do. I think it may be one of the most frustrating jobs in the world if he is under the unfair influence of someone who has more power than he does. That might be a producer, or a star upon whose name a film's financing depends. But a director working under optimum circumstances is in a very, very, very fortunate position, because he's a nonmilitant dictator.

MIKE NICHOLS

"It's a strange mistake to take
the kind of work I do seriously,
to think of it as important or
lasting. Plays are forgotten.
Film crumbles."

*There was always the impression with a Howard Hawks movie
that what really mattered was the life going on behind the cameras,
and that the movie which finally came out of it was an after-
thought. Hawks was able to animate a sort of private island life
within his company that made even a potboiler like* Hatari *seem
credible. Hawks was taking his friends and cast and crew on a
trip he wanted to make personally—and the film was both the
incidental excuse for and the record of that experience.*

*For Mike Nichols, too, directing is becoming a way of life.
From his start as a performer in improvisational cabaret at the
Compass Theater in Chicago, to his evolution into Broadway director and filmmaker, Nichols has regarded what he does as an
alternative to work. "It seemed better than getting a job," he
recalls of his Compass Theater days. "We didn't think of it as
work." He was improvising thirty to forty scenes a night for forty-
eight dollars.*

*The basis of Nichols' career is his concept of community—a
collaborative interplay between friends and colleagues. He is not
a loner. He is not a hustler. He is, in fact, disquieted by being in
vogue, being considered a Midas and a success.*

*"I'm really sick of the word success," he says. "Either I'm good,
or I'm pretty good, or I'm bad. But success seems to me beside
the point." He didn't take his Academy Award for* The Graduate
*seriously. He thought the film was a nice little comedy. And he
was startled and a little embarrassed by the furore which it caused.*

*"The things I've done," he has said, "are neither as good as the
people who carry on say they are, nor are they as bad as the reaction
to the reaction says they are. They're just sort of in-between."*

*Born in Berlin, November 1931, Nichols was raised in the United
States. After he was persuaded to be a director on the stage version
of* Barefoot in the Park, *he discovered he enjoyed the experience of
kibitzing with the actors and playwright and being a midwife to a*

*play. "If you're happy to be with the people you're doing it with,"
he says, "that's almost more important than what comes out."*

Nonetheless, working on seven plays was never as much agony as
Nichols felt while shooting his first two films. He panicked. By
Catch-22, though he still confided privately that he felt panic,
outwardly he appeared relaxed and he seemed to be enjoying the
filmmaking experience almost as much as working on a play.

"I don't think when I'm alone," he says. "That's why I'm a
director. I'm turned on by somebody else. A director works with
other people." Before leaving for Mexico, he sat for the following
interview in his penthouse duplex overlooking Central Park and
recollected a recent trip to Europe. It had been a business trip,
taken with members of the Catch-22 staff, to scout locations for the
scenes to be shot in Rome. While he was there, he auditioned the
local talent to choose two hundred whores for a big brothel scene.
"It's as much fun as I've had on any trip," he said.

Directing has become for Nichols a meaningful framework within
which he can travel with friends and create something in the process.
I suspect he is more interested in the process than the product.

Nichols is a reluctant superstar. With a record of seven hit plays
and two smash movies (The Graduate already having grossed upwards
of $50,000,000), he had the muscle to get $11,000,000 and total artistic
control of Catch-22. He can choose his projects and be assured of
financing, yet most of his personal pantheon of film directors—like
Buñuel, Renoir, Bergman, Fellini, Welles—were never popular with
mass audiences or the Hollywood moneymen. For so modest and astute
a sensibility, the irony is acutely discomfiting.

When Orson Welles came to Mexico at Nichols' invitation to
play General Dreedle in Catch-22, Nichols was deferential and
slightly apologetic. Welles had been trying for six years to buy the
screen rights to make the film himself but hadn't been able to get
the financing. His salary for the minor role in Catch-22 went to
pay for some trick shots in Dead Reckoning, which he was directing
in Europe. After working with Nichols, Welles said of him: "Nobody's
in his league with actors."

Another rare and significant tribute from a co-worker came from
cinematographer Robert Surtees. Writing in Action, the Directors
Guild publication, Surtees said of his experience on The Graduate:
"Mike was the boss. Nobody was going to come onto the set and
question what he did. They wouldn't dare; he wouldn't stand for
it. Which was nice for me. The only man I had to please was Mike
Nichols. The director runs the show. He makes the picture. You
have one allegiance—not to the studio, not to the producer, but

*to the director, and that's it. He's in charge of everything . . . The
picture is what the director makes it."*

A Nichols interview is a performance. Not being able to see and
hear him deliver his lines is to miss the inflection, the timing, the
arched eyebrow, the self-mocking tone, the interjections and ellipses
that get smoothed over in neat typography. He is not solemn or
pretentious about himself or his work and if this interview suggests
otherwise I fear it has done him an injustice. His reaction, for
instance, to a 7500-word analysis of The Graduate in The New
Yorker was that the young author of the article had thought more
about his film than he had.

FILMOGRAPHY:

WHO'S AFRAID OF VIRGINIA WOOLF? ('66)
THE GRADUATE ('67)
CATCH-22 ('70)

GELMIS: How are you going to make a movie out of a book which has been described by some as an anti-novel?

NICHOLS: Very slowly.

G: Why are you using Guaymas, Mexico, instead of a Mediterranean island?

N: We looked all over Sicily and Corsica, but all those places are just too developed now. Guaymas was perfect. We've built our own runway, base, and roads. We have the sixth largest air force in the world. We come right after France. We may take over Mexico.

G: What kind of preparations have you made on *Catch-22*? Did you see any war movies?

N: One or two.

G: Did you see anything useful?

N: Not useful. Because *Catch-22* isn't a literal rendering of what happened. It's a dream. And there's 60 or 70 per cent of it that I don't know how we're going to do. I just have certain sort of landmarks in it that I can see or hear. Certain people. The central thing of a picture for me is the rhythm of the atmosphere and the mood and how you get from one mood to another mood, or how you sustain the mood. And those are the things you just sort of feel around in yourself for, and the bunch of you find together when you're doing it.

G: You once told me the film is about dying.

N: Yes, it's about dying. And the theme is about when you get off. At what point do you draw the line beyond which you won't go?

G: Do you think of *Catch-22* as an anti-war film?

N: I suppose.

G: Does that word disturb you? Anti-war? Does it sound too pious?

N: Nobody wants to make a pro-war film. And I don't know what an anti-war film is. It's like "Fuck Hate." Nobody likes war. It'd be like making an anti-evil film. Or a pro-good film.

G: Yet John Wayne's *The Green Berets* glorified war and was a jingoistic defense of our tactics in Vietnam. It may have been the worst film of 1968, technically as well as morally, but it was a tremendous popular success in America.

N: I didn't see it. But it sounds like it's more of an article than a movie. *Catch-22* seems to me to have less to do with war, as I say, than with drawing the line. There's a book by Bruno Bettelheim about Jews in concentration camps during the war. Not the death camps but the work camps. To some extent, it changed my life.

He says that the people who asked, "Why me?" were lost. Because "Why me?" is the first step in a progression that takes you to agreeing with the people who are persecuting you. Only the people who kept their free choice survived, he says—and he was there, in the camp. Their only remaining choice was their opinion of what was being done to them. It couldn't be expressed, but they could hold on to it.

And he says that the people who drew the line for themselves— who said: "Beyond *this* point I will not go. If I'm asked to hurt another person, I will throw myself on the electric fence"—kept their sense of themselves and survived. The others, who didn't draw the line, who didn't say, "So far, and no further," quietly died after a few weeks. They just disintegrated and died. That's a big theme, but I hope that that's what *Catch-22* will be partially about: that you can't live unless you know what you'll stop at.

G: Do you look forward to the four months or so you'll be spending in a fairly hot, remote section of Mexico with the same people—some of whom may get temperamental during the filming?

N: The actual shooting of the film I dread. Even now, a week before I leave for Mexico, the panic has started. But I like the people who've been chosen for the film. And I like the kind of island life that you have on a movie. You're away from everything. You're away from evenings and dinners and parties and gossip. On *Catch-22* we all like each other. There isn't that weak link. There isn't that shmuck who makes everybody roll his eyes.

G: Why do you keep alternating between directing live theater and movies?

N: Mostly for the pleasure of rehearsing. I love rehearsing more than anything in work, with the possible exception of cutting a film. Those are the two best parts. I'm very happy in the theater with actors, fooling around. You have nothing but time. The luxury of being able to say, "Don't worry about it, we'll figure it out next week, next month. Let's leave this scene alone." Or to do a scene, and three days later to be able to say, "I know what we're doing wrong." Or, "I thought of something." That's such a luxury. It's like being on a huge double bed after being on this bed of nails.

G: What emotions do you have while you're making a movie? Are you bored by those tedious repetitions of changing the lights or setting up camera angles for the same scene?

N: I am never bored. I hate it, because it is almost constant pain. Until the cutting, which is almost constant pleasure. The reason one is very loving with actors and sympathetic with them when making a movie is that you all have a terrible sense that it's forever and that you'll never get another chance to do this minute, or two minutes, or thirty seconds. It causes grave anxiety and panic.

Different actors try to solve it in different ways. Some keep kidding around, to tell themselves it's really all right and to loosen up. Some stay intensely concentrated. But we all know that whichever take it is, that's it and we won't get another crack at it. That makes a knot in my stomach when I'm shooting a picture. So I don't enjoy it.

And there was another very unpleasant aspect to *Who's Afraid of Virginia Woolf?* for all of us. We had to keep coming back to the same damn room, over and over, every day. And the poor Burtons had to spit at each other for days and hit each other. They were very smart about it, in between. There was a lot of reading and eating and chewing of gum and jokes. But it was strange.

I said to someone while I was making *The Graduate*, "Remind me that I'm not enjoying this." I always forget afterwards. When I'm in the cutting room and we've got two reels together, it's wonderful. Or when you go to the first previews. We had two previews of *The Graduate*, and that first reaction of the audience astonished us all. I hadn't thought of it as either that funny or that rousing. I was very unnerved when they began to make noises and cheer at the end.

So, by then, I forget. It's the way women talk about having children. I hate it while I'm doing it. Every morning, I think, "Oh Christ, what am I going to do today?" That's perfectly true. It's not an illusion. Then in the cutting room it begins to be pleasure. And when it's over, I'm not entirely without some pride in it. And I forget that I hated doing it.

G: What is it about cutting that gives you so much pleasure?

N: You can take out things you hate. You can make things happen that never happened. You can have actors do things they never did. For instance, there was a scene in *Who's Afraid of Virginia Woolf?* that never happened. There was a long monologue of Elizabeth's that didn't work, through no fault of hers. And we took little tiny bits of it and put it on the soundtrack over that overhead shot of her yelling for George, going to the car, walking around the backyard, which had been a silent scene. We *made* a scene.

Another example is when you don't like the way an actor reads a line. So you take three words from one take and two words from another and a breath from a third and you finally hear the line the way you want to hear it. That's very much like tinkering with a play.

G: Sam O'Steen has been your editor on all three films. How did you get together with him?

N: He was a young guy who had only cut one or two pictures. And he was assigned to *Who's Afraid of Virginia Woolf?* to assist the big expert, Doan Harrison. I liked Doan very much, but we didn't understand each other too well. He was technically oriented and traditionally trained to thinking in terms of a shot which establishes everything, and so on and so forth. Sam and I just immediately hit it off. Doan soon left.

We had a great time telling the story from the actors' best moments and making our own cutting pattern. I picked the take, always. Sometimes I couldn't make up my mind until the weekend, and then we'd look again and then I'd pick the take. I'd tell him what I'd like to use and to cut to this and then to cut to that and so forth. Sometimes he did it. Sometimes he said, "That's dumb. Let me do it my way."

Often we'd argue about something. He'd cut something, and I'd say, "No, that's not what I was going to do when I shot this." And he'd insist, "Will you please just look at it." And, often as not, I'd end up agreeing. I'll give you an example of how people making a movie work with each other. That naked scene in *The Graduate*. I shot it for days, because I had a certain thing I was after. It had been an inspiration of Dick Sylbert, the art director.

Sylbert had said, "You know, that characteristic thing about California girls when you see the white marks where they don't get tanned, where the straps were, and the beginning of the brassiere where it gets white . . ." So I said, "Great, right, we've got to do that." And I shot all those patches of white skin and Sam and I had a hundred combinations of flashes of all that. And it didn't work and it didn't work and it didn't work. Until finally he called me and said, "Come here, I've got something for you to see."

He had found the one funny take, which was just Dustin, over Anne's shoulder, freaking out. And I said, "Of course, that's it, it's very simple." And then I added, "Now what if we put in quick flashes of what he sees. Look, look where his eyes go, and then he rolls them back. Why don't we stick in what he's reacted to before he rolls his eyes back?" That's an example of what I love most about making pictures. That's three guys now. Four, counting Dustin. And who did what is very hard to trace. We all did it together.

G: You seem to work best when you have someone you can bounce ideas off of—people like Elaine May, Neil Simon, Murray Schisgal, and, now, Buck Henry.

N: Yes, that's absolutely right. It's the only way I know to do it. Otherwise, I would be a writer. I need these other people. I need someone to turn me on. With certain people you find yourself thinking things you wouldn't be able to think without them. And the experience always is, with any of these collaborators, that each person blames himself first. The worst theater experience—the one I never understand—is where various people in Boston are screaming at each other, "If you'd only done this, and you hadn't done that."

The experience that I had with Elaine, with Simon, and with Buck and the others is if something isn't going right, the writer is always saying, "I've got to fix this." And I say, "No, no, no. I've got to restage it." And the actor says, "No, it's me. I've got to play it another way. Let me try something." You know, if you're happy to be with the people you're doing it with, that's almost more important than what comes out.

G: You've said that you hope to start a theater in New York where you could work with your old friends from the Compass Theater in Chicago.

N: Yes, I keep having this impulse to get everybody back together. Barbara Harris and all the people who worked together. We miss each other. And I find on everything I do that I prefer working with friends. So what we're going to do now in a very half-assed, unpressured way is that Elaine, Paul Sills, and I are starting a theater in New York. Paul stayed in Chicago with *Second City*. And he started a thing called Theater Games, a sort of community theater. We're still very close. Paul will do what he feels like doing at our theater in New York and if Elaine has time or I have time we'll do something together. It just seems important to me to close the circle, for the people who started out together to end up together.

G: What were those early days as a student at the University of Chicago like?

N: I had a lot of jobs. I was a night janitor in a children's nursery. And I eventually discovered that they didn't know when I was mopping the floor. So I just used to read all night. Then I worked for the post office. There were a lot of college guys there who would check in and go home and go to bed, get up in the morning, go back and sign out. I drove this huge three-ton truck and I would pull up to little old ladies and ask for help in finding addresses because I could never find any of them. I never did make a single delivery of any package. After a time, I was fired.

I was a desk clerk in a hotel. And I was a judge in a jingle contest. There are companies which judge jingle contests. And there's no decision ever made, really. I worked on a contest about a house where the first line was "This house has charms that grow and grow." First you eliminate all the ones that don't rhyme. That leaves you with 40 per cent. Then you drop the dirty ones. Then you eliminate all the ones that don't scan. Then you forget about the ones that make no sense of any kind. Finally, you are left with one jingle. And so nobody has to exercise an opinion.

G: How did you become a performer?

N: I came to New York and studied with Lee Strasberg. I couldn't get a job of any kind. As long as I could, I ate on extended credit at Chinese restaurants. But it got desperate and I was starving, starving. Once I ate a jar of mustard because that was all there was left in the fridge. I knew it was time to go back to Chicago. Then Elaine, Paul, Barbara, Alan Arkin, and I went to work in a restaurant cabaret called the Compass. My acting experience in New York hadn't been too practical. All I could really do was cry, which wasn't very useful.

We got thirty-five dollars a week and then went on strike and got forty-eight. It seemed better than getting a job. We didn't think of it as work. We would make up thirty or forty scenes a night. At first it was lousy. But then it got better and it finally ran about three years.

G: Though you've directed *Who's Afraid of Virginia Woolf?*, most people still think of you as a director of comedy because you began with *Barefoot in the Park* onstage and have been making audiences laugh since then. I know the reputation disturbs you.

N: It may be something wrong with me. But I can't understand that distinction: this is a comedy, this is a drama, this is a tragedy. How do you classify Samuel Beckett? Beckett is a laugh riot. Is it comedy? I don't know anything in the theater that's remarkable in which people don't laugh at certain points. It's like life.

People used to think that comedy meant talking very fast and running around and slamming doors a lot and saying the big lines right out to the audience. We were working on a scene in *Barefoot in the Park* and Elizabeth Ashley had this long monologue where her husband is coming up the six flights of stairs and she's saying, "Oh, your mother called and your sister's got a new boyfriend," and that sort of thing.

And then the gag at the end was that it wasn't her husband at all, and she gets embarrassed and you hear a door slam. We rehearsed that and I said, "Elizabeth, supposing in the play at the end of this exact same speech, a man comes in and kills you. Would you do the scene the same way?" And she said, "I guess not."

And it occurred to both of us that it's a mistake to do something a certain way just because it's a comedy. Why not talk the way people talk? Because people don't know what's going to happen next. And that's why I hate and refuse to make that distinction. Life is not a comedy and life is not a tragedy, whatever the hell it is. It may be both.

What the director is saying to his audience is, "This happened to me; did it happen to you too?" Metaphorically, almost always, not literally. The impulse is strong to say to whoever is watching, "You too?" So I don't think of the humor in, for instance, *The Graduate* as being manipulative but almost as a way of checking with other people. "Do you experience things as I do? Is it like that for you?"

G: Yet, W. C. Fields and the Marx Brothers were always exaggerations of life.

N: Yes, but they took a leap past reality as geniuses of that kind can.

G: Where do you land when you take that kind of leap? Supercharged reality?

N: I'm not sure where it is. Maybe it's caricature or surrealism. The Marx Brothers were completely surreal. I'm not saying it can't be done. What interests me is not making the distinction. Let them be like people, and if something funny happens, something funny happens. And if it makes you sad, it makes you sad. But why decide?

The first question is the one the audience asks: "Why are you telling me this?" And you have to know why. And then you ask the audience a question, the only question I know to ask. You say, "Is this like your life? Does this remind you of something? Does it seem familiar at all?" If you're lucky, it does.

G: How did you make the transition from theater to films?

N: Larry Turman, whom I had only met once or twice at parties, came to me with *The Graduate* when I was doing some play or other. I had thought about directing movies, and I had been offered Beverly Hills-type comedies. But nothing else. Larry brought the book to me. I read it and the next day I said I'd do it. And I was to do it rather soon. Then I was offered *Who's Afraid of Virginia Woolf?*, which I wanted very much to do. So Larry let me postpone *The Graduate*.

G: Why did you want to film *Who's Afraid of Virginia Woolf?*, since you realized that adapting a stage play imposes certain limitations?

N: I was a stage director. And a beginner, too. I think I'd been doing it for two or three years. And I loved *Who's Afraid of Virginia Woolf?* I thought it was a remarkable and interesting and funny play. I just thought, "What a great chance to do this material. Material like this may not come again in my lifetime." Why the hell not? How lucky to get a chance to do the movie, especially since I felt I understood it quite well. How lucky to get a chance to protect it, to some extent. To protect it from being turned into God knows what—"the child was real, but had committed suicide" or whatever else might have been done with it.

G: How do you account for the tremendous difference in styles between your first two films?

N: *Who's Afraid of Virginia Woolf?* and *The Graduate* seem to me two completely different problems. *Virginia Woolf* was a play that belonged very much to the man who'd written it. I liked the play and wanted to serve Albee and what he was concerned with. We did not try to "open it up," which is the popular idea of what a filmmaker does with a play. You know what happens? If you make a picture of a play, either you leave it as it was and people say, "You didn't open it up enough and it wasn't *filmic*," or you have some of it take place in various locations, and they say, "He lost the essential claustrophobic quality of the play."

Because a play usually takes place continuously, those are the two choices you have. In this case, the action occurs not only continuously but in one room. And I figured that people do not come home, sit down in their living room and start to talk to each other. I don't. And I don't know anybody who does. You come home. You take your shoes off. You go get something out of the ice box. You go to the bathroom. And it seemed to me that a film of *Virginia Woolf* could give that kind of freedom but that the real task was simply to examine those characters and the things that happen between them.

I know of no way to make *Who's Afraid of Virginia Woolf?* different in substance. I'll tell you something. There was a time when Lehman and I were working on it and I had a plan which grew out of my own feeling of claustrophobia. This was to make *Virginia Woolf* take place during Homecoming Week. There would be a kind of Walpurgis Nacht on the campus. Students burning things, racing this way and that. A kind of semi-real hell would be taking place. And I got, if not excited, at least interested in it for a week or two. I had various scenes worked out.

G: It sounds like an exciting idea.

N: It seemed exciting. One of the good things about collaboration is that it doesn't matter who's right as long as one of you is and both of you recognize it. In this case, Lehman was. And I knew it the minute he said it. He said, "They must be alone in the room. It must take place while everyone else is asleep. That's the kind of hell it is." It seemed to me unarguably right, and that was the end of my fires and burnings of effigies and so on.

G: Were you happy with the film?

N: I haven't seen *Who's Afraid of Virginia Woolf?* since it opened, but it seemed to me that there were certain things that I'm pleased with in it that have to do with what you can do on film and not on the stage. By which I mean, concentrating on the experience of one character. For instance, George going for the gun became *his* experience . . . When you take *Virginia Woolf* from the stage and put it in a movie, you lose one character: the audience. Because the audience, much more than in most other plays, is a character in that play.

If you and I are having a fight in front of an audience, every time I score off you and they laugh you get pissed off at me. They become part of the play. Then you have to get back at me. If you can get a laugh from them at me, you've won a point. And that sort of circus duel is a huge element of *Virginia Woolf*. But obviously you can't have it in the film.

G: What did the imaginary child represent for you?

N: I've always thought the child was a metaphor for a couple of things. One is for what exists between people when they love each other and what they build between each other. The worst thing that two people who've loved each other can do is to distort, to shit on the past. It is the single cruelest, and the one unforgivable thing that one lover can do to another. To say, "Not only don't we have it now. We never had it." That seems to me the most powerful thing the child is.

Then it also appears to be connected with George and Martha's hangup, which is one that I'm sympathetic with. Namely, the need to attack what is good. So that the child is also a metaphor for those strange people that you see occasionally, angels, that seem to pad around loving their friends, doing no harm. I think they exist. And I think they are invariably attacked and destroyed.

G: Some people explain the metaphoric child with the theory that *Who's Afraid of Virginia Woolf?* was written originally for four homosexuals but it was changed to heterosexual couples for Broadway.

N: I think that's nonsense. If Edward Albee wanted to write a play about four men, he would and he could. He wrote a play about two men, *The Zoo Story*. Also, when you're attacking the problem of the play, it becomes an insane idea. What do these people propose? That the son of the president of the university has lived for twenty-one years with his boy friend and he is entertaining for the evening the new science teacher with his boy friend? It has no meaning. The whole thing disintegrates.

So much of the play is about Martha's disappointment in George not living up to her father and not taking over the university. Do they assume that Albee tacked all this on because he was deprived of his original idea? Then at the end you would discover that the entire play was tacked on, because with the exception of that truthful thing about the child—that it's impossible for two men to have a child—there is nothing in the text to substantiate it.

It seems to me that there are things in *Virginia Woolf* that must be true in the lives of homosexuals. Things having to do with sado-masochism, with who's on top, with jockeying for position, with humiliating the partner. But that's not exclusive to them, Christ knows. Men and women know a lot about that too.

G: There were hardly any subliminal or subjective moments introduced from outside the material you were being so faithful to in *Virginia Woolf*, compared to the barrage you would use later in *The Graduate*. One of those moments involved the abandoned station wagon's eerily blinking directional signal, as if to infer something had gone out of control.

N: I have to go back. There was a wild scene that I put into the picture the moment after Martha leaves George in the parking lot. It was a bloodcurdling scene. It consisted of Martha driving the car, very upset, Nick sitting next to her and Honey lying down invisible in the back seat. They drove for a while. And Martha obviously made some kind of resolve. Her hand left the wheel and disappeared out of the frame in the direction of Nick's lap. Nick's head came up slightly and he shifted a little in his seat.

Then he turned around very sweetly to the back seat and said, "Are you all right, Honey?" And then he turned back. And his hand left the frame and Martha smiled slightly and they zoomed out of the shot. It was frightening. When I saw it, I said it had to go because the scene shouldn't be theirs, it's George's. This whole thing is happening to George and we must stay with George.

And what George sees when he has walked home is that Martha has drunkenly left the car half up on the sidewalk and the directional signal is going, because Martha is a slob, and also because there's a kind of call for help, which is Martha, all the time: "Stop me before I screw more."

G: Why did a film with four actors and a couple of sets cost $5,000,000?

N: I think it had mostly to do with the price of the property, which was immense, and the price of the Burtons. That was $2,500,000 right there. For the rest of it, it took us a long time. We ran into bad weather in Northampton and waited between two and three weeks and weren't able to shoot. If I had had any sense, we never would have gone to Northampton. We would have done it on a stage. For all you can see, there isn't that much visible difference. I still don't know whether I was right or wrong. I was certainly extravagant in wanting the actors to be on a real college in real winter with their breaths really showing and really at night. How much we gained from it, I couldn't tell you.

G: Why did you want to do it that way? Was it simply a way of coaxing genuine emotions out of your actors by placing them in an authentic academic environment?

N: In this case, yes. I had in mind a couple that I'd known at the University of Chicago all along when we built the set, when we picked the books, when we chose the bookshelves made of planks and bricks and so forth. And the cups, those green mugs this guy had at the University of Chicago. It seemed to me that for the actors it would be useful to be at a real college, to smell it and walk around it. It's the kind of thing that's a gamble. You can't measure what you've gotten from it.

G: Some critics felt that Elizabeth Taylor was too young at thirty-five for the role of a fifty-seven-year-old woman, despite the makeup. And that she was more strident than anguished.

N: When I found out that Elizabeth was going to play Martha, my first reaction was: "Yes, I can see it. I know what they mean. I absolutely can see something in Elizabeth that can play Martha." The age never concerned me.

G: Yet she is a beauty, and not the sort of Mary McCarthy-Elizabeth Hardwick intellectual one expected in the role.

N: The brilliant, over-educated, ball-cutting woman who also has womanly feelings and alternates between them is a very specific type. No movie star that I've ever known or heard of could be expected to capture that specific character element. It's that very specific poet's wife, or professor's wife, whose hair escapes from the knot at the back of her head, whose dress doesn't quite fit, who's read everything and laughs at Simone De Beauvoir, who says what, in effect, Martha said in the play: "abstruse in the sense of recondite. Don't you tell me words." That's very far outside most actresses' experience.

The fact is that Elizabeth *does* know about what you could call the center of the piece, which is the intimate and possibly painful connection between people. I think that's what she did, that's what she brought.

G: What did you do, exactly, when you first knew you'd direct a movie? Did you go back and read the textbooks, Pudovkin? Did you see a lot of movies at the Museum of Modern Art?

N: I started to read the books, but I couldn't make head or tail of any of them. You know what those books are: "For fear, put the camera low and shoot up . . ." I had been going to the movies a lot, anyway. And I started trying to see what they were doing, with great difficulty. Because I would keep starting to follow the story, and forget and would have to sit through it again. And I would ask friends who made or had been in movies: "Well, what would we do if we were just sitting here? How could it be shot?" I don't think I did much more to prepare, except worry. And, oh yes, I remember what else I did. I tried to run the movie in my mind before I made it.

G: In what sense?

N: I visualized what each scene would look like in advance.

G: Did you sketch at all?

N: Yes. I got a sketch artist. And he made a few sketches for me, and then I stopped him. I preferred to see it in my head. There were certain things, such as, for instance, George's going for the gun, or the car blinker light, or, most of all, I think, the parking lot, that I saw long before I started to work with Lehman on the script.

But I remember there was a day we did a makeup test. It was the first time I was ever behind a camera. The shot consisted of an actor coming in a door. I was also secretly trying to practice. And I really panicked. I thought, "Good Christ, I don't know how to bring them in the door. Where is the camera? If they open it, won't the door hit the camera? If it's so far back, do they walk into the camera?"

I didn't know any of those fundamental things. So I really froze. And I had advisors all over the place. I had Doan Harrison, who'd been lent me by Billy Wilder, and I had the sketch artist, and Haskell Wexler (the cameraman, who later won an Oscar for *Who's Afraid of Virginia Woolf?*). Haskell said, "Well, it would be interesting if they did this and then we'd see them disappear behind the wall as they were walking and then we'd see them again."

That was the hardest moment on the film for me. I felt, "I must decide. I can't do a shot just because Haskell Wexler says it's interesting. Only I know what's happening, and what will happen next." So I said to myself, "Shmuck, you don't know anything and you have to pretend that you do." And that was the worst hump I got over. After that, I don't know, I sort of made it up.

G: What were some of the films you studied?

N: I ran *8½* for the tenth time. And I watched a lot of movies, but I can't say I studied them.

G: You've been quoted as saying that you borrowed bits of style from various directors you admired. Could you elaborate? Who were the directors?

N: That was a tongue-in-cheek comment. I had been somewhat bugged by all the "influence" talk. A prominent critic said about both pictures that I was influenced by Kurosawa. He said that when he saw *Virginia Woolf* he thought he detected the influence of Kurosawa and that after seeing *The Graduate* he was sure. It wasn't a put-down. He thought it was wonderful. He was very pleased.

Now, I've seen just one Kurosawa picture, *Ikiru*, and I saw it *after* I finished with *The Graduate*, at Norman Jewison's house. It's a great film, but it's about Japanese people. I hadn't seen any Kurosawa. And then there was various attribution to this guy and to that guy. At which point I thought, I've been incredibly influenced, but you can't tell me by whom. I defy you to tell me by whom.

I've been influenced by Thomas Mann, you know, and Mozart and Pogo and, as it happens, George Stevens was very important to me. *A Place in the Sun* was the first American picture that really rocked me. I've seen it many times. There are technical things in *A Place in the Sun* that stayed in my mind and I think I used part of it.

G: Could you be specific with a few examples of technical things you remember?

N: Yes. There was a long dissolve in which the thing that remains gains extra meaning by hanging on. Like, he did it with the bar in the court. Clift was pretending to the Shelley Winters character, Alice Tripp by name, that they were going to be married. He knew the courthouse would be closed. And he and Shelley Winters stood in front of an empty courthouse, where you saw the bar, arguing about what they could do, how could they get married?

Clift says, "Let's go off for a picnic, then we'll get married tomorrow," meanwhile planning to kill her. And as Stevens did the dissolve of them driving to the lake, the bar—where he'll later be judged for her murder—is still lingering on the screen, just hanging there in that long, long dissolve.

That's one thing. Another thing is having something happen, something sexual happen, when it's so dark that you really have to make up what you think you're seeing physically. Stevens did a kind of novelistic thing with that whole picture. There are wonderful secrets in that picture that feed into the overall effect of it.

The great love theme is based on the horn of Elizabeth Taylor's Cadillac. The dogs, there's a thing with the dogs that's terrific. The first time Clift thinks vaguely about killing Shelley Winters, practically subliminally, you hear dogs barking. And from that point the dogs get louder and louder and after he's killed her he runs into some Boy Scouts whose dog yaps at him. And he goes right from that to the district attorney's German Shepherd, barking and snarling in his car. Those are nice private things that feed into the picture.

G: Feed in what sense? What is the effect or value of subliminal motifs?

N: The thing about something that's made right—whether it's a novel, or an opera, or a film—has to do with being hung on a spine. Why do composers go to all the truble of inverting what they did in the first act? Or basing, let's say, the score of *West Side Story* on five notes? And each song is a variation of this theme that Bernstein had in his head. Why is it useful? I think because the stronger the spine, the stronger the backbone of the thing that you're making, the more—whether openly or secretly—everything that happens is tied into that backbone. The more solid it is, maybe the truer it is.

When you work on a play you discover that every choice you make, every costume, every radiator on the set, the placement of everything, has to do with the spine that you've chosen. *Barefoot in the Park*, which couldn't be a lighter and more harmless comedy, seemed to me to be about the sexual awakening of a young girl and what proceeded out of that. If you make a decision like that about a play, it affects everything. Then the bedroom is central. Then the place you put the bedroom in the set is important, and so on.

Look, work is a series of problems that you try to solve whether you're good or not. And I'm convinced that was true for Shakespeare too. He was simply solving a problem. "This line, this foot. Next line." And that's all there is to it.

I think it's a strange mistake to take the kind of work I do seriously, to think of it as important or lasting. Plays are forgotten. Film crumbles. We all tend to make the mistake of thinking film is forever. For about fifty years. The prints disintegrate. Already now, there are great films of which no print exists. It's not forever.

There was a time when I really thought about this. And I concluded: "The biggest kind of shmuck wants to be remembered. And the next biggest kind of shmuck wants to remember you. And the least shmuck of all simply gathers information to take into his grave."

G: You've said that you resent being called a "success."

N: I loved rehearsing my first play, *Barefoot in the Park*. And I enjoyed thinking: "I think I can direct. This is fun. And I seem to be doing what I want to do." Then the reviews came out, and I was pleased. But I'm really sick of the word success. I'm insulted to be called a success. Either I'm good, or I'm pretty good, or I'm bad. But success seems to me beside the point. Nobody walks around a *success*.

I don't even know that I want to go on, at all. When I saw Kubrick, I said: "I don't know why the hell I do this. Tell me why you do it, because I'm not so sure I love doing it." And he said, "It's better to do it than not to do it." I suppose that's true. It explains why I keep making films though there are so many things involved that panic or distress me.

Film directors have very short working lives, with rare exceptions. You don't get to do it for very long. Whatever it is, I don't think it lasts. Since I'm not even sure I can *do* it to begin with, I'm constantly aware that it's going to go. Almost everyone I've admired comes to a point at which he seems to lose, I don't know, some sense of self-censorship or . . . it goes. I don't mean the vogue, or the reaction, because the reaction will be over next Monday. I mean the ability, whatever it is. If the ability exists, I'm not sure how long you hang on to it.

G: Can we talk about your use of sound in *The Graduate?* You used sound overlaps prominently, as in the sequence where Benjamin is still in the pool and the telephone is ringing in the next scene.

N: It was meant to be that the thing which you are seeing now leads to the one you are hearing. This boy in this diving suit at the bottom of this pool has been caused by this moment to call Mrs. Robinson.

There's another point to be made about the use of sound in *The Graduate*, which is that the audience is addressed at three separate points in the picture. In the opening of the picture, the first thing you hear is "Ladies and gentlemen, we're about to begin our descent into Los Angeles." It's a straight announcement. The second time there's a sound overlap, you hear, as Benjamin is walking towards his car, away from Mrs. Robinson: "Ladies and gentlemen, attention please for this afternoon's feature attraction . . ." and it's his father at the pool.

Then it happens when he's at the bottom of the pool. You hear him call Mrs. Robinson. And in each case, it was thought of as an organic thing: This thing that happens now leads to the next thing. They are the same. They are interlocked.

G: What story, if any, were you trying to tell with *The Graduate*?

N: I think it was the story of a not particularly bright, not particularly remarkable but worthy kid drowning among objects and things, committing moral suicide by allowing himself to be used finally like an object or a thing by Mrs. Robinson, because he doesn't have the moral or intellectual resources to do what a large percentage of other kids like him do—to rebel, to march, to demonstrate, to turn on. Just drowning.

Then finding himself to some extent, finding a part of himself that he hadn't found, through connection with a girl. Finding passion, because of impossibility. Impossibility always leads to passion, and vice versa. Going from passion to a kind of insanity. Saving himself temporarily from being an object, through the passion and insanity. Getting what he thinks he wanted and beginning to subside back into the same world in which he has to live, with not enough changed. I think that's the story.

G: William Hanley and Calder Willingham had each written scripts for *The Graduate* which you didn't like. How did you happen to get together with Buck Henry?

N: I knew that Buck was extraordinary and funny and incredibly intelligent underneath all that kidding around. So we hired him. He never read anything but the novel. He never read the earlier scripts. He wrote an excellent, very long first draft. And then he and I spent literally six months working five, six hours a day. Now, three of those hours were spent goofing off and screwing around and making up horrifying stage directions for what Benjamin might be doing while he was driving along, playing with himself.

I took advantage of Buck to really figure out ways of shooting things. Like that whole montage—out of the pool, into Mrs. Robinson's bed, back and forth, ending up leaping out of the water, landing on Mrs. Robinson—Buck and I did together over days and days and days. Discovering Benjamin in the diving suit was entirely Buck's. That was in his first draft.

G: What inspired him to see Benjy in a diving suit? Is that from the book?

N: Yes. In the book, there's a whole scene where he's given a present and told to go ahead and open it. But Buck figured how to use it in the picture—to announce the thing and to have him suddenly discovered in the suit moving out toward the pool.

G: How much of the book of *The Graduate* did you use?

N: A great deal of the dialogue is straight from the book. Another portion of the dialogue—the "plastics" and such scenes—is entirely Buck's. The change of emphasis and the environment, Charles Webb, the author, didn't concern himself with at all. Reading the book, you think, "What's the matter with Benjamin?" We knew from the beginning that one of the problems to solve was to make visible what was bugging him. But I get credit for a great many decisions and contributions that were Buck's.

G: Which came first, the song "Sounds of Silence" or *The Graduate*?

N: While I was in the middle of shooting *The Graduate*, and I had not made a decision yet about music, my brother came to visit me and brought me a Simon and Garfunkel album. I'd never heard them, except for one song on the radio. I started playing it in the bathroom in the morning, when I was showering and shaving. And the more I heard "Sounds of Silence," the more it sounded to me, as it happened, like what the picture was about.

I had already thought of the airport scene, with the announcement. But I kept thinking about the song. Then I decided we'd get Simon and Garfunkel. I wanted them because they sounded to me like the voice of Benjamin. Full of feeling and not very articulate. They touched me immensely, as they do personally. So we hired them and they wrote some other songs.

But we had already cut certain sections of the film to "Sounds of Silence" and "Scarborough Fair." And they seemed so right to Sam O'Steen and me that whatever Simon and Garfunkel wrote was never as right as those. So finally I said, "Well, screw it." I liked the idea of using existing music, anyway. If I ever use music in a picture again, I'd like it to be Bach or Vivaldi or Mozart or whatever seems to me to fit because at least it has some echoes of our lives, and also they're better composers than are available in Hollywood.

G: One of the things that *The Graduate* has been said to have is those Christ symbols which frequently get read into films. You've insisted in public that you never intended any such symbolism. Could you explain the lyric reference in the song "Mrs. Robinson" to Jesus—"Jesus loves you more than you will know"—coming out of nowhere? And at the end of the film, it's been noted that Benjy raises his arms in church and moans like a man being crucified. Later he uses a crucifix to beat the congregation and then to lock them in their church. And whenever he's upset, he says, "Jesus" or "Christ."

N: So do we all.

G: Was there a second level of some sort that you were trying to play off the Christ thing?

N: *Good Christ, no!* . . . The line was there, one, because Paul wrote it, two, because what it meant to me was a very specific attitude towards Mrs. Robinson. Do you remember when Salinger was talking about Seymour's mother-in-law? Do you remember that passage? He says, "She was born without a sense of the poetry that runs through life, all life, and yet she manages to go to matinees and have lunch with her friends and play cards. I find her unimaginably brave." And whatever "Jesus loves you more than you will know" meant to Paul, that's what it meant to me. And that's why I bought it for the picture.

Secondly, Benjamin's arms are not *outstretched*. They are *up*. He is pounding on the glass. There was an image that Buck and I had discussed. It came from endless talks between Sylbert and me about the essence of Beverly Hills and California and all the glass and all the water and all the artificial grass. There's all this nature, but you're completely separated from it by glass. We had in our minds certain images having to do with glass, with water, with being separated, with being cut off. And our thought about Benjamin up there in the church was like a moth fluttering at a window. That's all. I'm sorry everybody thinks of it that way.

G: And what about the crucifix?

N: Right. The crucifix is in the book. And I think it's very reasonably in the book because what the hell are you going to grab in a church if you're going to beat people off? You can't grab a priest. You can't grab a rock. The nearest thing was a giant metal crucifix. We had a technical problem. How's he going to keep all those hundreds of people from stopping him? Well, he's got to jam something in the door. What has he got in his hands? He's got the crucifix. Well, hey, why doesn't he just use it?

In the book, he just runs away. It's like "once out of the burning room." But I thought, "He's got to jam that door, or they're all going to follow him." Now, here's the point that should be made about all this. I suppose I must take the responsibility for all this Christ nonsense. Because if it's capable of being interpreted that way, I've got to take it. But it came about through a series of practical decisions and it crossed none of our minds.

G: There are no set speeches in a complex film like *The Graduate* to tell the audience what the author's point, or message, or intent, or stance is. Instead, you offer a juxtaposition of images which you put together partly in the script and partly, as you said earlier, created from nothing in a cutting room. Well, some images are more supercharged or symbol-laden than others, as in the case of a crucifix. So that people understandably get more visceral stimulation and inferences than the director consciously intended. Do you feel we lose or gain when the ambiguity of supercharged images or objects causes an audience to see meanings you never consciously put in the film?

N: We gain. And I think it's part of what gets us all about movies. It's that movies are more than they were, just by virtue of being on film. I think a film can easily be more than the people who made it. I agree with you.

G: If ambiguity is a natural outcome of these images which are put together, at what point does an audience ever know what the director, the writer, or the "guiding consciousness" had in mind?

N: Never. You don't know in a novel. You certainly don't know in a play. Possibly a novel is a bad example, because it's explicit whereas a play or movie is implicit by its nature. We will never know what a playwright had in his mind. And no one will ever know what a film director or a screen writer had in his mind. It either hangs together and joins your life and becomes part of you and you trust it, or it doesn't.

It's very much like a person. You either trust a person, or you don't. You don't know why. It has nothing to do with what they say. It has nothing to do with how they look. Nobody knows what it has to do with. You buy them or you don't. I think it's the same with films. And we'll never know about each other. You'll never know really what I mean. I'll never know exactly what you mean. It's a kind of electricity that can sometimes be set up where we both get the illusion that we're saying the same thing or that we mean the same thing.

G: Some critics felt *The Graduate* was brilliant in many ways but that it was structurally flawed, that the carefully constructed beginning was one kind of film, while the romance with the girl was another, bearing no relevance to it. Do you see any structural slippage?

N: It doesn't bother me, because it was deliberate on our parts. The picture changes in every way. The whole section with Mrs. Robinson is hard and glossy and Beverly Hills and cold and sexy in that way that things can be sexy when you get laid without a great deal of feeling. And with Elaine and his fantasy of Elaine, everything changes into a kind of fantasy prettiness.

My feelings about, for instance, the ending, what it means, who Elaine really is, what happens between her and Benjamin, are, at this point, just my feelings, and my opinion really doesn't have much more validity than anybody else's. Who's to say I'm right and somebody else is wrong? I have certain very specific thoughts about it. I've expressed them to kids and they've been stunned and enraged. In my mind, it's always been that in five miles she's going to say, "My God, I haven't got any clothes."

G: You'd said elsewhere that in five or ten years Benjy will be just like his parents.

N: It would be my guess. If the picture's any good, then it means that you guess about the characters as you do about people you know. I don't know what's going to happen to me. Who's going to leave whom? Who's going to marry whom? Who's going to commit suicide? Who's going to be ruined? We don't know those things. You make guesses about the people you care for, just as you make guesses about characters.

I'm just one of a whole lot of people who have an idea about the picture. A lot of us have the fantasy of breaking out, of dropping everything, of disappearing with that one girl, and extending a certain feeling forever, of taking the moment—let's say those three hours of your sitting with a girl and she's holding your foot and you think: "I would like her to go on holding my foot for the rest of my life. I don't want to go out and work. I don't want to go to dinner with those people I'm supposed to meet. I don't want to do anything. I want my life to be *this* and nothing else."

It's something everybody knows. And the fantasy of breaking through everything and living for that is a very powerful one. I think it can't be done. I think a lot of people, myself included, wish to God it could be done. And that's what the end means to me. That I'm moved by somebody who wants to try to do it and I'm pulling for them. But I don't know if they can make it.

G: That final scene, according to Dustin Hoffman, was shot in a strained atmosphere and both he and Katharine Ross were feeling exhausted and defeated so they didn't know whether to smile or to cry.

N: The end originally planned for the film was that they would get on the bus, turn, laugh, she would say, "Benjamin." He would say, "What?" which is all he ever said. She would kiss him and the bus would go off. I never questioned it. But something very odd happened to me the day we were shooting that scene. I was rotten to the two of them, really rotten. And I told them—and I don't usually do this—I said, "Now, listen, it's a big deal and we've stopped traffic for miles and we've got a police car. You get on that bus and you better laugh. You hear me?"

They had tears in their eyes, they were so terrified. They got on the bus and they tried to laugh, and we kept rolling, and they tried to laugh some more. And then they finally gave up, and they thought, "I don't know what the hell he wants me to do." And we rolled and we rolled and we rolled and we drove for miles. Then when I saw those rushes, I thought: "That's the end of the picture. They don't know what the hell to do, or to think, or to say to each other."

G: Do you consciously chart some sort of emotional curve in placing the scenes in sequence in the script, or in the editing, to achieve this building-up and relaxation cycle?

N: When I work on a play or a picture, I divide it into events, things that happen. It seems to me very important, for instance, to tell actors: "It's not over yet. No, you can't stop. It hasn't ended yet. Not yet. Not yet. Now it's over. Stop! Wait. Start the next thing." When I was working with Elaine, we used to have arguments about this. She was so much more prolific and could invent endlessly, make complete characters and carry them on for hours. I was unable to do this.

I just wasn't as good an actor. So I had to be concerned with moving it on, to the middle, and now to the end, to make a shape. So I'm very concerned with beginning, middle, and end. When is the beginning over? When is it time for the middle? When is the middle over? When do we start towards the end? And now it's the end. The shaping is essential.

G: You've stressed the importance of authenticity and detail in creating characters. Why is it vital? Does one define people by what they wear or the bric-a-brac in their home?

N: No. What you do when you think about a character is you have a secret person that you're thinking of, that you knew. The writer is thinking of one person, also. You don't ask him who it is. You think of another. I can't name a single character in anything I've done for whom I don't have a sort of reference person in my head. If she's got exactly the right kind of scarf and walks the same way and turns her head the same way, I recognize the person.

It's that thing I mentioned earlier about a Fellini picture. When he's on the button about Seraghina, I *know* he knew Seraghina and I know he re-created her accurately. I don't mean literally, but accurately. And when he got her accurately, I *remembered* her too, though I never met her. He had been so specific that he made us remember something that had never happened to us. I don't mean to be mystical. When you are specific, nobody else ever says, "Ah, look how specific."

But there is at least the chance, there's the hope that in some way you created somebody living that they will remember. It's like great moments in film which I've discovered—I've remembered—just before they happened. I'll give you an example. In *Belle de Jour*, remember when Deneuve's been with the Japanese guy and he leaves her and her head is down and her face is in the bed?

G: And there's blood and she looks like she's dead and we never find out what he had in that tiny box, buzzing away.

N: Exactly. And the maid comes in, and somebody starts to comfort her and she starts to raise her head. And you know she's going to be smiling. You *remember* it. Didn't that happen to you?

G: Yes.

N: That's what I mean. You can't aim for that. And you certainly don't think about it while you're working. But detail and accuracy and exactness seem to me the way to call out memory and feeling in other people. I think that when artists—and by that I mean writers and just a very few film directors—get something right, it touches on and becomes your own life, whether it literally corresponds or not. It can happen between friends. Richard Burton, for example, is the son of a Welsh miner. He had thirteen brothers and sisters. I'm a Jewish boy from Berlin with one brother. We have no experience in common. But at certain moments when we're drinking or talking, we are alike.

G: Who is Benjamin patterned after? You as a young boy?

N: Me right now. You know that whimper he does? He got that sound from me. I was told that I used to do that in meetings with Jack Warner. Somebody said, "When Mr. Warner is telling his jokes, you must stop whimpering." And I hadn't even realized I was doing it. So I told Dustin later and got him to do it.

You know, I was asked that question one of the two times I've talked to college kids at Yale. A girl with glasses and knee socks said, "Who is Benjamin, really?" And I said, "Well, you know what Flaubert said . . ." And she said, "About *The Graduate?*" And I said, "Forget it."

G: But you've just said that every character of yours was based on a person you knew. Who was Benjamin?

N: Benjamin was Charles Webb (author of the novel) first. Then he was Buck Henry (the scenarist). Then he was me. And then he was Dustin Hoffman. I have to guess, because I never discussed it with Webb, Henry, or Dustin, but I would bet that in each of our minds he's ourselves. Certainly in my mind, through the whole picture, he's both literally me and metaphorically me.

G: You're constantly being asked by young people for advice on how to break into filmmaking. What do you tell them?

N: I'm never quite sure what to tell them. I usually say, "Stick with your friends and let something come out of that." It seems to me that's the best way, rather than going out and pounding on doors and putting yourself on alien ground. It's like what we were talking about with men like Renoir—great films issue from extraordinary natures. Work like this I think should come out of your life, out of whom you're with.

They can make a community, whether it's two or four or ten. Whatever they want to do, whether it's plays or films or cabaret, should issue from what goes on in that group among the people they trust and the people who turn them on and allow them to think. I don't *think* when I'm alone. That's why I'm a director. I'm turned on by somebody else. A director works with other people. I don't have to sit in a room alone and plan things. I mean, I do, but it comes out of a connection with a group of people.

I think it's very important to start out in your own ground. I don't mean shoot what you know. But I mean I wouldn't be doing any of this if it wasn't for Chicago and a bunch of friends. We just wanted to do things together because we knew each other. We're still friends. It seems to me that's where it is, rather than going out among strangers who frighten you and don't allow you to be yourselves.

G: That sounds like it fits right in with the communal scene and with college life. People basically living with or for one another.

N: They're very lucky, if they're really living for one another. Then they've got it made. They'll make better movies than any of us have dreamt of, because they'll have forgotten about themselves. And what could be better than that?

STANLEY KUBRICK

"A director is a kind of idea and
taste machine; a movie is a series
of creative and technical decisions,
and it's the director's job to make
the right decisions as frequently
as possible."

*The most controversial film of 1968 was Stanley Kubrick's 2001:
A Space Odyssey. It started out as a $6,000,000 science fiction
movie and escalated into a $10,500,000 underground film. It polarized
critical and public opinion. Most of its young admirers considered
it a prophetic masterpiece. Its detractors praised the special effects
but found it confusing and pretentious as drama.*

*Despite Kubrick's own ready interpretation of the action, the
ending of 2001 was confusing to some people. The final scenes in
the alien "zoo" or heaven and the metamorphosis of the astronaut
into a star baby remained for many an enigmatic, purely emotional,
nonverbal experience. Understanding became a function of the emotions, rather than one's reasoning powers.*

*Less than half the film had dialogue. It was a reorganization of the
traditional dramatic structure. Process became more important than
plot. The tedium was the message. It was a film not about space
travel; it was space travel. "The truth of a thing is in the feel of it,
not the think of it," Kubrick asserted.*

*Kubrick traces some of his fascination with the fluid camera back
to Max Ophuls. His oeuvre, with the single exception of the optimistic
transfiguration in 2001, is a bleak skepticism and fatalism.*

*2001 was Kubrick's first experiment with restructuring the con-
ventions of the three-act drama. It's quite possible it started out
to be something entirely different. The book based on the original
screenplay by Arthur C. Clarke and Kubrick is literal, verbal,
explicit. The film, in its early stages, had a narrator's voice. It was
cut bit by bit and then eliminated completely, by virtue of which
2001 evolved as a nonverbal experience.*

*In his next film, Napoleon, Kubrick says he plans to return to the
use of a narrator and perhaps even animation or charts to illustrate
and explain the battle tactics and campaigns. Kubrick's personal interest in the aesthetics of a well-staged campaign goes back to his days
as a young chess hustler in Greenwich Village.*

Born July 1928 in the Bronx, Kubrick was introduced to still photography as a hobby by his father, who was a physician. He achieved a certain youthful prominence as his class photographer at Taft High School. Later, with a sixty-eight average, he was unable to compete with returning GIs for a place in college. So, "out of pity," he recalls, Look magazine hired him as a photographer.

Kubrick's early training in movies was with two documentaries. At twenty-five, he made his first feature film, the 35-mm Fear and Desire, for $9000—plus another $30,000 because he didn't know what he was doing with the soundtrack. He didn't make any money on his first four feature films. He has never earned a penny on The Killing and Paths of Glory, which some of his early fans still consider his best films.

The only film he disclaims is Spartacus. He says he worked on it as just a hired hand. Every other film he's directed he has made to suit himself, within prescribed bounds of existing community standards. He wishes Lolita had been more erotic. The lag time between conception and completion of his films is now up to an average of three years. In part, this is the result of his wish to handle every artistic and business function himself.

To concentrate all control in his own hands, Kubrick produces as well as directs his films. He originates, writes, researches, directs, edits, and even guides the publicity campaigns for his films. Though he gets his financing from the major studios, he is as independent as he was when he was raising his money from his father and uncle.

The following interview is the outcome of meetings that took place in 1968 in New York and London and of correspondence that continued through 1969. Kubrick lives near London. His third wife is Suzanne Christiane Harlan, a German actress who appeared briefly at the end of Paths of Glory.

FILMOGRAPHY:

DAY OF THE FIGHT (Documentary: '50)
FLYING PADRE (Documentary: '51)
FEAR AND DESIRE ('53)
KILLER'S KISS ('55)
THE KILLING ('56)
PATHS OF GLORY ('57)
SPARTACUS ('60)
LOLITA ('62)
DR. STRANGELOVE ('64)
2001: A SPACE ODYSSEY ('68)
NAPOLEON ('70)

GELMIS: 2001 took about three years to make—six months of preparation, four and a half months of working with the actors, and a year and a half of shooting special effects. How much time will *Napoleon* take out of your life?

KUBRICK: Considerably less. We hope to begin the actual production work by the winter of 1969, and the exterior shooting—battles, location shots, etc.—should be completed within two or three months. After that, the studio work shouldn't take more than another three or four months.

G: Where would the exteriors be shot? Actual sites?

K: I still haven't made a final decision, although there are several promising possibilities. Unfortunately, there are very, very few actual Napoleonic battlefields where we could still shoot; the land itself has either been taken over by industrial and urban development, preempted by historical trusts, or is so ringed by modern buildings that all kinds of anachronisms would present themselves—like a Hussars' charge with a Fiat plant in the background. We're now in the process of deciding the best places to shoot, and where it would be most feasible to obtain the troops we need for battle scenes. We intend to use a maximum of forty thousand infantry and ten thousand cavalry for the big battles, which means that we have to find a country which will hire out its own armed forces to us—you can just imagine the cost of fifty thousand extras over an extended period of time. Once we find a receptive environment, there are still great logistic problems—for example, a battle site would have to be contiguous to a city or town or barracks area where the troops we'd use are already bivouacked. Let's say we're working with forty thousand infantry—if we could get forty men into a truck, it would still require a thousand trucks to move them around. So in addition to finding the proper terrain, it has to be within marching distance of military barracks.

G: Aside from the Russian *War and Peace*, where they reportedly used sixty thousand of their own troops, has there ever been a film that used forty thousand men from somebody else's army?

K: I would doubt it.

G: Then how do you expect to persuade another government to give you as many as forty thousand soldiers?

к: One has to be an optimist about these things. If it turned out to be impossible I'd obviously have no other choice than to make do with a lesser number of men, but this would only be as a last resort. I wouldn't want to fake it with fewer troops because Napoleonic battles were out in the open, a vast tableau where the formations moved in an almost choreographic fashion. I want to capture this reality on film, and to do so it's necessary to re-create all the conditions of the battle with painstaking accuracy.

G: How many men did you use in the trench battle of *Paths of Glory*?

к: That was another story entirely. We employed approximately eight hundred men, all German police—at that time the German police received three years of military training, and were as good as regular soldiers for our purposes. We shot the film at Geiselgesteig Studios in Munich, and both the battle site and the château were within thirty-five to forty minutes of the studio.

G: If you can't use the actual battle sites, how will you approximate the terrain on the sites you do choose?

к: There are a number of ways this can be done and it's quite important to the accuracy of the film, since terrain is the decisive factor in the flow and outcome of a Napoleonic battle. We've researched all the battle sites exhaustively from paintings and sketches, and we're now in a position to approximate the terrain. And from a purely schematic point of view, Napoleonic battles are so beautiful, like vast lethal ballets, that it's worth making every effort to explain the configuration of forces to the audience. And it's not really as difficult as it at first appears.

G: How do you mean "explain"? With a narrator, or charts?

к: With a narrative voice-over at times, with animated maps and, most importantly, through the actual photography of the battles themselves. Let's say you want to explain that at the battle of Austerlitz the Austro-Russian forces attempted to cut Napoleon off from Vienna, and then extended the idea to a double envelopment and Napoleon countered by striking at their center and cutting their forces in half—well, this is not difficult to show by photography, maps and narration. I think it's extremely important to communicate the essence of these battles to the viewer, because they all have an aesthetic brilliance that doesn't require a military mind to appreciate. There's an aesthetic involved; it's almost like a great piece of music, or the purity of a mathematical formula. It's this quality I want to bring across, as well as the sordid reality of battle. You know, there's a weird disparity between the sheer visual and organizational beauty of the historical battles sufficiently far in the past, and their human consequences. It's rather like watching two golden eagles soaring through the sky from a distance; they may be tearing a dove to pieces, but if you are far enough away the scene is still beautiful.

G: Why are you making a movie about Napoleon?

K: That's a question it would really take this entire interview to answer. To begin with, he fascinates me. His life has been described as an epic poem of action. His sex life was worthy of Arthur Schnitzler. He was one of those rare men who move history and mold the destiny of their own times and of generations to come—in a very concrete sense, our own world is the result of Napoleon, just as the political and geographic map of postwar Europe is the result of World War Two. And, of course, there has never been a good or accurate movie about him. Also, I find that all the issues with which it concerns itself are oddly contemporary— the responsibilities and abuses of power, the dynamics of social revolution, the relationship of the individual to the state, war, militarism, etc., so this will not be just a dusty historic pageant but a film about the basic questions of our own times, as well as Napoleon's. But even apart from those aspects of the story, the sheer drama and force of Napoleon's life is a fantastic subject for a film biography. Forgetting everything else and just taking Napoleon's romantic involvement with Josephine, for example, here you have one of the great obsessional passions of all time.

G: How long a film biography are you contemplating?

K: It's obviously a huge story to film, since we're not just taking one segment of Napoleon's life, military or personal, but are attempting to encompass all the major events of his career. I haven't set down any rigid guidelines on length; I believe that if you have a truly interesting film it doesn't matter how long it is—providing, of course, you don't run on to such extremes that you numb the attention span of your audience. The longest film that has given consistent enjoyment to generations of viewers is *Gone With the Wind*, which would indicate that if a film is sufficiently interesting people will watch it for three hours and forty minutes. But in actual fact, the Napoleon film will probably be shorter.

G: What kind of research do you have going on right now?

K: The first step has been to read everything I could get my hands on about Napoleon, and totally immerse myself in his life. I guess I must have gone through several hundred books on the subject, from contemporary nineteenth-century English and French accounts to modern biographies. I've ransacked all these books for research material and broken it down into categories on everything from his food tastes to the weather on the day of a specific battle, and cross-indexed all the data in a comprehensive research file. In addition to my own reading, I've worked out a consultant arrangement with Professor Felix Markham of Oxford, a history don who has spent the past thirty-five years of his life studying Napoleon and is considered one of the world's leading Napoleonic experts. He's available to answer any questions that derive from my own reading or outside of it. We're also in the process of creating prototypes of vehicles, weapons, and costumes of the period which will subsequently be mass-produced, all copied from paintings and written descriptions of the time and accurate in every detail. We already have twenty people working full time on the preparatory stage of the film.

G: What movies on Napoleon have you gone back to see?

K: I've tried to see every film that was ever made on the subject, and I've got to say that I don't find any of them particularly impressive. I recently saw Abel Gance's movie, which has built up a reputation among film buffs over the years, and I found it really terrible. Technically he was ahead of his time and he introduced inventive new film techniques—in fact Eisenstein credited him with stimulating his initial interest in montage—but as far as story and performance goes it's a very crude picture.

G: What did you think about the Russian *War and Peace*?

K: It was a cut above the others, and did have some very good scenes, but I can't say I was overly impressed. There's one in particular I admired, where the Tsar entered a ballroom and everyone scurried in his wake to see what he was doing and then rushed out of his way when he returned. That seemed to me to capture the reality of such a situation. Of course, Tolstoy's view of Napoleon is so far removed from that of any objective historian's that I really can't fault the director for the way he was portrayed. It was a disappointing film, and doubly so because it had the potential to be otherwise.

G: Can you imagine yourself going down with just a cameraman and sound man and half a dozen people and shooting a film?

K: Sure I can. In fact, any contemporary story is best done just that way. The only time you need vast amounts of money and a huge crew is when you require complex special effects, as in 2001, or big battle or crowd scenes, as in the Napoleon film. But if you're just dealing with a story set in modern times, then you could do it very easily with both limited funds and a limited crew.

G: In your own case, *Lolita* was set in America, and yet you shot it on an English sound stage. Couldn't that film have been shot in this way, with just a handful of people on location?

K: Yes, it could certainly have been shot on location, although you'd still have needed more than a handful of people to do it.

G: Would you have done it that way if you were making the film now?

K: I would have done it at the time if the money to film had been available in America. But as it turned out the only funds I could raise for the film had to be spent in England. There's been such a revolution in Hollywood's treatment of sex over just the past few years that it's easy to forget that when I became interested in *Lolita* a lot of people felt that such a film couldn't be made—or at least couldn't be shown. As it turned out, we didn't have any problems, but there was a lot of fear and trembling. And filming in England we obviously had no choice but to rely mainly on studio shooting.

G: Obviously *Napoleon* wouldn't permit you to shoot with a small crew and flexible conditions on location. But in the foreseeable future do you see yourself shedding the shell of the studio superstructure and working simply again?

K: Yes, if I could find a contemporary story susceptible to such an approach which I liked enough to do. But I would certainly enjoy filming primarily on location. If you have the right story, it's a waste of time and energy to re-create conditions in a studio which exist outside. And if you make sensible arrangements, there are no technical difficulties about location shooting. Sound, which once presented problems, really doesn't anymore, since with skirt mikes you get a favorable voice-to-noise ratio. And in any case, background noise just adds to the verisimilitude of the scene. It's only when you're doing a period film that causes difficulties; in *Napoleon*, for example,

I'd hardly want a jet to fly overhead in the middle of the battle of Jena.

G: Your last film was about the twenty-first century. Your next film is about the nineteenth century. Do you think it's significant that you aren't very interested or satisfied with contemporary stories or themes of twentieth-century life?

K: It's not a question of my own satisfaction or lack of it, but of the basic purpose of a film, which I believe is one of illumination, of showing the viewer something he can't see any other way. And I think at times this can be best accomplished by staying away from his own immediate environment. This is particularly true when you're dealing in a primarily visual experience, and telling a story through the eyes. You don't find reality only in your own backyard, you know—in fact, sometimes that's the last place you find it. Another asset about dealing with themes that are either futuristic or historic is that it enables you to make a statement with which you're not personally blinded; it removes the environmental blinkers, in a sense, and gives you a deeper and more objective perspective.

G: In your last genuinely contemporary film, *Lolita*, you were frustrated in your efforts to make the movie as erotic as the novel, and there was some criticism that the girl was too old to play the nymphet of the novel.

K: She was actually just the right age. Lolita was twelve and a half in the book; Sue Lyon was thirteen. I think some people had a mental picture of a nine-year-old. I would fault myself in one area of the film, however; because of all the pressure over the Production Code and the Catholic Legion of Decency at the time, I believe I didn't sufficiently dramatize the erotic aspect of Humbert's relationship with Lolita, and because his sexual obsession was only barely hinted at, many people guessed too quickly that Humbert was in love with Lolita. Whereas in the novel this comes as a discovery at the end, when she is no longer a nymphet but a dowdy, pregnant suburban housewife; and it's this encounter, and his sudden realization of his love, that is one of the most poignant elements of the story. If I could do the film over again, I would have stressed the erotic component of their relationship with the same weight Nabokov did. But that is the only major area where I believe the film is susceptible to valid criticism.

G: At what point did you decide to structure the film so that Humbert is telling the story to the man he's going to shoot?

K: I discussed this approach with Nabokov at the very outset, and he liked it. One of the basic problems with the book, and with the film even in its modified form, is that the main narrative interest boils down to the question "Will Humbert get Lolita into bed?" And you find in the book that, despite the brilliant writing, the second half has a drop in narrative interest after he does. We wanted to avoid this problem in the film, and Nabokov and I agreed that if we had Humbert shoot Quilty without explanation at the beginning, then throughout the film the audience would wonder what Quilty was up to. Of course, you obviously sacrifice a great ending by opening with Quilty's murder, but I felt it served a worthwhile purpose.

G: Starting with *Lolita*, you've been making all your films abroad. Why?

K: Circumstances have just dictated it that way. As I explained earlier, it was necessary to make *Lolita* in England for financial reasons and to mitigate censorship problems, and in the case of *Dr. Strangelove*, Peter Sellers was in the process of getting a divorce and could not leave England for an extended period, so it was necessary to film there. By the time I decided to do 2001 I had gotten so acclimated to working in England that it would have been pointless to tear up roots and move everything to America. And with *Napoleon* we'll be doing a great deal of the shooting on the continent, so London is a convenient base of operations.

G: Are there any specific advantages to working in London?

K: Next to Hollywood, London is probably the second best place to make a film, because of the degree of technical expertise and facilities you find in England, and that isn't really a backhanded compliment.

G: Do you have any reluctance to work in Hollywood while the studio chiefs stand over the director's shoulder?

K: No, because I'm in the fortunate position where I can make a film without that kind of control. Ten years ago, of course, it would have been an entirely different story.

G: You don't consider yourself an expatriate then?

K: Not at all.

G: Why not? You've lived in England seven years and made your last three films there—even those which were set in America.

к: Yes, but there's nothing permanent about my working and living in England. Circumstances have kept me there until now, but it's quite possible I'll be making a film in America in the future. And in any case, I commute back and forth several times a year.

g: But always by ocean liner. You have a pilot's license but you don't like flying anymore. Why?

к: Call it enlightened cowardice, if you like. Actually, over the years I discovered that I just didn't enjoy flying, and I became aware of compromised safety margins in commercial aviation that are never mentioned in airline advertising. So I decided I'd rather travel by sea, and take my chances with the icebergs.

g: In your profession isn't it a problem not to fly?

к: It would be if I had to hop about all the time from spot to spot like many people do. But when I'm working on a film I'm tied down to one geographic area for long periods of time and I travel very little. And when I do, I find boats or railroads adequate and more relaxing.

g: *Dr. Strangelove* was a particularly word-oriented film, whereas *2001* seemed to be a total breakaway from what you'd done before.

к: Yes, I feel it was. *Strangelove* was a film where much of its impact hinged on the dialogue, the mode of expression, the euphemisms employed. As a result, it's a picture that is largely destroyed in translation or dubbing. *2001*, on the other hand, is basically a visual, nonverbal experience. It avoids intellectual verbalization and reaches the viewer's subconscious in a way that is essentially poetic and philosophic. The film thus becomes a subjective experience which hits the viewer at an inner level of consciousness, just as music does, or painting.

Actually, film operates on a level much closer to music and to painting than to the printed word, and, of course, movies present the opportunity to convey complex concepts and abstractions without the traditional reliance on words. I think that *2001*, like music, succeeds in short-circuiting the rigid surface cultural blocks that shackle our consciousness to narrowly limited areas of experience and is able to cut directly through to areas of emotional comprehension. In two hours and forty minutes of film there are only forty minutes of dialogue.

I think one of the areas where *2001* succeeds is in stimulating thoughts about man's destiny and role in the universe in the minds of people who in the normal course of their lives would never have considered such matters. Here again, you've got the resemblance to music; an Alabama truck driver, whose views in every other respect would be extremely narrow, is able to listen to a Beatles record on the same level of appreciation and perception as a young Cambridge intellectual, because their emotions and subconscious are far more similar than their intellects. The common bond is their subconscious emotional reaction; and I think that a film which can communicate on this level can have a more profound spectrum of impact than any form of traditional verbal communication.

The problem with movies is that since the talkies the film industry has historically been conservative and word-oriented. The three-act play has been the model. It's time to abandon the conventional view of the movie as an extension of the three-act play. Too many people over thirty are still word-oriented rather than picture-oriented.

For example, at one point in 2001 Dr. Floyd is asked where he's going and he replies, "I'm going to Clavius," which is a lunar crater. Following that statement you have more than fifteen shots of Floyd's spacecraft approaching and landing on the moon, but one critic expressed confusion because she thought Floyd's destination was a planet named Clavius. Young people, on the other hand, who are more visually oriented due to their new television environment, had no such problems. Kids all know he went to the moon. When you ask how they know they say, "Because we *saw* it."

So you have the problem that some people are only listening and not really paying attention with their eyes. Film is *not* theater—and until that basic lesson is learned I'm afraid we're going to be shackled to the past and miss some of the greatest potentialities of the medium.

G: Did you deliberately try for ambiguity as opposed to a specific meaning for any scene or image?

K: No, I didn't have to try for ambiguity; it was inevitable. And I think in a film like 2001, where each viewer brings his own emotions and perceptions to bear on the subject matter, a certain degree of ambiguity is valuable, because it allows the audience to "fill in" the visual experience themselves. In any case, once you're dealing on a nonverbal level, ambiguity is unavoidable. But it's the ambiguity of all art, of a fine piece of music or a painting—you don't need written instructions by the composer or painter accompanying such works to "explain" them. "Explaining" them contributes nothing but a superficial "cultural" value which has no value except for critics and teachers who have to earn a living. Reactions to art are always different because they are always deeply personal.

G: The final scenes of the film seemed more metaphorical than realistic. Will you discuss them—or would that be part of the "road map" you're trying to avoid?

K: No, I don't mind discussing it, on the *lowest* level, that is, straightforward explanation of the plot. You begin with an artifact left on earth four million years ago by extraterrestrial explorers who observed the behavior of the man-apes of the time and decided to influence their evolutionary progression. Then you have a second artifact buried on the lunar surface and programmed to signal word of man's first baby steps into the universe—a kind of cosmic burglar alarm. And finally there's a third artifact placed in orbit around Jupiter and waiting for the time when man has reached the outer rim of his own solar system.

When the surviving astronaut, Bowman, ultimately reaches Jupiter, this artifact sweeps him into a force field or star gate that hurls him on a journey through inner and outer space and finally transports him to another part of the galaxy, where he's placed in a human zoo approximating a hospital terrestrial environment drawn out of his own dreams and imagination. In a timeless state, his life passes from middle age to senescence to death. He is reborn, an enhanced being, a star child, an angel, a superman, if you like, and returns to earth prepared for the next leap forward of man's evolutionary destiny.

That is what happens on the film's simplest level. Since an encounter with an advanced interstellar intelligence would be incomprehensible within our present earthbound frames of reference, reactions to it will have elements of philosophy and metaphysics that have nothing to do with the bare plot outline itself.

G: What are those areas of meaning?

K: They are the areas I prefer not to discuss because they are highly subjective and will differ from viewer to viewer. In this sense, the film becomes anything the viewer sees in it. If the film stirs the emotions and penetrates the subconscious of the viewer, if it stimulates, however inchoately, his mythological and religious yearnings and impulses, then it has succeeded.

G: Why does 2001 seem so affirmative and religious a film? What has happened to the tough, disillusioned, cynical director of *The Killing, Spartacus, Paths of Glory*, and *Lolita*, and the sardonic black humorist of *Dr. Strangelove?*

K: The God concept is at the heart of this film. It's unavoidable that it would be, once you believe that the universe is seething with advanced forms of intelligent life. Just think about it for a moment. There are a hundred billion stars in the galaxy and a hundred billion galaxies in the visible universe. Each star is a sun, like our own, probably with planets around them. The evolution of life, it is widely believed, comes as an inevitable consequence of a certain amount of time on a planet in a stable orbit which is not too hot or too cold. First comes chemical evolution—chance rearrangements of basic matter, then biological evolution.

Think of the kind of life that may have evolved on those planets over the millennia, and think, too, what relatively giant technological strides man has made on earth in the six thousand years of his recorded civilization—a period that is less than a single grain of sand in the cosmic hourglass. At a time when man's distant evolutionary ancestors were just crawling out of the primordial ooze, there must have been civilizations in the universe sending out their starships to explore the farthest reaches of the cosmos and conquering all the secrets of nature. Such cosmic intelligences, growing in knowledge over the aeons, would be as far removed from man as we are from the ants. They could be in instantaneous telepathic communication throughout the universe; they might have achieved total mastery over matter so that they can telekinetically transport themselves instantly across billions of light years of space; in their ultimate form they might shed the corporeal shell entirely and exist as a disembodied immortal consciousness throughout the universe.

Once you begin discussing such possibilities, you realize that the religious implications are inevitable, because all the essential attributes of such extraterrestrial intelligences are the attributes we give to God. What we're really dealing with here is, in fact, a scientific definition of God. And if these beings of pure intelligence ever did intervene in the affairs of man, we could only understand it in terms of God or magic, so far removed would their powers be from our own understanding. How would a sentient ant view the foot that crushes his anthill—as the action of another being on a higher evolutionary scale than itself? Or as the divinely terrible intercession of God?

G: Although 2001 dealt with the first human contact with an alien civilization, we never did actually see an alien, though you communicated through the monoliths an experience of alien beings.

K: From the very outset of work on the film we all discussed means of photographically depicting an extraterrestrial creature in a manner that would be as mind-boggling as the being itself. And it soon became apparent that you cannot imagine the unimaginable. All you can do is try to represent it in an artistic manner that will convey something of its quality. That's why we settled on the black monolith—which is, of course, in itself something of a Jungian archetype, and also a pretty fair example of "minimal art."

G: Isn't a basic problem with science fiction films that alien life always looks like some Creature from the Black Lagoon, a plastic rubber monster?

K: Yes, and that's one of the reasons we stayed away from the depiction of biological entities, aside from the fact that truly advanced beings would probably have shed the chrysalis of a biological form at one stage of their evolution. You cannot design a biological entity that doesn't look either overly humanoid or like the traditional Bug-Eyed Monster of pulp science fiction.

G: The man-ape costumes in 2001 were impressive.

K: We spent an entire year trying to figure out how to make the ape-heads look convincing, and not just like a conventional makeup job. We finally constructed an entire sub-skull of extremely light and flexible plastic, to which we attached the equivalent of face muscles which pulled the lips back in a normal manner whenever the mouth was opened. The mouth itself took a great deal of work—it had artificial teeth and an artificial tongue which the actors could manipulate with tiny toggles to make the lips snarl in a lifelike fashion. Some of the masks even had built-in devices whereby the artificial muscles in the cheeks and beneath the eyes could be moved. All the apes except for two baby chimps were men, and most of them were dancers or mimes, which enabled them to move a little better than most movie apes.

G: Was the little girl Dr. Floyd telephoned from the orbital satellite one of your daughters?

K: Yes, my youngest girl, Vivian. She was six then. We didn't give her any billing, a fact I hope she won't decide to take up with me when she's older.

G: Why was Martin Balsam's voice as HAL, the computer, re-dubbed by Douglas Raine, the Canadian actor?

K: Well, we had some difficulty deciding exactly what HAL should sound like, and Marty just sounded a little bit too colloquially

American, whereas Raine had the kind of bland mid-Atlantic accent we felt was right for the part.

G: Some critics have detected in HAL's wheedling voice an undertone of homosexuality. Was that intended?

K: No. I think it's become something of a parlor game for some people to read that kind of thing into everything they encounter. HAL was a "straight" computer.

G: Why was the computer more emotional than the human beings?

K: This was a point that seemed to fascinate some negative critics, who felt that it was a failing of this section of the film that there was more interest in HAL than in the astronauts. In fact, of course, the computer is the central character of this segment of the story. If HAL had been a human being, it would have been obvious to everyone that he had the best part, and was the most interesting character; he took all the initiatives, and all the problems related to and were caused by him.

Some critics seemed to feel that because we were successful in making a voice, a camera lens, and a light come alive as a character this necessarily meant that the human characters failed dramatically. In fact, I believe that Keir Dullea and Gary Lockwood, the astronauts, reacted appropriately and realistically to their circumstances. One of the things we were trying to convey in this part of the film is the reality of a world populated—as ours soon will be—by machine entities who have as much, or more, intelligence as human beings, and who have the same emotional potentialities in their personalities as human beings. We wanted to stimulate people to think what it would be like to share a planet with such creatures.

In the specific case of HAL, he had an acute emotional crisis because he could not accept evidence of his own fallibility. The idea of neurotic computers is not uncommon—most advanced computer theorists believe that once you have a computer which is more intelligent than man and capable of learning by experience, it's inevitable that it will develop an equivalent range of emotional reactions—fear, love, hate, envy, etc. Such a machine could eventually become as incomprehensible as a human being, and could, of course, have a nervous breakdown—as HAL did in the film.

G: Since 2001 is a visual experience, what happened when your collaborator, Arthur C. Clarke, finally put the screenplay down in black and white in the novelization of the film?

ᴋ: It's a totally different kind of experience, of course, and there are a number of differences between the book and the movie. The novel, for example, attempts to explain things much more explicitly than the film does, which is inevitable in a verbal medium. The novel came about after we did a 130-page prose treatment of the film at the very outset. This initial treatment was subsequently changed in the screenplay, and the screenplay in turn was altered during the making of the film. But Arthur took all the existing material, plus an impression of some of the rushes, and wrote the novel. As a result, there's a difference between the novel and the film.

ɢ: To take one specific, in the novel the black monolith found by curious man-apes three million years ago does explicit things which it doesn't do in the film. In the movie, it has an apparent catalytic effect which enables the ape to discover how to use a bone as a weapon-tool. In the novel, the slab becomes milky and luminous and we're told it's a testing and teaching device used by higher intelligences to determine if the apes are worth helping. Was that in the original screenplay? When was it cut out of the film?

ᴋ: Yes, it was in the original treatment but I eventually decided that to depict the monolith in such an explicit manner would be to run the risk of making it appear no more than an advanced television teaching machine. You can get away with something so literal in print, but I felt that we could create a far more powerful and magical effect by representing it as we did in the film.

ɢ: Do you feel that the novel, written so explicitly, in some way diminishes the mysterious aspect of the film?

ᴋ: I think it gives you the opportunity of seeing two attempts in two different mediums, print and film, to express the same basic concept and story. In both cases, of course, the treatment must accommodate to the necessities of the medium. I think that the divergencies between the two works are interesting. Actually, it was an unprecedented situation for someone to do an essentially original literary work based on glimpses and segments of a film he had not yet seen in its entirety. In fact, *nobody* saw the film in its final form until eight days before we held the first press screening in April 1968, and the first time I saw the film completed with a proper soundtrack was one week before it opened. I completed the portion of the film in which we used actors in June 1966 and from then until the first week of March 1968 I spent most of my time working on the 205 special effects shots. The final shot was actually cut into the negative at M-G-M's Hollywood studios only days before the film was ready to open. There was nothing intentional about the fact that the film wasn't shown until the last minute. It just wasn't finished.

G: Why did you cut scenes from the film after it opened?

K: I always try to look at a completed film as if I had never seen it before. I usually have several weeks to run the film, alone and with audiences. Only in this way can you judge length. I've always done precisely that with my previous films; for example, after a screening of Dr. *Strangelove* I cut out a final scene in which the Russians and Americans in the War Room engage in a free-for-all fight with custard pies. I decided it was farce and not consistent with the satiric tone of the rest of the film. So there was nothing unusual about the cutting I did on *2001*, except for the eleventh-hour way in which I had to do it.

G: *Strangelove* was based on a serious book, *Red Alert*. At what point did you decide to make it a comedy?

K: I started work on the screenplay with every intention of making the film a serious treatment of the problem of accidental nuclear war. As I kept trying to imagine the way in which things would really happen, ideas kept coming to me which I would discard because they were so ludicrous. I kept saying to myself: "I can't do this. People will laugh." But after a month or so I began to realize that all the things I was throwing out were the things which were most truthful. After all, what could be more absurd than the very idea of two mega-powers willing to wipe out all human life because of an accident, spiced up by political differences that will seem as meaningless to people a hundred years from now as the theological conflicts of the Middle Ages appear to us today?

So it occurred to me that I was approaching the project in the wrong way. The only way to tell the story was as a black comedy or, better, a nightmare comedy, where the things you laugh at most are really the heart of the paradoxical postures that make a nuclear war possible. Most of the humor in *Strangelove* arises from the depiction of everyday human behavior in a nightmarish situation, like the Russian premier on the hot line who forgets the telephone number of his general staff headquarters and suggests the American President try Omsk information, or the reluctance of a U.S. officer to let a British officer smash open a Coca-Cola machine for change to phone the President about a crisis on the SAC base because of his conditioning about the sanctity of private property.

G: When you read a book like Red Alert which you're interested in turning into a film, do you right away say to yourself, this character should be played by such and such an actor?

K: Not usually. I first try to define the character fully as he will appear in the film and then try to think of the proper actor to play the role. When I'm in the process of casting a part I sit down with a list of actors I know. Of course, once you've narrowed the list down to several possibilities for each part then it becomes a question of who's currently available, and how the actor you choose to play one part will affect the peple you're considering for other parts.

G: How do you get a good performance from your actors?

K: The director's job is to know what emotional statement he wants a character to convey in his scene or his line, and to exercise taste and judgment in helping the actor give his best possible performance. By knowing the actor's personality and gauging his strengths and weaknesses a director can help him to overcome specific problems and realize his potential. But I think this aspect of directing is generally overemphasized. The director's taste and imagination play a much more crucial role in the making of a film. Is it meaningful? Is it believable? Is it interesting? Those are the questions that have to be answered several hundred times a day.

It's rare for a bad performance to result from an actor ignoring everything a director tells him. In fact it's very often just the opposite. After all, the director is the actor's sole audience for the months it takes to shoot a film, and an actor would have to possess supreme self-confidence and supreme contempt for the director to consistently defy his wishes. I think you'll find that most disappointing performances are the mutual fault of both the actor and the director.

G: Some directors don't let their actors see the daily rushes. Do you?

K: Yes. I've encountered very few actors who are so insecure or self-destructive that they're upset by the rushes or find their self-confidence undermined. Actually, most actors profit by seeing their rushes and examining them self-critically. In any case, a professional actor who's bothered by his own rushes just won't turn up to see them—particularly in my films, since we run the rushes at lunch time and unless an actor is really interested, he won't cut his lunch to half an hour.

G: On the first day of shooting on the set, how do you establish that rapport or fear or whatever relationship you want with your actors to keep them in the right frame of mind for the three months you'll be working with them?

K: Certainly not through fear. To establish a good working relationship I think all the actor has to know is that you respect his talent enough to want him in your film. He's obviously aware of that as long as *you've* hired him and he hasn't been foisted on you by the studio or the producer.

G: Do you rehearse at all?

K: There's really a limit to what you can do with rehearsals. They're very useful, of course, but I find that you can't rehearse effectively unless you have the physical reality of the set to work with. Unfortunately, sets are practically never ready until the last moment before you start shooting, and this significantly cuts down on your rehearsal time. Some actors, of course, need rehearsals more than others. Actors are essentially emotion-producing instruments, and some are always tuned and ready while others will reach a fantastic pitch on one take and never equal it again, no matter how hard they try. In *Strangelove*, for example, George Scott could do his scenes equally well take after take, whereas Peter Sellers was always incredibly good on one take, which was never equaled.

G: At what point do you know what take you're going to use?

K: On some occasions the take is so obviously superior you can tell immediately. But particularly when you're dealing with dialogue scenes, you have to look them over again and again and select portions of different takes and make the best use of them. The greatest amount of time in editing is this process of studying the takes and making notes and struggling to decide which segments you want to use; this takes ten times more time and effort than the actual cutting, which is a very quick process. Purely visual action scenes, of course, present far less of a problem; it's generally the dialogue scenes, where you've got several long takes printed on each angle on different actors, that are the most time-consuming to cut.

G: How much cutting are you responsible for, and how much is done by somebody you trust as an editor?

K: Nothing is cut without me. I'm in there every second, and for all practical purposes I cut my own film; I mark every frame,

select each segment, and have everything done exactly the way I
want it. Writing, shooting, *and* editing are what you have to do to
make a film.

G: Where did you learn film editing? You started out as a still
photographer.

K: Yes, but after I quit *Look* in 1950—where I had been a staff
photographer for five years, ever since I left high school—I took a
crack at films and made two documentaries, *Day of the Fight*,
about prize fighter Walter Cartier, and *The Flying Padre*, a silly
thing about a priest in the Southwest who flew to his isolated
parishes in a small airplane. I did all the work on those two films,
and all the work on my first two feature films, *Fear and Desire*
and *Killer's Kiss*. I was cameraman, director, editor, assistant editor,
sound effects man—you name it, I did it. And it was invaluable
experience, because being forced to do everything myself I gained
a sound and comprehensive grasp of all the technical aspects of
filmmaking.

G: How old were you when you decided to make movies?

K: I was around twenty-one. I'd had my job with *Look* since I
was seventeen, and I'd always been interested in films, but it never
actually occurred to me to make a film on my own until I had a
talk with a friend from high school, Alex Singer, who wanted to be
a director himself (and has subsequently become one) and had
plans for a film version of the *Iliad*. Alex was working as an office
boy for "The March of Time" in those days, and he told me they
spent forty thousand dollars making a one-reel documentary. A
bit of simple calculation indicated that I could make a one-reel
documentary for about fifteen hundred. That's what gave me the
financial confidence to make *Day of the Fight*.

I was rather optimistic about expenses; the film cost me thirty-nine
hundred. I sold it to RKO-Pathé for four thousand dollars, a hun-
dred-dollar profit. They told me that was the most they'd ever paid
for a short. I then discovered that "The March of Time" itself was
going out of business. I made one more short for RKO, *The Flying
Padre*, on which I just barely broke even. It was at this point that I
formally quit my job at *Look* to work full time on filmmaking. I
then managed to raise ten thousand dollars, and shot my first feature
film, *Fear and Desire*.

G: What was your own experience making your first feature film?

K: *Fear and Desire* was made in the San Gabriel Mountains

outside Los Angeles. I was the camera operator and director and just about everything else. Our "crew" consisted of three Mexican laborers who carried all the equipment. The film was shot in 35 mm without a soundtrack and then dubbed by a post-synchronized technique. The dubbing was a big mistake on my part; the actual shooting cost of the film was nine thousand dollars but because I didn't know what I was doing with the soundtrack it cost me another thirty thousand. There were other things I did expensively and foolishly, because I just didn't have enough experience to know the proper and economical approach. *Fear and Desire* played the art house circuits and some of the reviews were amazingly good, but it's not a film I remember with any pride, except for the fact it was finished.

G: After *Fear and Desire* failed to pay back the investors, how did you get the money to make your next film, *Killer's Kiss?*

K: *Fear and Desire* was financed mainly by my friends and relatives, whom I've since paid back, needless to say. Different people gave me backing for *Killer's Kiss*, which also lost half of its forty-thousand-dollar budget. I've subsequently repaid those backers also. After *Killer's Kiss* I met Jim Harris, who was interested in getting into films, and we formed a production company together. Our first property was *The Killing*, based on Lionel White's story "The Clean Break." This time we could afford good actors, such as Sterling Hayden, and a professional crew. The budget was larger than the earlier films—$320,000—but still very low for a Hollywood production. Our next film was *Paths of Glory*, which nobody in Hollywood wanted to do at all, even though we had a very low budget. Finally Kirk Douglas saw the script and liked it. Once he agreed to appear in the film United Artists was willing to make it.

G: How'd you get that great performance out of Douglas?

K: A director can't get anything out of an actor that he doesn't already have. You can't start an acting school in the middle of making a film. Kirk is a good actor.

G: What did you do after *Paths of Glory?*

K: I did two scripts that no one wanted. A year went by and my finances were rather rocky. I received no salary for *The Killing* or *Paths of Glory* but had worked on 100 per cent deferred salary— and since the films didn't make any money, I had received nothing from either of them. I subsisted on loans from my partner, Jim

Harris. Next I spent six months working on a screenplay for a Western, *One-Eyed Jacks*, with Marlon Brando and Calder Willingham. Our relationship ended amicably a few weeks before Marlon began directing the film himself. By the time I had left Brando I had spent two years doing nothing. At this point, I was hired to direct *Spartacus* with Kirk Douglas. It was the only one of my films over which I did not have complete control; although I was the director, mine was only one of many voices to which Kirk listened. I am disappointed in the film. It had everything but a good story.

G: What do you consider the director's role?

K: A director is a kind of idea and taste machine; a movie is a series of creative and technical decisions, and it's the director's job to make the right decisions as frequently as possible. Shooting a movie is the worst milieu for creative work ever devised by man. It is a noisy, physical apparatus; it is difficult to concentrate—and you have to do it from eight-thirty to six-thirty, five days a week. It's not an environment an artist would ever choose to work in. The only advantage it has is that you must do it, and you can't procrastinate.

G: How did you learn to actually *make* the films, since you'd had no experience?

K: Well, my experience in photography was very helpful. For my two documentaries I'd used a small 35-mm hand camera called an Eyemo, a daylight loading camera which was very simple to operate. The first time I used a Mitchell camera was on *Fear and Desire*. I went to the Camera Equipment Company, at 1600 Broadway, and the owner, Bert Zucker, spent a Saturday morning showing me how to load and operate it. So that was the extent of my formal training in movie camera technique.

G: As a beginner, you mean you just walked cold into a rental outfit and had them give you a cram course in using movie equipment?

K: Bert Zucker, who has subsequently been killed in an airline crash, was a young man, in his early thirties, and he was very sympathetic. Anyway, it was a sensible thing for them to do. I was paying for the equipment. At that time I also learned how to do cutting. Once somebody showed me how to use a Movieola and synchronizer and how to make a splice I had no trouble at all. The technical fundamentals of moviemaking are not difficult.

G: What kind of movies did you go to in those days?

K: I used to want to see almost anything. In fact, the bad films were what really encouraged me to start out on my own. I'd keep seeing lousy films and saying to myself, "I don't know anything about moviemaking but I *couldn't* do anything worse than this."

G: You had technical skills and audacity, but what made you think you could get a good performance out of an actor?

K: Well, in the beginning I really didn't get especially good performances, either in *Fear and Desire* or *Killer's Kiss*. They were both amateurish films. But I did learn a great deal from making them, experience which helped me greatly in my subsequent films. The best way to learn is to do—and this is something few people manage to get the opportunity to try. I was also helped a great deal by studying Stanislavski's books, as well as an excellent book about him, *Stanislavski Directs*, which contains a great deal of highly illustrative material on how he worked with actors. Between those books and the painful lessons I learned from my own mistakes I accumulated the basic experience needed to start to do good work.

G: Did you also read film theory books?

K: I read Eisenstein's books at the time, and to this day I still don't really understand them. The most instructive book on film aesthetics I came across was Pudovkin's *Film Technique*, which simply explained that editing was the aspect of the film art form which was completely unique, and which separated it from all other art forms. The ability to show a simple action like a man cutting wheat from a number of angles in a brief moment, to be able to see it in a special way not possible except through film—that this is what it was all about. This is obvious, of course, but it's so important it cannot be too strongly stressed. Pudovkin gives many clear examples of how good film editing enhances a scene, and I would recommend his book to anyone seriously interested in film technique.

G: But you weren't impressed by Eisenstein's books. What do you think of his films?

K: Well, I have a mixed opinion. Eisenstein's greatest achievement is the beautiful visual composition of his shots, and his editing. But as far as content is concerned, his films are silly, his actors are wooden and operatic. I sometimes suspect that Eisenstein's acting style derives from his desire to keep the actors framed within his compositions for as long as possible; they move very slowly, as if under water. Interesting to note, a lot of his work was being done concurrently with Stanislavski's work. Actually, anyone seriously interested in comparative film techniques should study the differences in approach of two directors, Eisenstein and Chaplin. Eisenstein is all form and no content, whereas Chaplin is content and no form. Of course, a director's style is partly the result of the manner in which he imposes his mind on the semicontrollable conditions that exist on any given day—the responsiveness and talent of actors, the realism of the set, time factors, even weather.

G: You've been quoted as saying that Max Ophuls' films fascinated you when you were starting out as a director.

K: Yes, he did some brilliant work. I particularly admired his fluid camera techniques. I saw a great many films at that time at the Museum of Modern Art and in movie theaters, and I learned far more by seeing films than from reading heavy tomes on film aesthetics.

G: If you were nineteen and starting out again, would you go to film school?

K: The best education in film is to make one. I would advise any neophyte director to try to make a film by himself. A three-minute short will teach him a lot. I know that all the things I did at the beginning were, in microcosm, the things I'm doing now as a director and producer. There are a lot of noncreative aspects to filmmaking which have to be overcome, and you will experience them all when you make even the simplest film: business, organization, taxes, etc., etc. It is rare to be able to have uncluttered, artistic environment when you make a film, and being able to accept this is essential.

The point to stress is that anyone seriously interested in making a film should find as much money as he can as quickly as he can and go out and do it. And this is no longer as difficult as it once was. When I began making movies as an independent in the early 1950s I received a fair amount of publicity because I was something of a freak in an industry dominated by a handful of huge studios. Everyone was amazed that it could be done at all. But anyone can make a movie who has a little knowledge of cameras and tape recorders, a lot of ambition and—hopefully—talent. It's gotten down to the pencil and paper level. We're really on the threshold of a revolutionary new era in film.

K46